Gunnar's Learning Curves

A Memoir By
Gunnar S. Jenson

To: VAdm. Michael H. Miller '74
in Chicago on 10/28/11
"Ex Scientia Tridens"
And from reading this
memoir, More Knowledge.
With every good wish,

Bru '56

Gunnar S Jenson
1920 Rockne Dr
South Bend IN 46617-2243

ISBN: 1-4392-5347-1

ISBN-13: 9781439253472

Gunnar's Learning Curves

If the United States Navy
were managed by patent attorneys,
our warships would still have sails!

I have tried to help.

Memoirs

by

Gunnar S. Jenson

Money isn't everything,
as long as you have some.

John Jenson, my Dad, said that. Often.

It's a great life,
if you don't weaken.

He often said that, too.

Was you there, Charlie?

Nelly's (Mom's) favorite
good-natured closing argument.

The old forget.
The young don't know.

I am trying hard to remember.

Gunnar

Making a lot of money
did not attract me ... enough.
Lodged in my subconscious was a concern that
I could acquire too much money,
too quickly,
get lazy, soft, lose perspectives,
and give up on pursuing life's
more meaningful challenges:
Like
strengthening legitimate avenues
for the impoverished to improve theirs
and the lives of others.

How would I propose for them to do that?

Via their new writings
and discoveries, of course.

After all,
one cannot be accused of stealing
if one's writings and discoveries are
deemed entirely new;
and
perhaps one need not remain impoverished
if they have commercial value.

Gunnar

The great and glorious masterpiece of
man is to know how to live to purpose.

Michel de Montaigne

There are two things to aim
for in life: first, to get what
you want; and, after that, to
enjoy it. Only the wisest of
mankind achieve the second.

Logan Pearsall Smith

I have lived as many would if they could.
A little luck, now and then?
Where would anyone be without it!

Gunnar

Doing it
when you feel an urge to do it
can overcome procrastination.

However,
having the ability to generate interest
in doing whatever needs to be done
whenever it is needed,
can be a good and useful leadership trait.

Finding contentment
in a day's work well done
when it represents only a portion
of the whole undertaking can also be useful.

GUNNAR S. JENSON

CONTENTS

CHAPTER:

FRONT PAGE: Author and son standing south of the White House south lawn, August 1971.

BACK COVER: Author aboard USS Bon Homme Richard (CVA-31) in Western Pacific, 1961.

Remembering

Alaska Representative-at-Large Nick Begich
House Democratic Leader Hale Boggs
of Louisiana
and two members of their flight crew
who disappeared on a flight from Anchorage
to Juneau, Alaska on October 16, 1972

and

United States Senator Philip A. Hart
from Michigan
who died of Cancer on December 26, 1976

CHAPTER 1

SWEDISH PARENTS, SWEDISH ANCESTORS, TO SWEDEN AND BACK

When one is only four years old and walks out into a howling, gale-force wind on the wet main deck of an ocean liner in the middle of the Atlantic Ocean at noon during a storm so severe that one must look up in order to see the tops of huge, towering waves as they surge closer to roll and pitch the ship, the scene can last a good long time in a little boy's memory. So it has lasted for me, since sometime in 1937. I'm really not certain of the exact crossing time. But it was after my Swedish immigrant, naturalized U.S. citizen parents had decided to send me from Chicago Heights, Illinois, to live with my maternal grandparents in Sweden for a few years. That turned out also to be shortly before Hitler absorbed Austria (in 1938) and moved his troops into Czechoslovakia, a year later.

Observing from the Gripsholm's main deck, on the way over, I developed a peculiar liking for that bluish water and whitish foam that forms on the smooth backsides of waves in high wind conditions, the remains of spent white caps, I believe. That affinity remains even to this day. As waves crest, daylight shines through and brings out the blue in the water, while foam also leaves a trail on the otherwise smooth backs and troughs of waves. It seems to happen best in salty ocean water, miles from shore. And the higher the wind and waves, the better and more foam. What a sight! What sounds! What smells! Somewhat different than inland lakes, perhaps due to water depth and salinity. Of course, having the wherewithal just to venture out onto the ocean in stormy conditions to witness such ocean phenomenon may be part of the fascination.

The Swedish liner, Gripsholm, was about the same size as her sister ship, the Kungsholm, that I would be returning aboard, in 1939, after Hitler's sudden invasion of Poland. A German submarine would challenge and stop us in mid-ocean on that return voyage.

Dad's father had passed away when dad was about fourteen years old (because he had worked himself to death, according to dad), and dad's mother had remarried afterwards. Dad had not gotten along with his step-father or her, after she remarried, according to what my mother had whispered to me, in secret, one day. Outwardly, in the presence of my dad, I was encouraged not to go and visit her, once I had arrived in Sweden. After all, dad hadn't gone to see his mother in her nursing home, either, during his several return visits to Sweden! But my mother took me aside, before I left, and instructed me in hushed tones that it would be appropriate, OK and good for me (and her) to visit her, if I could. Indeed, I was taken to visit Mrs. Westberg, once, and found her a most gracious lady and very friendly towards me! My one and only contact with my paternal grandmother. Relationships with my maternal grandparents, on the other hand, were something else again.

The original plan was for me to get at least a few years of Swedish schooling, possibly as much as through sixth grade, before returning to the United States. My mother, who had the equivalent of a high school education, and my father, who had not quite made it through what we in the U.S. would qualify as eighth grade, believed that Swedish schools were the best. They, and their many other (naturalized) immigrant friends that I can recall growing up around in the Chicago area also agreed with the philosophy that "others may be able to take your material possessions away from you, but they can't ever take away your education! And the more educated you can become, the better!" (Through experience I have come to believe in that advice. It's as valid today as it seemed to be then!) Thus, it was intended that I receive as much education in Sweden as possible, before being returned to the U.S., and to the vicinity of Harvey, Illinois, where I was born.

While my parents were not exactly poor, they weren't rich either. Middle class, possibly. They had arrived in the U.S. around 1925 and lived through the Depression, prospering during it, actually. (My father had joined with another Swede named Brackman in the car repair business.) By 1937, my folks thought they would share their only child with their parents "back in the old country"; while also working and saving some money during his absence. I was only four and alone during the crossing in 1937, except for an accompanying nurse. A youngster traveling alone without his parents, but with an accompanying nurse across the Atlantic on an ocean liner can attract a lot of ooohh's and aaahh's. Thus, one stormy day, the captain extended an invitation for me to join him and his guests for dinner at his table in the dining room.

Boy! What an honor, I thought! Young as I was, I really did value that courtesy. Perhaps the captain had invited me because I had endured the rough seas while other adults were ill in their cabins or standing in breezeways or holding on to railings getting ready to (you know what). I remember wanting to make the captain proud and glad for having invited me.

Perhaps I would be invited back to his table again, sometime. Or back up to the bridge, once more.

That was not to be, unfortunately.

You guessed it. Let's just say that my turn for taking on a case of the seasickness came just moments after the captain and all of his head table guests had been seated, served their salads, and had eaten some of them. What a way to go! I never saw that captain again. I stayed out of his way for the remainder of the trip to Sweden! Good riddance! But, I don't remember getting seasick again, either!

*   *

When you "can't speak the language," and you're a little boy standing for the first time in the living room of your grandfather's house surrounded by very vocal, well wishing, adult relatives whom you cannot understand at all - and you really, really, NEED to go #1, what do you do? Easy! Just naturally let your legs cross (without even being aware of it) and someone with a reasonable understanding of body language will get the message. Thank you, Ester Arvidsson, mother's sister-in-law! With a big, broad smile, she took my hand and led me straight to a small closet under a staircase where there was a pot. We became friends for life.

Grandfather's and grandmother's little red house with white trim in the country was built of wood. I had first noticed that when I glanced around the closet under the unpainted stairs beside the living room that first evening. Later, on Christmas Eve, as young as I was, I had sense enough to realize the dangers involved when candles were lighted in holders attached to branches all over that evergreen Christmas tree in the middle of the living room! But, it turned out OK. The little wax collector plate on the bottom of each holder prevented wax from dripping onto the tree branches and thence to the floor; and the candle holders, themselves, seemed to be firmly affixed, each one keeping each candle at or very near to a true verticle and away from any overhanging branches.

When New Year's Eve rolled around, many, many adult friends and relatives were in attendance. It was a joyous occasion. Doubly so for me, because part of the 12 o'clock midnight celebration became the dismantling and tossing out of that worrisome candle-lit Christmas tree!

Lapland, way up in northern Sweden, was as cold and snowy as travel brochures suggest. My maternal grandfather, Otto Arvidsson, took me up there, once. We may have also been accompanied by my namesake, Gunnar Arvidsson, my mother's brother. (The name Gunnar, by the way, is reportedly as common in Sweden as, say, Bob or Bill is in the U.S.)

As I recall them, the Lapps were dressed just as you see them pictured in brochures, today: colorful, with some "busy" patterns and designs. I still have two knives from there, crudely made by hand by Lapps, with sheaths and handles fashioned from parts of deer antlers, and with carved designs added. Not much is wasted by the Lapps. They don't seem to have much to begin with, except a lot of very cold air, snow, ice, their deer herds, and what must be a very satisfying life-style. They all seemed to smile a lot. Good-natured people!

Back in Skutskar (closer to Stockholm), and constructed behind that little red and white Swedish house of my grandfather's, was something else you might have to travel far to see: a man-made timber transport canal. Made of thick wooden planks forming a V-shaped cross section, it stood about one-story high above ground, was equipped with a walkway at the top along one side, and had phone-booth-sized observation "shacks," each with a door and windows on three sides and were strategically placed so as to allow the men manning them the best opportunities for surveillance up and down the canal and around all of its turns. Logs in the canal could jam. Attendants would then have to come quickly from their "shacks" carrying their long poles with hooks on the ends to pry the logs loose.

Before having to abide by instructions to stay away from that canal, I was taken up for a tour along its walkway to see the floating logs and to watch the men with their long poles "keeping things moving." The "shack" closest to grandfather Otto's little red and white house had a waist-high table shelf in it, at which workmen stood and ate their brown bag lunches and drank coffee from their thermos bottles while monitoring the progress of logs drifting along with the canal's controlled water flow. Incidentally, the water flow could be reduced to a mere trickle when there were no logs to transport (down to the mills).

There came a time when grandfather Otto built his own fishing boat from scratch on the upper floor of the red and white two-story barn that was located on the other side of his house from the canal. I was allowed up to see it and smell its pleasant varnish and caulking odors, now and then. A big, lapstrake, lifeboat is what it looked like to me. Grandfather Otto seemed to have it all pretty well under control - until it came time to get the boat out of the hayloft! The boat was then observed to be much wider and taller than the doors at either end of the loft. Fortunately, as capable a carpenter as my grandfather was - after all, he had built that boat from scratch - he was also able then to remove the wood siding and wall studs from one end of the barn and to roll the boat out on logs and down a temporary wooden rail ramp that he also erected.

Embarrassed? A little, maybe, but nothing major. After all, he hadn't experienced the loss of the enamel on all of his teeth at an early age for nothing! Seems, to do that, he had bet some of his buddies in a restaurant that he could eat his porcelain coffee cup. Yep! You guessed it. He won that bet, but had to replace all of his teeth with dentures, afterwards! A stubborn Swede? Hmmmm. Come to think of it, he probably built that barn (and house), to begin with, all by himself, as well. He definitely could persevere.

In front of the house and barn was a paved road. The road also had lanes reserved for bicycles only. It was along that road that fishermen came with fresh fish to sell (very) early every weekday morning, fish they had already netted at or before dawn. Although I don't recall seeing it in operation, I was told my grandfather's new boat had joined that nearby fishing fleet.

Children were sent to first grade at the age of seven, in Sweden. Thus, I was too young yet to attend. But I quickly learned to speak Swedish from the many adults around me.

Ester (mother's sister-in-law) and several others brought me along to the countryside, one day, to joyfully gather hay and load it into huge piles on horse-drawn wagons. I say joyful because that's how I remember everyone being, at the time. We used long, hand-made (of course), wooden rakes, with wooden pegs for prongs. (It was a matter of pride for carpenters to have made the pegs to fit properly.) And there were other memorable outings.

One day, my grandfather, Otto, decided to take me for a walk deep into a nearby woods. Suddenly and unexpectedly we came face to face with one huge old moose, with antlers that seemed as wide as he was long! "Don't move!" whispered grandfather. We were standing in the shade of some towering evergreens and on the matted surface of accumulated (reddish brown) pine needles. After chewing for awhile and looking straight ahead at both of us for about as long as he had wanted, the moose turned and pranced away.

At that time, there also were many nations in Europe wishing that Hitler would turn his attentions away from them as well. He had quietly absorbed Austria in 1938. In 1939, German troops also marched into Czechoslovakia. But I was totally unaware of impending world events that would soon cause my parents and relatives to mobilize their activities towards getting me back to the U.S.

The road near Otto's red and white house gave a hint, one day, of developments that were taking place elsewhere in the world, particularly in Europe. That road was usually not traveled much, by cars OR bicycles. However, one day, I heard humming sounds while inside the house that seemed to come from the road and that became louder and more prolonged than any I remembered ever hearing before. Looking out a window, I then saw something I'd never seen before, either: a convoy of army trucks was speeding by, one after another, after another. I had never SEEN so MANY trucks. In fact, as a youngster, I found it hard to fathom that there could even BE so many trucks - in the whole WORLD. Not to mention, also, that some of those army trucks were disregarding the bicycle lane markers and actually driving in the bicycle lanes! Some were even weaving back and forth in and out of the bike and motor vehicle lanes. Don't they follow rules?, I wondered. But, next, the thought quickly crystallized that these, being Swedish Army soldiers, could probably do whatever they wanted. After all, who could stop them? Certainly not the local police. That army convoy was an ultimate force.

It wasn't long after that when a telegram arrived that really ignited some pandemonium. It had just been announced to the world on September 1, 1939, that Hitler had invaded Poland. Upon learning of it, my parents had rushed to send a telegram from Chicago and to somehow provide for my immediate return passage aboard the Kungsholm. It was to be the very last vessel carrying civilians to depart from Sweden for the U.S., and, if I couldn't get aboard, I would have to remain in Sweden for the duration of what looked to the informed like a long, upcoming, world war. By then, I had definitely learned to speak Swedish, fluently, but had forgotten English as well. There had been no one around to speak English with. I had bonded with almost everyone. Parting would be difficult.

Everyone pitched in (to make the going away as easy as possible), and they did somehow manage to get me and my belongings aboard that last departing ship in time for the passage.

*   *

Another nurse (I believe, but I can't remember with accuracy) awoke me in our little stateroom aboard the Kungsholm, after we had been at sea for several days. Our little stateroom had a porthole. It was beside my upper bunk, but a metal cover was bolted over it so I was not immediately aware of the time of day or night. "We must put on our life jackets and hurry up on deck," said the nurse, in a no-nonsense tone of voice. I remember jumping down from my upper berth and feeling the warm metal deck plating under foot. It gave way a little, as I landed on it with both feet. The ship was steady as a rock, I quickly noticed; stopped in the water. There were none of the usual machinery vibrations or noises; but sounds of people talking and some of them shouting to one another arose from the corridor outside. They were easily heard through the slats in our stateroom door. "I don't need a life jacket," I said. "I know how to swim!" But she persisted, and I obeyed, threading my arms through the jacket and helping with fastening the straps. Soon, my nurse and I were in the corridors and climbing ladders (stairs) with the other passengers, arriving, at last, on one of the upper decks, from which we might easily climb into one of the lifeboats hanging just above us.

It was daytime, but very foggy. Early morning, more than likely. Gawking around at the fog and looking at the people and lifeboats on that upper deck, I didn't bother to look down at the water, until the nurse exclaimed suddenly, "Look! Over there on the water! A German submarine! It's flashing a signal light at us!" There! I saw it, too. The water between us and the submarine was as smooth and black as polished marble. We were stopped, dead in the water, and so was the submarine. It was just sitting on the surface (off our port beam), aligned almost parallel with us but turned slightly towards us. Both vessels were very close to each other. Fog surrounded everything. All we could see was the submarine and the water between us.

The signal light on the sub's sail bridge continued flashing, pointing up towards our bridge. The signalman and one or two others could be seen on the bridge of the sub. I turned to my right, looked up, and could see our signalman flashing back and using a light mounted on the flying bridge railing, almost a quarter of the way out from the pilot house. Soon, passengers learned that we had been stopped and asked who we were, where we had come from, where we were headed, and if we were carrying troops or munitions of any kind. Fortunately, for everyone aboard, we were eventually allowed to continue. Just how we could have been stopped that way in so much fog was never explained to me. I probably didn't think to ask, either. More than likely, the fog must have developed after we and the sub had come to a stop.

It had been a strain on everybody to have had such a close call, and we happened to be near Iceland. So, the captain decided to steer for Iceland and to let everyone go ashore for a few hours of rest and relaxation in the warm afternoon sunshine and to stand on solid ground for awhile.

As little boys (and daring young men) are apt to do, they can push the safety envelope beyond reasonable limits. That's what happened to me during that Iceland stop. I don't know his name, but one of the passengers saved my life during that brief stopover.

It was a bright, sunny day as passengers walked onto land, stood around talking to one another and, generally, enjoyed "unwinding" after their close call with the sub. I looked around, saw a steep hill with a huge boulder at the base of it, and, impulsively, ran over and began to scale it. The higher I climbed, the steeper became the hill's incline. Eventually, it became very steep.

After climbing high enough to be able to see a lot and becoming somewhat tired of climbing, I stopped to gaze around once more at everyone below and all else in view (which included the harbor). Out of the corner of my eye, I also happened to notice one of the ship's heavy set male passengers, dressed in a short-sleeved white shirt and tie. He made a sudden, slight movement in my direction, moving slightly away from the circle of passengers he was standing with, as if reading my mind and (correctly) anticipating what I was about to do.

An overwhelming urge to go ahead and experience what it would be like to try to run down that steep hill took hold of me. Instinctively, I knew that running almost straight down would be a very fast trip, that my feet probably would have a hard time keeping up. But I wanted to try it. I also sensed, as I leaned downward and foolishly started to run (almost diving) that the huge boulder staring up at me from the base of the hill was quickly becoming hard if not impossible to steer away from. My running feet soon began to fall behind my body as I raced headlong towards that boulder. With head turned upward, I was looking straight at it with eyes wide open and I almost fell running towards it, out of control!

After he had begun edging himself towards the base of the hill, my fateful rescuer made a break for it just as I began the lunge, running towards the front side of the boulder I was "headed" for. He was coming really fast, despite having a long way to run. Like a professional football player going for a touchdown pass, he literally intercepted me just as I was about to impact headfirst with the boulder. He came running from my left, grabbed me firmly around the waist from slightly be-hind, and we both were swung towards the boulder and then around counterclockwise. I just missed the boulder by inches, and we both fell to the ground some distance away. It was a relatively safe and gentle stop, considering. I surely must have had sense enough to thank him; but I never have found men-tion in any family records of his name. Likely deceased by now, I still offer thanks to him, whoever he was and wherever he might be, for saving my life!

*   *

Arriving outside of New York City's harbor, our ship dropped anchor within sight of two suspension bridge towers (part of a planned railroad bridge never completed, but at today's Verrazano Narrows Bridge site). The tops of some New York City skyscrapers could be seen in the background, to the right of the towers. We were still a ways out in the ocean, I thought. I hoped there would be no more German submarines to challenge us. As it turned out, we had to remain anchored for quite some time; for several days, as I recall. For some reason, we were quarantined and had to wait it out for awhile, there, within sight of our "safe looking" destination. I shudder, still, when thinking about what the little traveling boy did next to satisfy his curiosity.

Our cabin was below the main deck - quite a ways. It had a porthole. The porthole had a metal cover bolted on to it. A wrench that looked like it would fit the porthole nuts was clipped to the bulkhead beside the porthole. Now that the ship had stopped and the sea was calm and the little boy traveler found himself alone in his cabin with nothing to do, he decided to try his hand at removing the porthole cover.

A bit of effort was required to unscrew the first bolt, then the second, and so on, and the cover was finally loosened. No water came gushing in, just daylight around the cover's edges. A little lifting and twisting and the cover eventually came off, revealing a glass window underneath. The glass was so dirty and full of dried salt crystals that only blurred vision was possible to the outside.

To a six year old, of course, it only made sense to also remove the dirty porthole glass if one was to have a look outside.

It was a good thing the ship was anchored and in calm water! The glass port bolts came unscrewed about as easily as the cover bolts. And, finally, the bottom of the window was pulled out and raised up about the hinges at the top. Without giving attention to much else, I quickly stuck my head out to see what I could see. Wow! It seemed that I could have reached out and almost touched the water! That's how close to the water-line that porthole was! I could have sunk the ship, I thought, if the porthole had been only a little lower (or the ship a little heavier). I twisted my neck for a quick look around. I could barely see the tops of a few New York City skyscrapers way off in the distance and to the right of the suspension bridge towers. Then, the awesome, scary, starboard side of our ship came into view. As I strained to look up higher, the side of our ship appeared steeper and taller. It was monstrous! Huge! And I was at the bottom of it, in the shade of the ship, almost at the water-line. If a wave were to come along, I reasoned, the water could rise and flood my stateroom! What's wrong with you, boy! Get that porthole window and cover back on! And hurry!!

Fortunately, I was able to replace the window and cover without incident. I don't remember mentioning what I had done to anyone, afterwards, either, until this writing.

After a day or two, which had seemed like an eternity, the quarantine was ended and our ship was allowed to proceed into New York Harbor. We docked and I looked forward to my father's arrival to pick me up. But he wasn't there. Everyone else seemed to be leaving the ship with their baggage but me. I had to wait for my dad, and he was nowhere in sight. We had been held up at the harbor entrance for quite some time, after all, and he should have had plenty of time to get to New York from Chicago. But, where was he?

Funny thing about being left alone on a ship in a strange city, when your father does finally arrive to pick you up with a big smile on his face, you forgive and forget. I only remember disembarking with my dad and walking amongst many other passengers, stevedores, policemen and hawkers of various services, through the dock building to the street. We entered a cab to begin our journey back to Chicago (by train), and that's about all I can remember, except that we made it safely, of course, and that I then spoke only Swedish, having forgotten English.

My mother was delighted to see me again, naturally. She truly appreciated that I could speak Swedish so well. A decision was made and a family agreement then voiced that we would all consciously speak Swedish around the house from then on, so I might retain it into adulthood. First, however, I had to learn to speak English again. What I can recall about that was that after hearing a little English spoken again, once I had made my mind up to relearn it, I was soon able to imitate a few words, shortly after which, like a flood, all the English I had known before leaving, came back to me. All of this happened within a day or two of my return. It was as if the English language had been stored somewhere in my brain and I had gained total recall.

Speaking Swedish at home as much as possible to please my mother worked for awhile, but everyone gradually drifted back to speaking English. We were, after all, Americans! Were we ever! And World War II for Americans would soon begin.

CHAPTER 2

JENSON'S ONE STOP SERVICE

"Stop there once and you'll never stop again!" was frequently offered in jest, even by church member friends
of dad's. My father showed a daring sense of humor with that
sign -in neon lights- mounted directly above his Mobil gas station office door entrance, at the inside corner of the L-shaped
garage building. But business WAS good. People DID stop.
More than once. As regular customers. Many gas customers
were memorable, as were some who came for repairs.

One of the easiest gas purchasers to remember drove a
black '41 Chevrolet four-door sedan, was always well dressed
(in a suit, usually, and tie) and was named Sam. Sam was
a frequent customer, a very likeable man who would usually
step out of his car, stand around making small talk, while I
pumped his gas, cleaned the windshield and checked the water
and oil under the hood for him. Sam always chewed gum, it
seemed, and he would actually hand me a stick of Wrigley's
Spearmint or Doublemint Gum every time he came in! Say
what you want, but nobody else did that. In fact, no one else
that I can remember ever gave me anything except payment for
their gas, oil, and whatever else they'd bought from the station.
That gum was a "gift!" Sam's car was always clean. I liked
Sam. Years later, I was told that Sam worked for the mafia.
Maybe so, maybe not, but I still liked and appreciated the way

he had treated me. And I learned that small tokens can often be quite effective in garnering friendships and good will.

During WWII's rationing period, many shortages developed. My father seemed to have sources for some items that not many others had. One memorable incident involved Jack Benny's chauffeur, Rochester. On the Jack Benny programs, Rochester always drove an old, noisy, broken down jalopy of some kind. But, hey! Not in real life!

One day, I returned from school in the late afternoon, assumed my gas pumping duties at the filling station, and I just happened to glance through the big windows and see something unusual parked in the car wash rack. The car was so unusual, in fact, that I found myself rushing through the office and out onto the wash rack area. There, I stopped and became awestruck by what was parked in front of me --- an automobile like I had never seen before...and I had seen many cars!

The year was around 1945. The car was a 1941 Cadillac Fleetwood Special that looked even better than a new one, with a special paint job and color. Chrome: not a scratch on it anywhere, and it appeared to have the shine and thickness of sterling silver. As far as I was concerned, that car was perfect! Who could ask for anything more!

But, it really wasn't...perfect. At least not then. It needed a new radiator core, something my father was able to find and have his radiator men "recore" for Rochester's four-door Cadillac sedan. Within a few days, the car with what could have been 15 coats of metallic maroon lacquer paint was gone; back on the road, or headed for Eddie "Rochester" Anderson's garage in Hollywood where it might have best belonged. Perhaps it's in a museum, somewhere, today. What a car!

When I returned to Chicago Heights from Sweden in 1939, mother and dad had moved into a downstairs apartment about one block away from the apartment we had lived in prior to my leaving. This new apartment building had four apartments in it and had been purchased by my father during my absence. Our new home was also located only about 50 yards away from dad's filling station, which he had also purchased during my absence. If you walked out the back door of our apartment, down the porch steps, turned right and passed the other downstairs apartment heading out across an empty lot, and across Emerald Avenue, you'd then find yourself on the filling station drive with an island of gas pumps in the middle. A little further and you'd reach the station building. If it were absolutely necessary, one could park eight or nine cars overnight inside that building. It had five overhead doors, one allowing entry to a wash rack that was lined on one side with windows (where Rochester's car was parked). Behind the station, a short distance to the east, the Chicago & Eastern Illinois Railroad tracks ran by atop about twenty five feet of embankment. The engines were steam driven, puffed black, gray and white smoke, and blew some pretty loud whistles as they passed by and approached some road crossings and the train station in downtown Chicago Heights, where they would often stop.

At the age of nine, I drove a car for the first time, into Dad's station - literally. In fact, I drove it into the very stall that Rochester's Cadillac would eventually be parked in. Well, maybe one could call it a glancing blow to the left door frame.

The station owned a 1932 Pontiac 4-door sedan, with a wooden plank fastened to the front bumper. It was used for push-starting cars. The brakes were mechanical (which meant the driver's brake pedal was connected directly to the brake shoes in each wheel via wire cables suspended and routed under the car). Hydraulic brakes (with power added) have long since replaced those mechanical brakes and for good reasons. Even with really well adjusted mechanical brakes and very strong legs and feet, one could not count on short stopping distances. And, if those cables were left alone (unadjusted) for any length of time, you would soon realize one of the fundamental reasons for down shifting through the gears, in those early years. Downshifting would permit the engine to share in slowing the vehicle when brakes alone were not enough.

At any rate, when Dad said to me for the very first time late one afternoon that I could drive the Pontiac in for the night, I charged out of the office and ran to where the car and trailers were parked. Surveying the area, I decided to take as much advantage as possible of that first invitation to actually drive a car alone - by driving it as far as possible!

Behind the station, where the Pontiac was parked, there was a lot full of parked semi-truck trailers, owned by Keeshin Trucking, Inc. Here and there, a space was left between trailers, large enough for a car to fit between and pass through. After looking things over, I put the Pontiac in neutral and pushed it as far back between two of those trailers as possible. Driving another 50-60 feet became meaningful when the whole "trip" amounted to only about 200 feet or so.

"Bud, the mechanic," as we called him, was sent out to monitor. Bud walked with a crutch under his right arm and had just a stump for a left arm protruding from his left shoulder. In his younger days, Bud had been driving a convertible with the top down and was having a good time, as he later described it, with his left arm hanging out and resting on the door. He was side-swiped by an on-coming auto and lost his arm. "It could have been worse," he readily admitted, "It was a damn foolish way for me to have been driving." The crutch and braces on both legs resulted from polio. I cannot ever remember Bud being late for work, nor can I remember much that he could not do. He was a bit slow getting around, but he seemed to make up for any lost time once he had gotten to where he was needed and could begin working.

Bud came out and stood beside the opened overhead door leading into the wash rack while I scrambled to the back lot. I finally got into that '32 Pontiac sedan, turned the ignition key on and disappeared from view as my foot reached down to depress the starter pedal. It may have been possible to adjust the front seat, but I don't remember wanting to take time to figure out how, just then. I made the best of what there was, though, finding that I could either sit up and hold on to the steering wheel and see through the windshield and side windows to steer, or I could slip down and disappear from view in order to be able to depress the pedals. It was one or the other.

Finally, I got the car started, into first gear, and gradually released the clutch. Moving past the trailers towards the wash rack was thrilling - and then some! Bud was standing to the left of the doorway with a brick wall behind him. As I maneuvered around from behind the station, turned, stopped and backed to the edge of the street, I was lined up for a straight run into that wash rack stall. There were cars parked inside, ahead of where I was to stop, so I was acutely aware of needing to stop, once inside.

Bud was a patient man. Not a word came out of him, as I took aim for the door and gradually released the clutch to begin a slow approach at idle on a slight upgrade to the doorway. The closer I came to the door, the more nervous I became. It was going to be close! Too close!! Squeak! The side of the left front fender went against the door frame as I reached it. Just as quickly, though, I lurched down and depressed both the clutch and brake with both feet. The car stopped almost immediately, the black fender pressed against the white painted wood door frame. The fender was creased a bit on the side, but not seriously. (I later straightened and repainted it myself).

Here is where I became indebted to "Bud, the mechanic" for a lifetime, in my opinion, (and to my dad, of course, for leaving us alone out there). Many men could have hollered for me to get out of the car, and they might have then taken over and added insult to injury by urging that I take up driving after more years of practice, or some such. But not Bud. "Try it again," was all he said. And I did; this time, fitting that proverbial thread through the needle, successfully! Through the doorway we went (the car and I) until the parked car ahead suddenly began to look like it was getting too close. Down I scrambled, to push on the brake pedal. I pushed, but the car kept moving. It slowed a bit, but then seemed to lurch forward again. So I pressed both feet down on the brake pedal with all the strength I could muster. The car slowed, but still moved. I grabbed the lower part of the steering wheel with both hands and lifted so my feet could push even harder on the brake pedal. The car finally then stopped, as the motor died. Whew! But, Dummy Me! I had forgotten to engage the clutch! The good news, though, was that the Pontiac had stopped exactly where it belonged, a few inches from the car ahead of it, and in the middle of the stall! Thinking about it as I write this more than 50 years later, I probably felt as "psyched up" about proper line-up and getting through the "narrows" of that doorway as I did, later in life, when making that very first landing on an aircraft carrier some 85 miles south of Pensacola, Florida, in a Navy F9F8-T (Cougar) jet trainer. More about that later.

The Jeeps that are still manufactured by the Chrysler Corporation in the 21st Century had their origins in WWII, were produced by several manufacturers then, but were first introduced by the Willys-Overland Corp. Willys also manufactured cars.

Somehow, my father acquired a Willys dealership right there at the filling station and just prior to the outbreak of WWII. He took possession of a new 1941 or '42 model Willys demonstrator business coupe. (A business coupe had only front seating for three, if they squeezed into it, a small storage space was created up behind the front seat, and it had a long and what thereby became a relatively large trunk, for salesmen to carry samples, presumably.) There were only a few 1942 model cars manufactured before the Japanese attacked Pearl Harbor on December 7, 1941, and only a few more '42 models were produced after that, mostly for the government, and most of those lacked chrome. Their otherwise chromed and stainless steel body parts were painted the same color as the rest of the car, usually, as is commonly done again today, come to think of it. All of the car makers were soon totally involved with producing ships, airplanes, tanks, trucks, bombs, guns and everything else that became essential for "the war effort."

Car owners were issued A-Cards, B-Cards, C-Cards, D-Cards and E-Cards for their rationed gasoline purchases. A holder of an A-Card with all of its gallon stamps that would have to last a month, for example, was also issued a decal with a white capital A on a black background for mounting on the windshield. That way, one could spot who was the more important to the war effort with the use of his car. I don't recall any official reasons for the decals. But, by then, I had attended school enough to be able to read them. Those very first few days at Jefferson school were quite memorable! Some would even say embarrassing.

Swedish children were first enrolled in school at age seven; going on six, I was too young. In the U.S., however, the starting age was six (if six by a cut-off date, around September 1). My sixth birthday came on September 20th. It also happened that I returned to the U.S. late in the year, several months after school had started. Mother was quite conscious of my "standing," in school and in the community, so she and my father arranged for me to start off as a second grader, that following year. I was about as old and as big and strong as some of my fellow classmates in second grade on that memorable first day; quite proud of having returned to the U.S. speaking only Swedish and having been able in a very short time to switch back to English. And, on that very first day, when the teacher asked everyone to get out their reading books, I can still recall telling myself that if someone else could be called on first to do a little reading, I would pick it up quickly and become a reader, myself; so that if called upon after that, I, too, would be able to read aloud to the class. Well, guess who was called upon to read first!!

It was back to first grade for me on that very first day of school; but my parents did arrange for me to have a chance later to skip from the middle of second grade to the middle of third, which I eventually did accomplish. That allowed my mother to often claim: "He skipped a grade."

One other "incident" arising from my not fully understanding the English language yet after living in Sweden arose soon after being dropped back to first grade. Sitting in that school desk chair with the books under me, I developed an urge to go #1. I raised my hand and asked to go to the bathroom. The teacher asked, "Is it necessary?" Too proud to let on that I didn't know what the word necessary meant, I answered emphatically, "No!" "Well, stay in your seat, then," she said.

Hmmmmm. I did, but after a while, I couldn't hold it any longer. All I knew was to just let it go...and I did. After some time, a water puddle started forming on the floor around my chair, expanding outward in every direction. It might have gone unnoticed a bit longer except that it was making a dark stain on a light-colored wood floor that had had the varnish pretty well worn off of it. After one or two of my fellow students happened to glance in my direction and catch sight of what was happening on the floor beneath me, my just sitting there, stoic, and looking straight ahead at the teacher didn't hold them back much. They soon roared with laughter, and I was the one sent home - to change my clothes. And, thanks to the teacher, no doubt, not another word was said about it that I could remember, afterwards.

Sweden had opted for bicycles with the skinny tires and wheels by the time of my visit. As a going away (back to America) present, my grandparents and other relatives had generously chipped in to buy and send along with me a new, skinny wheeled, boys bike. I rode it to Jefferson School, even mounted a large wooden basket up front and delivered papers with it.

In those days, the bike to own was a Schwinn with balloon tires and a spring action front fork. How I yearned to even ride one of those, much less be able to own one. (I haven't ridden one yet, by the way.) While the big balloon tired bikes were considered macho (rightly so, perhaps, for they did take extra muscle power to keep them moving), anything with those "skinny" tires was thought by my peer group to be the equivalent of being owned/ridden by a wimp.

Gradually, then, being friendly and willing to play games with some of my peers wasn't enough. I began having to defend myself physically (and verbally), usually on the way home. I didn't look for trouble, often going a different route, not to avoid anyone, but simply to enjoy some stimulating variety. But, one afternoon, shortly after school had let out, I was challenged.

About two blocks from school, I rounded a corner at the bottom of a hill, walking home. I don't recall what month of the year it was, but the grass was green and leaves were on the trees. Suddenly, and to my surprise, there emerged from behind a big bush four or five school chums, led by one Robert Davis, whom I had considered a bully, slightly older and bigger than I. He challenged me to a fight, right then and there. Without hesitation, I accepted.

Approaching one another on someone else's front lawn, he promptly pushed me. Hard. As I began to fall backwards, I instinctively extended my right arm to catch the fall. In an instant, the palm side of my hand hit the grass and transferred the load of my falling body to my elbow. I heard something and felt something.

In a moment, I had become engaged in a fight and just as suddenly I found myself in pain and unable to bend my right elbow. I immediately called a halt to the fight and in the same breath rescheduled it for a specific time and day about a week later, I think it was, and to take place behind or beside a Clubhouse in a nearby park. It seemed to come naturally to do that so as to avoid being declared the loser, I guess. Who wants that reputation? Thankfully, in due course, I made short work of beating the bully in the "scheduled" fight. More important, to me, however, was that I was never again bothered or challenged to another (street) fight, by Davis or anyone else.

Washington Junior High for 7th and 8th grades was about twice as far away from home and in almost the opposite direction. I then walked even a bit further, to an intersection beyond the school, to assume crossing guard duties, for awhile. I can remember developing a sense of public service and responsibility as a crossing guard, wearing a white belt identifier which my mother was quick to wash and want to keep clean for me.

Also there was (and still is, I think) a 4-6 inch thick concrete foundation wall that drops off about 2 feet on the one alley side but has a 5 to 6 foot drop-off on the other side, to wall-in a school trash-can-deposit area. We used to stand on that wall, face one another, and try to knock off opponents - towards the deep drop-off side, of course.

The auditorium had a respectable stage, I was told. It was used for school functions, mainly; but, also, once a year during the winter, members of the Kiwanis Club would rehearse and put on well received by grown ups and children, alike, Minstrel Shows, for charity. Carl Hirsch, the undertaker father of a boyhood friend of mine, Bob, and Bob's uncle, Ed Hirsch, were two perennial leaders of and stars in those productions.

The Hirsch West End Funeral Home had an ambulance or two, in those days, as did most funeral homes. In fact, if not for funeral homes providing them, there would have been no ambulance services. For laughs, I often said one could consider a possible motive for not getting patients to hospitals in time: to promote another ride, in a hearse next time? Just kidding, of course. I observed many speeding ambulances driven by practiced drivers intent on saving the lives of their passengers.

West End had two Packard limousines, a 1937 and 1941 model. Thanks to Bob, I was permitted to tour the insides of those two beautiful, black limos, on an occasion or two. The Packard brake and clutch pedals were larger than any others I'd seen; and rectangular; and the limos had what were called jump seats, behind the front seats.

Snows and cold weather could envelop the outside of that Washington School Auditorium at night, but, during Minstrel Shows, roars of laughter and good will would emanate from within, as persons otherwise unknown and usually unseen in Chicago Heights would set aside their demeanors and perform for the sake of cheers and laughter.

Afterwards, people could wander out and down the street to the corner on Chicago Road and Sixteenth Street to have some ice cream, coffee, cocoa, banana splits, fudge sundaes, and the like, in a new facility built on that corner just for that. It had tall windows looking out to the north, mostly, and to the east. There, a red traffic light would one day play an important part in my life.

CHAPTER 3

POST WWII OPPORTUNITIES

Dad had been a Willys dealer just before WWII started. I can remember him taking delivery of only one car, though. After WWII ended, it was around 1946-47 when he became a Packard dealer, in a large red brick building only a block from the filling station, towards downtown Chicago Heights. The structure had a long, wide, glass-fronted show-room that faced Emerald Avenue on the west, capable of easily displaying a half dozen cars, or more. The ceiling must have been ten or twelve feet high, and there was a layer of one-story apartments resting on top of it. The showroom floor had a massive number of small white six-sided ceramic tiles that seemed to extend as far as the eye could see. A servicing area was at the rear. Meanwhile, the filling station, radiator repair and welding business had been taken over by another Swedish immigrant and family friend, Herman Peterson.

My father had become a Packard dealer in partnership with a Jewish survivor of the Auschwitz concentration camp, Kappel Asher. They sometimes called him Capital Ash, in jest. I was young and out of respect always called him Mr. Asher. A likeable, gregarious person, Mr. Asher showed me the large, uneven identification numbers the Germans had tattooed onto his wrist. He told me he figured he had been within a week or two of being killed when the war ended. He then looked at me and said, "Something like that should not be allowed to happen ever again." I looked him back in the eye and said I agreed and would do what I could to prevent it.

Cap always spoke well of his wife. He claimed she owned the apartment building (with a considerable number of units) that they lived in on the west side of Chicago Heights adjacent to Lincoln Highway. And he credited her with giving him the brand new Lincoln Continental that he drove (and which I knew to have had an advertised price of $10,000; big money in those days). I never met Mrs. Asher, but they sent me $5 as a gift for Christmas every year for many years, until they passed away.

Packards, at that time and as before the outbreak of WWII, were considered equal in luxury and status to Lincolns, Chryslers, and Cadillacs. All of them had been more or less tied for first place until the 1948 Cadillac made its debut. Its body design (especially its tail light fins, as they came to be affectionately called) launched Cadillac towards becoming America's (and the world's) #1 luxury production-line car. Next, a year later, in 1949, Cadillac and Oldsmobile introduced a new V-8 overhead valve engine designed by Charles Kettering. Just to hear the exhaust sounds from a car with a new Kettering engine at idle was thrilling. But to hear a '49 Olds 88 or 98 accelerate from a standing start and see its Fisher Body rise up and appear to move forward during that initial acceleration was even more captivating.

About two years after becoming a Packard dealer, my father became a Nash dealer, and without a partner - that I knew of, at least. He purchased a building at 1644 Chicago Road (near Washington Junior High School) that had previously housed a Chevrolet agency before and during WWII. It had been owned and operated by Oscar Yanson. Across the street from it was a vacant lot about as wide and deep as the 50- by 150-foot garage.

The Nash Ambassador was truly a comfortable car, to drive and work on. With Overdrive, one could shift into third gear and accelerate a bit more before releasing foot pressure on the accelerator so the engine could return to idle. That would kick it into Overdrive (the equivalent of fourth gear). Later, when decelerating, merely depressing the clutch pedal would kick out the Overdrive. The engine had large pistons, was an overhead valve straight 6 with 7 main bearings for maximum crankshaft support. The lower priced models had smaller engines: flat L-heads that developed less power but gave excellent fuel economy. Only Nash cars had one-piece body frames that were welded together, not bolted, for strength and to avoid onset of body squeaks and rattles.

Another feature that no other car maker offered at that time was called the Weathereye. It consisted of an exterior air scoop permanently mounted in the center just ahead of the windshield, behind the hood. The Weathereye allowed a continuous flow of air into the car unless it was shut off from the inside. Fresh air passed directly over the heater coils which were warmed or not warmed by the driver's adjustment of the liquid flow to the coils of engine coolant. I do not recall our ever having had to fix a customer's Weathereye.

From riding a skinny two-wheeled bike to driving Buick Roadmasters, Chryslers, Chevys, Fords and just about any car you can name had taken only a few years, it seemed.

As September 20, 1949, rolled around, I became old enough to obtain a driver's license: 16. Dad sent me to Chicago with one of his garage men for my first driver's test. And he lent me one of the used cars on one of his lots, a gray 1947 Buick Roadmaster sedan. What a car! Had no trouble passing either the written or the driver's test. What a day to celebrate! After all, I had been driving (illegally) since I was 9.

The longest trip had been to Minnesota and back in a 1941 Ford 2-door sedan. I sat on an air-inflated, yellow plastic o-ring so as to appear taller and older, while mother and her friend, Ellen Peterson, rode along for some 1,300 miles, round trip. I was eleven or twelve at the time. Mother and Ellen seemed to think nothing of it. They talked to each other the whole way.

Driving a '32 Ford roadster hot rod that could accelerate from zero to sixty in about five and a half seconds became another source of memorable experiences. Dad had purchased it at the Dyer (Indiana) Auto Auction for $1,000, which was quite a sum, around 1949; but only a fraction of the $5,500 that was claimed as the actual cost of building it. The car had come from California, I was told. Dad acquired it to attract buyers to his Nash dealership and used car lot. I don't recall him driving it more than twice; but I did.

One of the rod's peculiarities, shall we call it, involved its steering. When accelerating, steering was normal. But, if the accelerator pedal were released abruptly, the rod tended to lose steering control. An abnormal amount of play would be introduced into the steering mechanism and a driver would wind up having to move the steering wheel quite a bit from one side to the other in order to attempt to stay on the road. Depending on the speed attained when that loss of control happened, the rod could easily wander back and forth across two to four lanes of highway.

The cure (almost) that I eventually found useful was to let up on the accelerator pedal slowly after accelerating; and to gradually ease up on the pedal when wanting to use the unwinding engine to decelerate and before applying the brakes. When using this technique, the rod still had a slight tendency to wander to the right and left, but it was manageable enough for one to be able to stay in one lane. A passing midget race car driver put it almost to the ultimate test, one day, on Governor's Highway.

Governor's was a four-lane concrete highway located a few miles west of Chicago Heights and, back then, there were only farm fields on both sides of it between Lincoln Highway and Vollmer Road. A few school buddies and I had gone out there and measured a quarter mile exactly with a tape measure and painted marks on the side of the pavement at each end. Then, one would stand beside the road at the starting point and bring down his arm as I passed by. Another, at the finish line, would use that signal to start a stop watch, turn and face across the highway and stop the watch as he observed me passing by.

The initial start-up could commence after clearing a five-way-stop at the Lincoln Highway intersection to the south. The Governor's Highway "course" then headed north northeastward and allowed about one mile for accelerating before reaching the starting line. After the measured quarter mile there was about another half mile of four-lane pavement afforded before coming to Vollmer Road, a paved asphalt two-lane country road with a stop sign. Vollmer Road crossed Governor's Highway at a slight angle and therefore required that one go a bit further and take a bit longer to cross Governor's Highway; but, being out in the country, not much traffic was usually encountered on either Governor's Highway or Vollmer Road - until the day when a midget race car driver came along pulling his racer on a trailer behind his pick-up truck. Headed south, he had pulled off of Governor's Highway and onto the grass shoulder and parked just behind the rod, near where my two buddies and I were standing. We had clocked a run, or two, around

6-7 seconds, or so, and had done the math to calculate speed: usually around 130 MPH, as I can recall it, now.

The midget driver emerged slowly from his truck and looked the car over with admiration. Who could blame him? The roadster body had some fifteen coats of light metallic maroon lacquer paint on it. The Firestone dead rubber racing tires were taller and wider in the back than the smaller and narrower ones in front. There were no fenders on the front wheels and only short, specially made fenders, covered the upper front portions of the rear wheels. There was no hood, just a radiator encased in its original grille, no fan to see, just a chromed generator hanging on one side of the engine. There were two chromed air cleaners atop two Stromberg 97 carburetors, mounted on a Weiand polished aluminum intake manifold, flanked by a pair of Weiand polished aluminum finned heads. The '48 Mercury V-8 block was bored, ported, relieved and painted red. Its underside had a chrome plated oil pan. Shiny stainless steel exhaust pipes were bent rearward, joined and connected to chromed mufflers and tail pipes. On the ends of the two tail pipes were chromed cans about three inches in diameter and some six to eight inches long. A 3/4 inch diameter chromed steel rod had been fashioned into what looked like a bumper; but it was too close to the body and almost too high to be considered much more than ornamental. A couple of tear drop shaped tail lights were also mounted on the rear body panel, with round blue lenses mounted in them that could be seen when the brakes were applied. Quite a car!

The midget driver took it all in. Then, he looked up at me and asked, "Could I drive it?" "Sure," I said, almost impulsively. The man, after all, must have been a race car driver. He was towing a midget race car. I would keep it until he returned with my rod. So, I described our "routine" and invited him to see what speed he could be clocked at. The rod's speedometer was only accurate enough to obtain approximate speeds, so we volunteered to time him.

A slight rise in the Governor's Highway pavement towards the Lincoln Highway starting point prevented us from observing his turnaround. Eventually, though, we heard him coming and saw him appear over the rise at about the same time. He was accelerating and moving right along. Since I had always been driving, this opportunity to observe from a distance was a new experience for me to enjoy. The starting "line" came and went and he quickly zoomed across the finish line, too. We turned to watch him go by and then saw something unexpected that put fright into all of us: A car had stopped and had begun to cross Governor's Highway at the Vollmer Road intersection from (our) right to left. The midget driver abruptly took his foot off the accelerator and tromped on the brakes. He had been in the inner passing lane going north, but, in a fraction of a second, the rod moved left, all the way to the edge of the 4-lane pavement. Fortunately, there was no oncoming traffic. Then, just as quickly, he drifted back all the way across four lanes to the right-hand edge of the pavement, then back to the left and right again, before gradually straightening out and moving past and beyond the car crossing Governor's on Vollmer and appeared, after that, to slow down and almost disappear on down the road.

My friends and I drew sighs of relief. Nothing like that had ever happened to us. It had been a close call.

Eventually, and I mean by that several minutes later that seemed like an hour, the midget driver returned. He coasted off the pavement and parked behind his trailer. No movement, no words. He just sat there for awhile. I looked him over and saw that his face was as white as a sheet. And it stayed white.

Slowly, then, he opened the door, got out, walked past all of us and to the cab of his truck. He got in, sat there for awhile, started it up, and slowly drove off. He uttered not a single word. To anyone. We never saw him again.

Bloom Township High School was built during the 1929 depression era. It was quite a facility. Distinctive looking - even today.

One design feature was that it had a cafeteria on the top floor with windows on opposite sides and running east and west almost the full length of the building, so one could look to the north or south from just about any table. Being some five or six stories above ground afforded some distant viewing.

It also had a basketball gymnasium with bleacher seats on both sides of the court. Original plans had called for the floor to be built so that it could part in the middle to reveal an Olympic-sized swimming pool; but there had been cuts, made necessary by the Depression.

My dad played the accordion, so I, in turn, had taken accordion lessons in the basement of a music store on Illinois Street in downtown Chicago Heights, for a year or more. Later, as a Bloom High School sophomore, I volunteered my small band to play for an after-school dance. The teachers assigned to that extra-curricular dance activity did not want us to play for the dance, claiming we didn't know and couldn't play enough numbers, we couldn't last long enough. I argued with them and won; but, boy, were they ever right! Fortunately, they had conditioned the blow by having a record player brought along with lots of records. My band and I played every tune we had rehearsed. However, when we were about out of music to play, that's when the dancers began arriving in droves. When last seen, that little portable record player on a small table on one side of the (basketball court) dance floor and hooked to the loudspeaker system, had sure come in handy.

Friday nights in the Fall brought football fans out to the portable stands to watch games under the lights. Our perennial arch-rival was Thornton High School, nearby. I had gone out for football and my big challenge had been to run the required laps around the track during after school practice sessions and then to survive what seemed like endless blocking, tackling and running to catch passes. Eventually, I decided that football was best left to others. While supportive of the team, I was quite satisfied to watch from the sidelines. But I also gave some of the players free and exciting rides in cars.

With two lots full of used cars, my dad allowed that he probably would not miss one of them if it was gone for only a day - and if, while I had it, I would fix or schedule to have fixed whatever I detected to be wrong with a car. So, the routine developed whereby I would change cars at noon every day except Sunday. Cars that I did not care for were turned in after school, and I would get another. I thought of myself as kind of a test driver.

Besides the varying handling characteristics one had to contend with when racing around the Village of Flossmoor in different cars, there also were some interesting differences in speedometer readings that I was able to detect while making timed runs on the Governor's Highway measured quarter mile strip.

Up to about 50-55 MPH, all cars seemed to register the correct speeds; but above 55-60, many fluctuations developed. Generally, Chrysler products seemed to register higher speeds than a car's actual speed when driving above 55 MPH. As I can recall now, one '48 Chrysler Town & Country 4-door station wagon (made with real wood) showed 110 MPH on the speedometer while being clocked at 78. Next and more accurate were Fords. But GM cars from Chevrolets to Cadillacs seemed fairly accurate up to 60 and then did not falsely rise as much at speeds over 60 as the others.

One of Bloom's star football players was named Billy Graham (no relation to the now famous reverend). He had two brothers, Rolla and Robert. They happened to live near my father's Nash garage. What an exciting ride we shared one morning, after I picked them up to give them a ride to school!

As we drove along Dixie Highway heading back to school, after a brief tour of nearby Flossmoor, we were in a 1947 Buick Roadmaster 4-door sedan. I approached a slightly banked 45-degree left turn at Vollmer Road on the 4-lane asphalt pavement at 55 MPH (as I can recall it, now), trusting the speedometer's accuracy. I had made that turn before at 50 MPH in cars with higher centers of gravity; so I felt that 55 in a lower slung and heavier Buick (with 4 passengers) would not be a problem.

The pavement may have been slightly wet from morning dew. About half way into the turn, the car just seemed to rise up and float into a counterclockwise spin. It happened so quickly that the car had spun a full 360 degrees and come to a rolling stop before I could react. The motor had stalled. We were still headed in the desired direction. I pushed the clutch pedal down and engaged the starter. Only a little extra time was needed before the motor was running again. I shifted it into first and off we went. The Graham brothers said nothing. Neither did I. Bloom's tall architectural tower landmark soon came into view. Back then, which was shortly after the end of WWII and when car productions had just restarted, Buick advertised that "When better cars are built, Buick will build them." I'd have to say that that 1947 Roadmaster model was already well built.

Bloom had whites and blacks and boys and girls whose immigrant parents had come from nearly every country on earth. There were only a few blacks, and I had one of them in my band. There seemed to be many Italians. The father of one of them owned and operated an Indian motorcycle franchise on East Sixteenth Street. His son, Monty, who was about my age, showed up at Bloom one day riding a new Indian motorcycle. It appeared smaller than previously known Indian motorcycles, but it certainly was faster. On a street in front of the school, we watched him do wheelies in several gears from a standing start as he merely depressed a foot pedal to shift into a higher gear. Awesome!

So, one day, at about high noon, Monty and I happened to meet beside Bloom High School. He was on his Indian, I was in the rod. The sun shone brightly overhead. We were side by side and headed away from school in the northbound lanes of Dixie Highway, rolling along slowly at little more than a walking pace so Monty could keep his balance on the bike. We had wondered about the comparative speeds, but neither of us could say for sure one way or the other, so we were going to find out for ourselves. There was no other traffic. I counted aloud for a start and then Monty's front wheel rose a foot or more from the concrete pavement right beside me, as I, too, squealed ahead. Then, Monty's bike did another wheelie, then another and another. His front wheel rose only about six inches off the pavement at the higher speeds, but he was still doing wheelies! We stayed about even, with only slight relative movement, about six inches, back and forth. Monty merely depressed a pedal to shift gears, but I had to coordinate clutch, throttle, and gear shifting so as to be able to accelerate as fast as possible and minimize loss of acceleration momentum.

As we approached 60 MPH, the rod was just beginning to move out in third (high) gear. Monty was still beside me, but, then, very suddenly, he dropped back and away. It was as if he had applied the brakes. In our debriefing, it was agreed that Monty's Indian had merely run out of gears. His bike was long on acceleration but short on high speed.

It can be added here that most, if not all, motorcycles, back then, including Harley-Davidsons and full-sized Indians, required riders to depress clutch pedals before moving shift knobs from gear to gear. Therefore, we found it easy to view Monty's new bike as revolutionary in that regard. And fast, too.

There were homework assignments at Bloom, but I usually came home, put all of the books I was carrying from school on a table beside the back door; and I would pick them up again on the way out in the morning. My dear mother, after a time, would station herself at the door as I left and ask, as I picked up the books, "Have you studied and done your homework?" I would answer with something like, "It's easy. I'll get it in class." Awhile after that, I found her greeting me at the door as I came home from school. She would ask me to "Please do your homework before you go out." I would find some excuse not to and leave. Again, in the morning, I would pick up the books while en route to school.

My mother had come from Sweden where education was (and is) considered important and valuable. So had my father, for that matter, but he was not as outspoken about education. There were times, however, when my parents and other Swedish immigrant family friends would try to impress upon me the importance of getting an education by repeating, "They can take anything and everything away from you, but not your education. That is something that will stay with you forever." There may be more truth to that than we realize.

Down the street from where we lived was a Ford dealer named C.W. John. My father seemed to be having some sort of discussions with Mr. C.W. John that I eventually deduced as having to do with getting me to attend the Culver Military Academy in Culver, Indiana. Mr. John also had a son, and his son was already a cadet at Culver. In time, my father was recruited and so was I.

The 85-mile drive to Culver was uninspiring on one of the Midwest's classic cold, cloudy, winter days. The tests took a long time to complete. I learned, later, that I had not really met the school's minimum academic standards. It was felt, however, that I was capable of improving - sufficiently to be allowed entrance to Culver as a Second Classman (high school junior). I would first have to complete sophomore year at Bloom, however.

Leaving the rod behind was made easier by my father promising not to sell it while I was gone. He parked it in the showroom with even its clear plastic hood strapped on to cover the engine. Dad's business was good. Very good, in fact. After the war, new cars were in great demand and the supply was limited. Used cars sold well, too.

Dad and I had worked out an arrangement whereby I would attend the Dyer Auto Auction with him, pick out a car that I wanted, and he would buy it for me. I was too young and not officially a dealer as far as the Auction house was concerned. Then, I would later pay my dad for the car, fix it up, and leave it on one of his lots to be sold. People were interested in selling their older cars and buying newer ones. Mine sold quickly. I was glad and grateful because I was limited to having only one car at a time. As a young man still in high school and without a bank account, I wound up carrying a lot of cash around in my pocket. One day, that would help me post bond and avoid being arrested for speeding in the rod.

The Village of Flossmoor had a small population of around 2,500 people, but they lived in beautiful custom-built homes with expansive yards, usually. So the geographic area covered by the village was larger than what one might think would be necessary for such a small population. Many of my friends lived there and had their own cars, or access to some pretty fancy ones owned by their parents.

Buddy Lederer had a dark blue 7-passenger Buick limo. I think it was a 1941 model. His family also had a new Kaiser and a new Fraser. But the most impressive car of all that I can remember from those days was a black 1948 Cadillac Fleetwood sedan that was driven by Barry Freeman and owned by his father, an attorney for, among others, the singer, Vic Damone. That Cadillac had soft, fragrant, genuine black leather seats that smoothed the ride that was already made smooth by a heavy, low slung, Cadillac chassis fitted with a Fisher Body.

Down Western Avenue and at Vollmer Road lived another friend, Michael Hammond. Mike attended Morgan Park Military Academy, but, when he was home, he had access to three cars, a Willys Jeep station wagon, a '49 Ford convertible and his father's gray '48 Cadillac sedan with a telephone in it. (Not much to brag about now, but it sure was unusual to have one then.) Mike's father was the CEO of Whiting Steel in nearby Harvey, Illinois, and thus needed the phone for business.

With all of these and other friends and their cars, it had become almost natural to race one another around the village, after school. Since they usually had to drive the same car every day, I could often detect differences in the various cars I drove from one day to the next. I don't remember ever seeing any small children out playing in their yards, so from that perspective I suppose you could say we were safe. But I did, at the time, and still do feel remorse for disturbing the neighborhoods with sounds of squealing tires as we rounded many corners.

One afternoon, I was alone and driving the rod east on Flossmoor Road from the village shopping center and train station. I stopped for a red light at Western Avenue. When the light turned green, I made a right turn onto Western to head south and began slowly accelerating up to the speed limit, around 40 MPH. After clearing the intersection, I glanced up into the rear view mirror and noticed that behind a group of bushes on the far northeast corner of that intersection a police car had been hiding. Mostly I could see the light on its roof, but it was parked about two car lengths east from the edge of Western Avenue and was faced perpendicular to it. I continued watching. After a few moments, it slowly began to move towards Western Avenue. I had done nothing wrong, but it looked like it was going to follow me. Police hiding behind bushes seemed wrong to me, but I also thought it would be hard to prove him wrong. In an instant, I decided if he can be wrong, so can I!

My foot tromped down on the accelerator impulsively, in third gear, yet! I soon passed the Flossmoor Country Club entrance at over 100 MPH. A glance in the mirror told me the squad car had been left way back there; but he had activated his flashing red light and was making an effort to chase me.

After going down and up again in a prolonged dip in the road, I was approaching Vollmer when the pursuing squad car had just disappeared from view at the start of the dip.

He couldn't see me as I slowed and carefully negotiated a right turn onto Vollmer Road and accelerated back up to speed. It may have taken him a few extra moments to stop and try to determine if I had turned right or left on Vollmer, perhaps trying to hear the roar from my exhaust or tire squeals.

By about that time, I had made another left turn on the other side of the Illinois Central Railroad embankment which gave me some shielding, accelerated up to around 70-80, and cut the engine to begin coasting. There would be no more sounds for him to detect.

After coasting all the way to Lincoln Highway, I restarted the rod and drove back to my father's dealership, some 4-5 miles, at normal, to below normal, speeds. After parking and getting out of the rod, I approached the front office where my father came out to speak with me. He sort of ambled up to walk along next to me and we then stopped and turned to almost face each other squarely. "I've just had a phone call," he said, "from the Chief of Police in Flossmoor. They recognized the car but didn't know who was driving it."

"I was driving it," I responded. "What should I do?"

"Well, you'd better go over there and straighten it out," he said.

"O.K.," I said. But I took a "regular" car.

The Flossmoor Police Chief looked somewhat surprised when I arrived. He showed no animosity towards me. Perhaps he had not been driving the squad car in pursuit of a little hot rod earlier in the day, or perhaps he was surprised by my timely appearance or by my appearing at all. In any case, he asked me to sit down beside his desk and proceeded to ask me a few pertinent questions, which I willingly and truthfully answered. Then came the decision as what to do with me. I was given a future court date and time and told that bail would be $350 until then. (It may have been $450; but I know it was at least $350.)

As I said earlier, for lack of a bank account, I carried fairly large sums of money. By the Police Chief's reactions, he was taken completely by surprise when I reached into one of my pockets, pulled out a wad of money, and proceeded to count out the necessary amount for bail. But I also want to add that my impression all along after meeting him was that the Chief respected me. I never once felt that he wanted to do me any harm. If anything, I sensed that he held me in some kind of awe.

My father then clued me in on another lesson, once I had returned and related to him what had happened. I wanted his estimate as to how much the fine might eventually be. His answer: At least as much as you just gave them. They know they can fine you that amount because they already have it. That's why it pays to try for the lowest bail possible. Hmmm. Sure enough. In due course, he was proven correct. I do not recall the Court appearance, but I must have honored it. I do not recall getting any money back, nor having to pay more. The policeman may have been wrong for stalking, but I had also been wrong for driving too fast. Fortunately, no one was involved in an accident of any kind. Still, to use the vernacular, two wrongs hadn't made a right.

CHAPTER 4

A-TENN-HUT!

S tanding outside at attention, in rain, snow, daylight and darkness, was definitely a new way to function. We mustered outside in formations for breakfast, noon meal and evening meal before marching to the Mess Hall. The food was good. Menus were prepared by a nutritionist charged with feeding some 650 young males all of the nutrients their growing bodies and minds could need.

On Wednesdays and Sundays, we drilled and marched on Culver's parade grounds. While cadets assigned to the Infantry marched on Sundays, others in the Cavalry rode horses, drove and rode in tanks, and still others in the Artillery manned trucks that pulled 105 mm howitzers. Cadets in the marching Band, of course, played their instruments so members of the Infantry could march in step and they also played for everyone else to hear.

Parents often came and watched our Sunday parades from the grandstand in front of a huge riding hall. The hall was large enough for indoor polo games and more. In inclement weather, parades were often held inside that hall. Parents and other visitors could observe from bleachers high up on the north side.

The Academy is located beside Lake Maxinkuckee, one of the deepest lakes in Indiana. Its waters can feel cold, especially in the Spring, if one falls out of a crew shell after catching a crab with an oar. Of all people for that to happen to, one of the Benson brothers from Alaska didn't rotate his long oar and get it up and out of the water in time. The other seven of us pulled on our oars at decent boat speed and Benson was quickly pushed (by his oar) off his seat and over the side into Lake Maxinkuckee. Fortunately, he was not struck by any of the oar lock extensions protruding out from the sides of the boat. They passed over him. The crew coach, Colonel Roberts, saw what had happened from his speedboat nearby and proceeded to the rescue. Benson was taken promptly to the Academy hospital where he remained for over a week, as I recall. We kidded Benson that since he was from Alaska, we expected him to be conditioned to cold water. But he wasn't, any more than the rest of us were.

Eventually, we became qualified enough to take on the University of Wisconsin sophomores on a lake within sight of Madison. I can easily recall the big waves and high winds, on that race day. We started well and stayed one or two boat lengths ahead for almost the entire one-mile course. Catching a crab was easy, in those conditions. If any one of us failed to get our oar up, out and swung around for another stroke, the boat would practically stop dead in the water before we could get it going again. Avoiding that kind of error allowed us to stay out in front for most of the race. However, we had trained for standard high school half-mile races. Doing a whole (college) mile and in those conditions began to take its toll when we neared the finish line. With only about five boat lengths to go, the Wisconsin team got moving and had pulled ahead of us by almost two boat lengths when we, ourselves, crossed the finish line. Col. Roberts took his Culver crew out for a steak dinner at one of Madison's best restaurants, that evening, at his own expense, it was rumored. We felt like staying and racing them again, after that.

The Academy is adjacent to the town of Culver, truly out in the country. Two thoughts came to mind after I had entered and commenced formal training as a cadet, followed by a third. I shared the third thought with a few friends: "Whoever wants to go AWOL tonight, meet me at the Logansport gate at 8:30." Several of us met under the lights and were on the verge of walking out and becoming absent without leave. We had no plan except to leave. Then, as I came to within a foot or two of passing between the pillars, a question struck me. I asked aloud, "Will my father still have to pay my tuition if I leave?" "Yes," someone answered, emphatically, "I know for sure he'll still have to pay for the whole year." "Well," I thought aloud, "I can't do that to my father. I'm going back." All of us went back. I remain sincerely grateful to this day to whoever it was who had the right answer that night. "The gem cannot be polished without friction, nor man perfected without trials," according to a Chinese proverb. According to Helen Keller, "Character cannot be developed in ease and quiet. Only through the experience of trial and suffering can the soul be strengthened, vision cleared, ambition inspired, and success achieved." Aristotle? He offered, "I count him braver who overcomes his desires than him who conquers his enemies; for the hardest victory is over self."

As for the other two thoughts, let's just call them observations. The first was: No cadet at Culver was allowed to have a car; the second: At night, each of us had homework to do and we had to be quiet and in our rooms to do it from about 8 to 10 PM.

Punishments resulted from being placed "On Report" by upper classmen, usually. Demerits were assigned (and kept track of). Extra Duty involved marching back and forth or around a triangle area and carrying an M-1 rifle for whatever number of hours serving out the punishment required. Extra Duty marches took place when others went out for afternoon intramural athletics or on Saturday afternoons when one could otherwise be at the movies in a little theater in town or doing something else more productive. I had my share of demerits and then some. I was even demoted and later reinstated before graduation.

During First Class (senior) year, I had been promoted to the rank of Lance Corporal, the highest rank I could attain in the Cadet Corps by attending Culver for only two of its four-year curriculum. Also, I had been placed in charge of holding room inspections on my hallway in the mornings just before breakfast formations. Rooms and lockers had to be squared away; beds made; and M-1 rifles field stripped with the rifle parts cleaned and displayed atop the tightened bed blankets once or twice a week.

One morning, as I was inspecting his room, a cadet started muttering aloud enough for me to hear some challenging words that were disrespectful and insulting, not just to me personally, but to the inspection routine. And he kept it up, after I tried to just ignore him. After many wrestling team victories and weight lifting sessions, I found it easy to grab him by the shirt and necktie knot with one hand and to lift him up against the wall beside the door in his room. He STILL gave me lip. So, I slapped both sides of his face several times with the other hand. That changed his attitude completely and immediately. He began to cry. He was going to report me, he said, sobbing. And so he did.

Colonel Benson soon called for me to appear before him and I told him what had happened. He understood my actions, but I should have limited them to only putting that cadet on report for insubordination/disrespect, etc. The Colonel had to demote me because physical force used like that was also a violation of rules and regulations. I respected Colonel Benson and so that was that. Besides, what else could I do?

The American Bar Association published a book in the 1950s that was filled with contributions from previous ABA presidents and members. One of them offered that our system of laws and justice here in the U.S. is tolerated mainly because we are allowed to appeal court decisions to higher courts, and, ultimately, to the Supreme Court. Indeed, I tend to agree. Fortunately, or unfortunately, miscarriages of justice can occur in the military; but appeals are usually improbable unless a court-martial is involved.

There were few to no distractions at Culver. I could complain to myself about having to do "homework," but I would also have to reason that everyone else had their homework to do, too. So, it wasn't like I was being singled out. One wasn't behind or being punished with homework. Also, we needed to do our homework because occasionally a test could be expected on it at the start of the very next classroom session. Only after test answers had been collected would teachers then answer any and all questions on a previous night's homework.

Our classes were small, sometimes only 8 to 10 cadets per class. Teachers would go to extraordinary lengths, at times, to find answers to just about any question a cadet might ask. On any subject.

Fifty years after graduating, we learned more about our various activities in life after Culver. One of my roommates, Donald Eichstaedt, among other things, directed the design, building, testing and service support (for 14 years) of the 1972 Lincoln presidential limousine used by Presidents Nixon, Ford,

Carter and Reagan. That limousine was credited with helping to save Reagan's life during the assassination attempt in
1981.

Another roommate of mine was Jose Alfredo Tabush from
Guatemala City, Guatemala. "Freddie" had never touched
snow in his life until one day when it snowed at Culver, Fred
took one fast look at it from our second-floor window and ran
down and out onto the lawn that was covered by about an inch
of wet snow. He dove onto the ground and rolled over several times in the snow wearing only his pants, a cotton long
sleeved shirt and tie. No coat. Twenty some years after graduation, I tried to contact him, only to learn he had been killed
in the crash of a private plane in New York State in April 1961.
I had liked cheerful and optimistic "Freddie" Tabush. He was
smart, too. Here's an example:

Teardrop-like cars were being designed, built and raced
on the Utah Salt Flats at that time. One of them had literally become airborne and rolled over in high speed flight.
I subscribed to a car magazine and showed Freddie a side view
picture of the car taken before it crashed. He immediately di-
agnosed the problem and then showed me the reason why that
car could not remain on the Flats at high speeds. He reached
for a ruler and pencil. Then he drew a line from the very front
edge of the wing-like car body to the farthest part of the car
body at the rear. From front to rear, that line sloped downward.
Therefore, Freddie explained, that up angle caused the car to
want to fly. Had that line from front to back been horizontal
or slightly up in back, the car would have inherently wanted
to stay on the Salt Flats. It is easily explained and understood
with conventional wisdom today, but, back then, I considered
it a reflection of Freddie's intelligence and practical common
sense that he could figure that out. And so quickly!

Culver has an impressive and memorable walk through the Iron Gate ritual to conclude graduation ceremonies. Fifty years later, I was honored (alive and able) to pass through the Iron Gate again in a new protocol that was introduced in 2000. What it did for me, mostly, was raise my awareness of how quickly 50 years had gone by; and that 50 years HAD gone by! It brought to mind what my mother had said before she passed away (at age 83). We were celebrating her 76th birthday when she turned to me and said, as if almost stunned, "I didn't realize so much time had passed! Has it been 76 years already?" How short human lifespans truly are, in terms of the universe. But, to many, 76 orbits around the Sun can seem like a long time, too.

Before joining the Navy, at my own expense I took a few flying lessons at what was named Governor's Park Airport. You guessed it. It was located adjacent to Governor's Highway, but several miles south of the measured quarter mile. Eventually, I would become a Naval Aviator. The Navy didn't train pilots, it trained Naval Aviators. I wanted to prepare myself for Navy Flight Training but not overdo it, so I would not have to undo any bad habits.

My instructor had gained a little experience in WWII, shall we say, and had two sons who were crop duster pilots. His only fault as far as I was concerned was that he couldn't keep a fire going in his cigar for very long, having to persistently re-light it. His cigar also became a motivator for me to pay attention and to fly solo as soon as possible.

Today, however, if I were a cadet and flight training were available, I would want to learn to fly under the direction of experienced, FAA-certified instructors at Fleet Field, Culver's private airport. Culver is the only high school in the country with its own airport. That was not an option available to me, but I have since landed and taken off from Fleet Field in my corporate Beech Bonanza. The main runway is paved. They have a hanger and classrooms. Excellent facilities.

The same room as Don Eichstaedt and I shared at Culver during our first year there was occupied by a young cadet from Taiwan, when I returned "50 years later." I met the young lad and enjoyed watching his reactions when he learned I had once lived in his room. He was even more surprised, I think, when I told him about having served aboard a Navy Destroyer in the Formosa Straits in the 1950s. What had been our mission, he wondered, his eyes opened wide. I told him about discovering a sunken burned out wooden hull of a Chinese junk floating just beneath the surface and in the middle of the Straits. Also, we patrolled and were alert for any possible invasion of Formosa (Taiwan, now) by a massing of Chinese junks along the mainland coastline. All of that had occurred long before he was born, but he seemed seriously concerned and interested. It must be challenging for him to live in Taiwan and not know if or when mainland China might eventually decide to claim it as its own.

Kaohsiung (pronounced cow-shung) Formosa, in early 1957, had air raid sirens and loud speakers mounted high up on posts and buildings all around the city that were activated at eight o'clock every morning. The national anthem could even be heard aboard our ship anchored way out in the harbor. A fighter jet would simulate attacks on the city. If we took the time to look, we could observe anti-aircraft guns on various rooftops tracking the jet through each of its attack runs.

Most striking, during a trip ashore, one day, was seeing a light green 1955 Buick Special 4-door sedan with an ivory colored top. It was parked in an open area that was unpaved and dark brown to black so the car's bright colors made it stand out dramatically. That car was even considered new in the U.S., at that time, and probably sold new for about $2,500 in the U.S. I asked someone who was familiar with internal Formosa affairs how much that Buick might cost to license for a year. Not many cars could be seen in all of Formosa at that time. There were not many roads on which to drive them, either. So the license fee was intentionally restrictive: about $1,345/year for that Buick, I was told.

On reflection, now, it tells quite a story about what I thought was an old room at Culver when I first lived in it in 1949-50. It may have been old then (and is even older today), but it was well built, certainly. And then for me to travel half way around the world and back and to return to it some 50 years later and find another young cadet living in it who came to it from that same country half way around the Earth that I had visited and helped defend, well, it was an unusual surprise and discovery for both of us, I think. It was a pleasant realization of how citizens of the world can relate to one another, given opportunities. What might another 50 years bring?

Two grandsons of the R.J. Reynolds tobacco founder, Richard "Josh" Reynolds III and his younger brother, Patrick, were to graduate one year or more after I did.

Unfortunately, "Josh," the likeable intramural boxer would succumb at age 60 to emphysema and congestive heart failure caused by smoking.

Patrick has offered that his grandfather, the company's founder, died in 1918 of cancer that may have been caused by chewing tobacco. His father, R.J. Reynolds Jr., died of emphysema, as did "Josh." Two other brothers live quiet lives with their families and support Patrick's efforts to discourage smoking.

Even after watching his father die, Patrick started smoking at age 19; and it took him 17 years to quit. Most smokers, according to Patrick, start by age 14 and are hooked by age 19. "Almost nobody starts smoking after age 19. The tobacco companies know this." While it is normal for teen-agers to want to break away from their parents during their transition from childhood to adulthood, Patrick advises his young audiences that it is "not appropriate, not cool to put a cigarette into your mouth."

Patrick sold all of his stock in the R.J. Reynolds Company in 1979 and, to his credit, has continued making public appearances to speak out against smoking: "My grandfather and my dad didn't know their own product would cause people to die an entirely preventable death. When my grandfather started the tobacco company, he had no idea smoking would kill hundreds of millions of people around the world. Now it's important to me to tell you the truth and get you ... not to smoke."

Weekends at Culver had invited an assortment of people and cars; but graduation ceremonies brought all of them together at once, it seemed. Moments before or after the ceremonies, I can't remember exactly when, now, but one of my classmates, Chuck Norris, I believe, coaxed me out to the boathouse parking lot. There, stood a huge black Lincoln roadster (of 1920s era) with the top down that looked like it was practically showroom new. A 2-seater with the rumble seat closed down in back, it had the large diameter wooden spoke wheels. What a car! Chuck was shorter than I, but that was not going to stop him from driving his "new car." Quite a graduation present! Perhaps he still has it.

Another unusual car parked nearby was a shiny new (1951) light tan Cadillac limousine with a long chromed air horn (usually reserved for trucks) mounted on each side of the hood. The family in that limo, I believe, owned the company that made the air horns.

Actor Dick Powell and his wife, June Allyson, were present. June Allyson's brother, Art Peters, was also graduating. He had been in the Infantry for four years while I was in the Artillery for only two. So we really did not have much chance to meet until at our 50th Reunion.

After saying good bye to Freddie Tabush (for the last time, as it turned out), aside from having actually graduated from the renowned Culver Military Academy, to my surprise and delight also was the reappearance of a certain '32 Ford roadster I had come to know. It was mighty but small amongst the many "big" luxury cars clogging the roadways on and off the Academy grounds, on that memorable graduation day.

Eventually, I was following behind my parents' car en route back to Chicago Heights. When about half way there, I passed them doing a bit over 100 mph while they cruised along at about 65. My father saw me coming and must have said something to my mother. I heard her scream through the open windows as I passed them. She may have been expressing both fear and joy. I was coming home to help run the business and, eventually, take it over, I thought. And I truly felt adequately schooled - for life.

CHAPTER 5

HIGH SCHOOLS WERE EASIER

The hot rod became less important to me as I assumed responsibilities in my father's Nash dealership and used car lot organization. The rod was parked in the showroom and sort of left there to gather dust.

There were two mechanics and a parts man placed in my charge as the new Service Manager. I tried to keep all customers and those workmen happy and satisfied. Also, salesmen and office workers were scattered about who answered mostly to my father. I washed a few cars, if necessary now and then, using a unique wash rack that had come with the garage. It consisted of raised concrete around its perimeter that sloped down to a large cast iron grate placed over a drain in the center, over which a car being washed was parked. Unless the drain was plugged, which happened only occasionally, a car washer could avoid having to stand in water.

During that summer of 1951, a customer from nearby Flossmoor handed me a fairly large booklet, published by The International Harvester Company, his employer. He chiefly wanted me to read about the importance of people in any organization. While I understood and agreed with his point of view and was grateful for his attention and the gift of a book, I felt drawn more towards trying to understand science and engineering and I wanted to help create some of the "things" I felt we were still in need of, at that time. Getting a patent or two in the process was also inspiring. Even my grandfather, Otto Arvidsson, when he had visited us from Sweden after WWII had said several times, "Get a patent and live on the royalties for the rest of your life!"

Americans are often accused of being materialistic. My reaction to that is to say experience has revealed to me that one can become less "materialistic" after acquiring sufficient "materials" with which to work and live comfortably. That's how it seems to have worked out for me, at any rate.

The cheerful International Harvester man returned several times and, each time, while waiting for his car, he would seek me out and mention again the importance of people and knowing how to manage them effectively. I was the Service Manager and every man working in that garage was 20-40 years older than I and obligated to follow my lead. The IH book had organizational charts applicable to very large organizations, I thought. What I faced and was having to deal with successfully on a daily basis was a small organization consisting of older men who can resent a younger man trying to lead them - particularly when the younger man in charge is related to the business owner. One must earn respect, and I tried very hard to do just that.

Dairy Queen was relatively new, back then, and one had just been opened near our apartment building. On a summer evening, as I stood at the end of a long line that curved around from the front window counter, under yellow (bug detracting) fluorescent lights, a new, black, 4-door Cadillac sedan with its headlights on swung around and parked almost beside me. A short, stocky, well-dressed (in a suit), black man got out and stood in line behind me. His well-dressed wife in the front seat and two well-dressed children in the back seat were also illuminated in yellow light. Soon, we struck up a conversation. He was a lawyer. That was his family. He was likeable and offered me some advice concerning the treatment of blacks that I can still recall: Don't bother trying to help them, he said. For, no matter how much help you give them, there are some (negroes) who just will not work to improve themselves. Both you and they will be better off if they are left alone. Interesting, I thought, but I still found (and still find) myself motivated to try to help the underdog, almost any underdog, black, white, or whatever.

As Labor Day approached, I could sense being left out of the usual school start-ups. So, I applied myself even more to doing a good job as a Nash garage Service Manager.

Then one day, a customer drove in for some regular service. It was a few minutes after 12 o'clock noon when I finished writing up a work order. The mechanics and parts man had already "knocked off" for lunch. But, considering myself always on duty, I would forgo lunch completely if necessary, particularly if I could help a customer.

"Can I drive you to your office?" I then asked.

"Sure," he answered. "Why don't you drive," he suggested, as we approached his car.

So I got in behind the wheel and headed north on Chicago Road. Until then, I had had no reason to doubt that I had had an adequate to superior education. Friends at the Swedish Evangelical Mission Covenant Church that my parents (and I) attended with devotion and with an almost flawless attendance record (for over thirteen years) had asked if I ever intended to go to college. I had answered, "No. I believe Culver gave me as much of an education as I'll ever need. More than enough, in fact."

Well, about a quarter of a mile down Chicago Road, the light turned red at 16th Street, beside the ice cream parlor, down the hill from the Washington Junior High School auditorium. As we sat there for a few moments waiting for a green light, the customer spoke briefly about some of his engineering office activities. He used terms that were obviously common to him; but new to me. For the first time since graduating from Culver, I heard words and phrases that I could not recall ever having heard before. He expressed himself easily. I could follow the gist of his comments; but he used words and phrases that I had no previous knowledge of, lots of them; too many, in fact! As that traffic light changed to green, and as I gradually applied pressure on the accelerator, I realized that I needed and wanted to go back to school. I wanted to learn what I had not already learned; and I was aware that the longer I waited, the harder it would become to do it. I would have to attend college as soon as possible, I told myself. (I remain indebted to that gentleman to this day.)

My father's reaction, upon hearing of my interest in going to college was, "Okay. See what you can do." He said nothing more. But I took his OK to also mean that I could be relieved of my duties as his Service Manager.

Having graduated from Culver meant a lot to college entrance examiners. I somehow contacted the University of Illinois at Navy Pier in Chicago and was invited to go there and enroll.

Navy Pier has since been modified and improved; but I recall sitting in a school chair with that sort of desk pad on the right side, to fill out forms. I had been left alone in a classroom that was, shall we say, "original," very old and abused. It was positioned over the waters of Lake Michigan on the south side of Navy Pier's center line but not very far from the shoreline entrance. That classroom had been white washed from the bottom of its wooden walls to the beams in the ceiling. There was a blackboard along one wall. The floor was uneven, made of wood that had long since lost its varnish and probably had been warped by frequent rains entering through the open or broken dormer type windows on the roof ceiling above, the only windows in the room. It was a cloudy day and no lights had been turned on, so there wasn't much light for reading and filling out forms. But what mattered most, I thought, would be the knowledge I could acquire from professors, textbooks and presentations. Welcome to IU at Navy Pier! I wanted to get as much of an education as I could afford, expecting that I would have to pay my own way through college. The fee for IU Navy Pier had seemed reasonable and affordable. The threat of not finding a parking place close to the school and of having to drive back and forth a good distance from Chicago Heights every day, however, lurked in the back of my mind. But not for long.

Until that time, Dad had furnished me with a new Nash Rambler 2-door sedan to commute with; but I expected to have to commute via the Illinois Central (IC) Railroad, eventually, and walk several miles a day to and from stations. Driving and parking and even commuting by IC were not to become problems, however.

Dinner in the kitchen of our apartment with my parents had barely started, after my first day of filling out forms at Navy Pier. My father looked over at me and said, "You're really serious about wanting to go to college, aren't you."

"Yes, I am," I answered.

"Well," he continued, "I may not know much and I may be just an immigrant, but I learned a long time ago that if you're going to go to college, you should go to a good one and preferably one that is well known. Do you think you could get yourself into Northwestern?"

"I might," I replied. "But I can't afford it."

"I'll pay for it (he paused) if you can get in."

Although I had not checked it out first hand, I had previously surmised when I considered college options on my own that tuition at Northwestern University in Evanston was more than anything I, personally, could afford. So, Dad's offer was recognized immediately for what it was worth financially and I was truly appreciative. So, I promptly said, "Thank you. I'll see what I can do."

Northwestern had fraternities and sororities and dormitories, too. And I had a car. Again, having graduated from Culver seemed to delight entrance examiners. Having financial means probably didn't hurt much, either. I was promptly accepted into the graduating Class of 1955. Pledge Week was nearly over. I was encouraged to look around, introduce myself and find a fraternity that would have me if I wanted one, but as soon as possible. I could live in a dormitory, in the meantime, or for the whole year. That was up to me.

Actually, since I knew nothing about fraternities, their identities, letters, logos, histories, all Greek to me, I was seriously considering moving permanently into a dormitory when I happened to meet a sophomore named Larry Attebury. Larry became very helpful, even taking me to have dinner one evening with his family in their home in nearby Kenilworth. He belonged to one of the fraternities (Theta Psi, I believe) and wanted to help me become a fraternity brother. I was grateful and then able to focus more on Northwestern's campus, its facilities, courses and professors.

Culver's buildings had been separated from each other; but those at Northwestern seemed to have even wider expanses of lawns between them. In turn, there were many students walking hither and yon, and they all seemed to be dressed differently. They weren't wearing uniforms, that was for certain. And they weren't walking very fast or with much determination, either, I thought. I wasn't immediately aware of it, but, subconsciously, I began to lose patience with how much time everyone seemed to be wasting. An unfair evaluation, perhaps, when school had not yet officially begun. But, it really bothered me to see so many couples walking around, holding hands and holding on to each other. Had they come for romance, to learn something, or what? Did they not realize how expensive it was to be here? Nice campus, otherwise, I thought; but another unsettling event was in store that surprised even me.

There was an auditorium filled with noisy students and one professor on stage at a lectern. It was to be the first and last class I attended at Northwestern University. I can't recall the subject matter. What I can recall, however, is instantly disliking the lecturer. I saw him as egotistical and seeming not to care whether his audience paid attention to him, or not. He read from his prepared text, which can be justified, but he did so without any apparent concern for whether or not his audience could hear or understand him. His conduct implied that it was up to students in the audience to "get it." If they didn't "get it" by listening to him read, they could "get it" by reading their own texts. In fact, he may have said that. He struck me as having no desire to appeal for the attentions of his student audience, not even a little. Should I copy that?

After that "lecture," I concluded that I had not benefited from it. Further, right or wrong, I could not imagine needing to hang around for any more of them - certainly not at any great expense.

Promptly, I made my way to the Dean's Office, I think it was. He seemed interested and decent. Once I was seated beside his desk, he gently asked me, "What's on your mind?"

"If I were to leave Northwestern right now, would my father have to pay for the whole year?" I asked him.

"No," was his answer. "He wouldn't have to pay anything, since you've only been here barely a week."

"Good!" I announced. "I'm leaving."

"Wait," he replied. "But why? You must give me a reason for leaving. I can't release you without one."

As much as I tried to avoid having to declare what was on my mind, at that time, there was to be no permission granted for me to leave without my declaring a reason. So, when that finally became sufficiently clear to me, I confessed to having concluded that it would be a waste of my time and the university's if I were to spend four years there "going downhill."

Enough! I was immediately allowed to leave. In fact, you could say I was promptly ushered out of the office.

So, I returned to being a Nash garage Service Manager. At least I had a job.

My father, when I was growing up, had hinted, now and then when we were among friends, that he was grooming me to someday take over his business, so he and mother could retire. As I was returning home from Northwestern, the thought arose in the back of my mind that, perhaps, it was meant to be that I should now try to develop beyond being a Service Manager into handling new and used car sales and the whole dealership. My father was still fairly young, I thought, and probably not yet ready to retire; but I could give it a try.

A month or so later, I began to feel imprisoned. No one was to be blamed but me. It was as if I had been transformed into becoming an unthinking, uninspired, robot. I went about my job as Service Manager with an eye towards relieving dad of the entire dealership. Whenever that thought came to mind, however, I instantly sensed being too young for it. My dad, too, was too young to retire.

We went to church on Sunday mornings, usually returning home shortly after 12 o'clock noon. One Sunday, we pulled into our driveway and stopped, to let mother out so she could unlock and enter through the front door. I was driving dad's new, black Nash Ambassador 4-door sedan. After mother had gotten out, dad and I proceeded back and made a left turn onto our backyard parking spot. Dad would usually have his passenger side door opened before I could bring the car to a complete stop; but not on this particular day. He just sat there, staring straight ahead. So, I, too, sat quietly.

After some silence, he asked this question: "I don't know for sure if I can do it, but if I could get you an appointment to West Point, would you go?"

Now came my turn to be silent. After digesting the surprise, I reasoned that I knew how tough it would be, since I had endured Plebe Year at Culver, whose routine was advertised as having been patterned after West Point's. But, I also knew from experience that a civilian college or university was not to my liking, either. So, if I was serious about wanting a college education, I decided the answer would have to be: "Yes."

Nothing more was said. We immediately opened the car doors, walked to the base of the backyard stairs, climbed them, entered our apartment through the kitchen and proceeded to enjoy more of Sunday and some lunch, after mother prepared it.

Not long after that, dad suggested that I could help my chances of getting an appointment to West Point by meeting the wife of a local doctor and making a good impression.

She was a senior citizen, in her 80's, perhaps, and had been active in Republican politics for many years. What a delightful person! And talkative! After we had conversed for awhile, she "announced" to me that United States Senator Everett Dirksen was coming to attend a function nearby and she wanted to bring me along so she could introduce me to him and make an appeal on my behalf for an appointment to West Point.

When that time came, I was brought before the Senator and introduced. It may have been on a gymnasium floor, somewhere, as I can recall it. He had a twinkle in his eye, white hair, and extended a soft little hand that I firmly grasped and shook. Little did I know how frequently that hand might have had to endure being squeezed and how sore it might therefore have become. But Senator Dirksen showed no sign of pain or annoyance. He was gracious and calmly explained to my faithful Republican advocate and me that my name should be submitted to his office. I would then be tested and entered into competition with others for an appointment. Sounded fair to me. In due course, I proceeded to Chicago's Main Post Office, downtown, and joined others in taking the required tests. The room used for testing reminded me a lot of Navy Pier.

Meanwhile, dad soon came along with yet another opportunity. One day he asked me to go with him to Chicago. He wanted me to meet a man there who might help with getting an appointment to West Point. "Look presentable," he suggested, "to make a good impression."

So, we proceeded to an office somewhere on North Wells Street in Chicago. I met the man, answered a few questions, and that seemed to be that.

The cold and snow of Winter arrived. Loved to drive. Who doesn't? But an icy road almost killed me, one Sunday afternoon, while I waited for word about an appointment.

Along about late Fall in 1951-52, I went for a drive in the country in a yellow (bottom) and medium brown (top) two-door Nash Rambler that I had been driving for awhile. It was new when I got it from my dad on loan to drive as a fringe benefit, I guess, for my having taken on the job of being the Service Manager in his Nash dealership. I don't recall having been placed on the company's payroll. On that cold but clear Sunday afternoon with about 12 inches of snow everywhere on the ground except on the roads which were essentially cleared and dry, I ventured westward towards Joliet. On that particular day, I also mimicked a well known (at the time) masculine, male, movie actor by smoking a small stogie. It didn't take long before I had to give up on the stogie.

After driving for an hour, or so, I turned around and headed back home, eastward, on a dry concrete-paved country road, with the sun setting behind me. No one else was in sight, so I accelerated up to around 70, intending to hold it there for awhile to blow any accumulated carbon deposits out of the engine. What happened next will take much longer to tell about than the time required for the event, itself. It was a close call.

After cruising along comfortably for awhile and taking in some beautiful and serene farmland sights, I seemed to detect movement off to the right. Turning my head and focusing on the source of that movement, I immediately saw two cars, one behind the other and separated by only a car length or two, approaching at high speed at a right angle to the road I was on and, if they didn't begin to slow in the next instant, would cross my path ahead. They weren't slowing!

I hit the brakes; but nothing happened. Then I saw I had moved onto a solid sheet of ice that covered the oncoming lane, too. The whole road was covered with shiny gray ice all the way to the corner way up ahead where there was a

stop sign. I released the brakes. There was no reaction from
the wheels having been locked and then unlocked. The car
continued moving straight ahead as if I hadn't done anything.
At least it wasn't beginning to slide. I had released the throttle,
but not much speed was lost. The road's embankment dropped
down steeply on the right to a ditch at the bottom. The ditch
ran ahead to a big drain pipe going under the other high embankment carrying the road with the two oncoming cars on it.
Impossible to turn right to go down the embankment anyhow.
No traction on the ice; I'm too close to the intersection. I could
not steer more than to maintain going straight ahead. I was
resigned to facing whatever was going to happen next. I could
do nothing.

Did they slow down or speed up? Did they see me? As the
seconds and fractions of seconds ticked by before they reached
the intersection, I judged that neither car changed speed at all.
Neither of them must have seen me.

The first car flashed by, directly in front of me. I sped
through; and the second car came on as if chasing the back of
my car, almost hitting it. We crossed within a few feet of each
other. Moments later, I looked back expecting to see at least
one of the cars slowing down to recover from what had been
a near collision, but they merely proceeded on, as if nothing
had happened. Could they truly not have seen me? After all,
I had passed from their left to their right only a few feet ahead
of that second car. I turned and glanced at the speedometer.
I may have been doing around 55 when I went through that
intersection!

Perhaps, while driving along at about 50 or 60 you would
not detect another car crossing a few feet in front of you at 55
miles per hour. Intent as I was, I had glimpsed the first car
flash by in front of me in a partial blur of shiny chrome on

a deep black car body. After it passed by, my field of vision instantly leaped ahead to the road ahead and its flat, snow covered farm fields on each side. Those other cars just seemed to continue driving north without any perceptible speed changes, as if nothing had happened. Wow!

As I drove eastward on dry pavement at about 35 MPH for awhile, I reviewed what had just happened. If I had hit either one of those cars, I would likely have been killed; and I would also have likely caused the death of some or all persons in the car I hit. Stunning. Not to be taken lightly. Just think, I mulled, as I turned to look eastward again, at this moment I could be back there dead in the wreckage of this car. And some of those other people could lie dead in their wrecked car. Honestly. If I failed to be aware of living on borrowed or gifted time, I should have my head examined. Of course, as I write this more than half a century later, some of those folks were just as lucky. They just weren't as aware of it as I. It was another moment when, in gratitude, I again pledged to try to use my time left on earth for useful, constructive purposes.

My father came with a report: "I've got news for you." That was one of his favorite attention getters. He appeared a bit reluctant, however, just before giving me the "news." "What if I can't get you an appointment to West Point?" He paused and then asked, somewhat sheepishly, "Would you go to Annapolis, instead? It seems," he went on, "there are no more appointments available this year for West Point; but I can get you a Second Alternate appointment to Annapolis, if you want it." He then explained that, as a Second Alternate, I could be appointed only if the person with the Principal appointment failed his academic or physical tests AND if the person with the First Alternate appointment also failed one or both of his tests AND provided I had passed both tests. "Yes, I'll take it," was my answer. I did, after all, like ships and had crossed the Atlantic. Twice.

Thanksgiving passed and Christmas was coming when it was agreed that Gunnar needed to brush up on his academics in order to pass Naval Academy Entrance Exams. Soon, dad discovered another Northwestern. This time, it was the Northwestern Preparatory School, in Minneapolis, Minnesota; dedicated by its owner-operator-professor to helping young men prepare for entrance exams. to Annapolis, West Point, the Coast Guard and Merchant Marine Academies. Mr. Roddy's school year had started back in September; but, again, thanks to Culver, I was allowed a mid-term entry that commenced around the middle of January 1952. The Exam was scheduled for the 23rd or 26th of March, as I recall, and at the Minneapolis Post Office.

In just two months, Mr. Roddy took a room full of young men through all of the math I had ever been taught. We started promptly at 8 a.m. every morning except Sundays and continued straight through until noon with no breaks. After an hour and a half break for lunch, which we ate right there in his mansion's dining room, we then reviewed English for another two and a half hours. Some studied History.

Mr. Roddy's sister was the school business manager and administrator. A very large black and white television set could be viewed downstairs at the living room entrance and was left on until 8 o'clock. My folks did not have a television set at home, yet, so watching Dave Garroway and his monkey on what later was recognized as the historic beginnings of NBC's "TODAY" show was a first for me and appreciated.

Mr. Roddy, according to rumors I was privy to, had attended West Point for several years, but did not graduate, for some reason. His parents left him their old mansion at

310 Groveland Avenue and some considerable wealth. He, in turn, eventually turned the house into Northwestern Prep.

One of the most unusual features I can easily visualize was in the coach house, behind the mansion. There were living quarters above on the second floor; but the main floor was built of wooden timbers with a circular turntable cut out near the entrance. A coach could be pulled into the coach house, the horse or horses unhitched and taken away, and a carriage could then be turned around while still inside by rotating the circular floor. Pretty fancy.

Groveland Avenue was built on hilly terrain just south of downtown Minneapolis and was lined on both sides with one mansion after another. A street light, up the hill a few houses, caught my attention on several nights when I was out walking in zero to twenty below temperatures. There was a new 1952 black Cadillac sedan parked beneath it. A clean, black car, by itself, can be dazzling; but that Cadillac was special, somehow. Parked beside an ornate street light, it showed no signs of frost anywhere on its roof, hood, or trunk lid, as one might expect. The street was covered with several inches of snow packed down by passing cars. As they drove by, vehicles sounded like the severe cold was causing the snow and ice to grip the tires and provide traction.

It was unusual and memorable to have a chance to spend one Sunday afternoon with Buddy Lederer up there, a long way from Flossmoor. Attending school in the area, he had left his '41 Buick limo at home in favor of driving a new Kaiser sedan instead. Buddy gave me a short afternoon tour of the Twin-Cities; not much daytime up there in Winter. Had it not been for him, I would not have known about nor seen the 3M (Minnesota Mining and Manufacturing) air force hangered down the hill from downtown St. Paul. The Mississippi River swings almost a half turn around the St. Paul Municipal Airport where several large hangers had quite a number of 4-engine company planes belonging to 3M in them. Impressive.

On another Sunday afternoon, I decided to walk all the way out to the Minneapolis Airport and back, alone. It was a welcome challenge; cold, too. Airports can be inspiring, especially to a young man interested in becoming a pilot someday. I reached Lindbergh Field from the north and promptly entered the terminal for warmth and a good look out the windows at the airfield. Just to the north, was the end of what looked like a main runway. Off the very end of it a horizontal mound of dirt was embedded with a horizontal row of lights, each about two to three times the diameter of car headlights and all were pointed down the runway.

Some twelve and a half years later, those very same lights would still be there as I taxied out one night to take off in a company Beech Bonanza. Those lights were off and I had completely forgotten about them. The tower cleared me for take-off. I had taxied out to the middle of the runway and, as I applied full power to begin a take-off roll, lights came on from behind and lit up my plane and the runway on both sides and ahead of me. Instantly, I imagined another plane was making an approach and had turned on its landing lights just before touching down on the runway. It was going to land on top of us! I had two neighbor friends along in the plane with me to go fishing at Herman and Agnes Peterson's resort in northern Minnesota, Marty Braverman and Bernie Gunsberg.

Power back; hard right brake to turn right! Turned almost 90 degrees; looking back. What's coming? Damn! It was those horizontal lights! They were turned on to light up the runway for planes taking off! Promptly, I straightened out, accelerated down the runway and took off. That was my first and last use of Lindbergh Field with an airplane. That was also my first and last encounter with lights lighting up a runway like that.

Academy Entrance Exams were finally given and I then proceeded to the Great Lakes Naval Training Center north of Chicago for the relatively easy (for me) physicals.

"I've got news for you," announced my father again, towards the end of June, but this time there was enthusiasm in his voice and demeanor. "The Principal passed the mental tests; but failed his physical. The First Alternate passed his physical; but failed the mental. You passed both mental and physical tests. YOU'RE IN!!"

Thanks, Dad.

CHAPTER 6

LET'S SEA & AIR

My orders were to report to the Naval Academy on a certain date which I don't recall exactly, now, but it may have been July 2, 1952. Most of the Class of '56 had arrived on June 30th. I had made it from the airport to the bus station in Washington, D.C., and boarded the bus for Annapolis. Either I was early or the bus was late; but I had to sit in the bus at the station for quite some time, peering out the open window beside me. That section of our nation's capitol looked and felt sleepy in the hot, humid, early afternoon sun. A two-story apartment building across the wide street from my bus window had an old brick wall with a few windows and had been painted white a long time ago. A tree now and then shaded the uneven brick sidewalk next to it. Occasionally, a black man or woman would stroll along in the shade under those trees. It looked something like what I had imagined the Old South to look like.

After landing at Washington National Airport in a 4-engine Douglas DC-4 or DC-6 (or a 4-engine Lockheed Constellation with the slightly curved fuselage and triple vertical rudders, I don't remember which; but I would be riding all of them a lot in coming years), I had taken a cab to the bus station. The observations at the bus station and some distant views of the Washington Monument and the Capitol Dome during the cab ride were my introductions to the District of Columbia. I would see a lot more of it, in due course; beginning in earnest about six and a half months later, in January 1953, when the Brigade of Midshipmen would join others and march in President Eisenhower's Inaugural Parade.

At the Academy, once sworn in with a few other late comers, under the encased flag in Memorial Hall inscribed with "Don't give up the ship," we were assigned temporary rooms, laundry numbers and issued stencils with our names punched out on them. We then applied the stencils and black ink to our uniforms as per written directions also issued. I still have a wooden case containing drafting tools that also bears my stenciled name on it. Through the years, those drafting tools have been useful. They were paid for, like everything else issued to us at that time, by government loans which we repaid automatically a little at a time over four years before graduating.

The first two months consisted of being introduced to every known sport and playing a little of each one by its applicable rules; learning to sail; doing close order drills; and attending classroom sessions.

Some seamanship drills and classes were led by one of the Navy's few remaining old salts, a sandblower (short) but easily heard Chief Petty Officer. He also reminded us of the sailing ships of yore and their marlinespikes, fore topmasts, main shrouds, capstans, blocks, sheaves, heaving line knots, and a host of other nautical terms and descriptions.

On climbing into a bunk bed to spend one of my first nights at the Academy, I remember peering up at the bed springs and straps above, hearing the quiet all around after taps, and feeling assured that no one was going to call on me to do anything more, at least until reveille. There was also a solid feel to

Bancroft Hall. No vibrations anywhere, in the floors or walls. Well built. Sleep came easily and was welcome.

Shortly after Labor Day, the upper classmen returned and life became tougher. They had been home for 30 days after being away for two months mostly on cruises aboard Navy combatants. As plebes (fourth classmen, freshmen; all the same) we had to earn our places in the Brigade, just as upper classmen had done before us.

Bancroft Hall was our dormitory, the largest in the world. There were almost 3,800 of us living in it at that time. Plebes had to march down the middle of hallways and do square corners at every turn. We had sinks and showers in our rooms; but, to go to the bathroom, for example, plebes had to march straight out their door to the center of the (wide) hallway and do a square corner before marching down the middle of the hallway. Once abeam the door to the head, one would turn another square corner and march to and through its doorway.

Plebes had many challenges. I will describe only a few of them here. There were basic routines that everyone followed: Attending classes, participating in afternoon sports, and doing regular evening studies of assigned homework. Then a bit more, particularly for plebes.

At meals, seating was assigned at each table so that plebes could serve the upper classmen. Plebes had to sit erect on the front edges of their chairs. Upper classmen could ask a plebe a question about ships, the Navy, sports, about anything; i.e., What's the displacement of a Fletcher Class destroyer, Mr. Jenson? How long is the barrel of a 5 inch 38? What percentage of the Earth's surface is covered by water? How high is Mt. Fuji? When was the League of Nations organized and by whom? When did Joseph Stalin become the head of the Soviet Union?

A plebe was not allowed to say, "I don't know, Sir." If he didn't know the answer to a question, a plebe would have to reply, "I'll find out, Sir." The plebe would then have until the next meal to look up an answer and be ready to give it. Also, plebes were not permitted to take notes. All questions and answers had to be committed to memory.

Towards the end of plebe year, I tried to estimate the number of questions I had been averaging and came up with about 6.5 per breakfast, 6.5 per noon meal, and 6.5 more per every evening meal. That aspect of plebe year was, indeed, challenging. If a question had been forgotten or not researched sufficiently to derive an answer before the next meal, the standard procedure was for the plebe to be told, "Come-around to Room #–– after dinner, Mr. Jenson," or after study hall, or whenever an upper classman directed.

A "come-around" was issued by a First or Second Classman, usually, to any plebe at any time and for just about any reason; but typically was for some noticed infraction of Naval Academy Rules or Regulations. Failure to show up could result in being placed on report and/or receiving a bunch more of come-arounds.

Being placed "On Report" led to Extra Duty marching with an M-1 rifle on a shoulder; a few hours at a time but for as many total hours as might be accumulated.

Navy won the Army-Navy football game in the fall of 1952 and what a blessing that was for Navy's plebes! We were allowed to carry-on, dispensing with all plebe routines - including questions at meals - until after Christmas leave. We thereby also gained impressions of what life could become after finishing plebe year.

Meanwhile, I cannot overlook a telephone call made to my father some two to four weeks after the upper classmen had returned. Bancroft Hall had one room near the Rotunda that was filled with pay telephone booths. It also had a window. I remember the warmth and brightness of the sunshine coming through that window one morning when I called my father to report: "This is not for me. I've had enough. I'm going to resign and leave."

"That's OK," he answered.

I repeated, wondering if he had heard me correctly: "This is not for me. I've had it. I'm going to resign."

"That's OK," he answered again, and then added emphatically; "But don't come home!" Hmmm.

A few moments of silence later, my head cleared.

Mulling it over, I resented what I had begun to perceive as mind-altering experiences at the Academy. Having to endure punishments in the process became just another reason to leave; but I had quickly been jolted into regaining sense enough to finish what I had started. My father may have been just an immigrant with the equivalent of an eighth-grade education, and a graduate of the school of hard knocks, as he often labeled himself; but he had more talent and wisdom than he gave himself credit for.

The Battleship Missouri had just returned from Korea in the Spring of 1953. It anchored out from the Academy in Chesapeake Bay and waited for those of us assigned to her to come aboard via motor launches. We sailed in the afternoon for Norfolk. Two days later we departed Norfolk in the company of other ships and proceeded to Panama; then to Rio de Janeiro; back to Guantanamo Bay, Cuba; Norfolk, Virginia; and, finally, a troop transport, APA, returned us to Annapolis. When the 192 foot high Chapel Dome was sighted - the one with the John Paul Jones crypt directly beneath it - tradition allowed us to become youngsters (3rd classmen). Plebe year was over! A 30 day leave, to be spent back home in Chicago Heights, was soon to follow.

The cruise had been interesting and inspiring. On our way down, the Colon, Panama, stop had allowed us enough time to ride the railroad across the isthmus, through the jungle, literally, to Panama City and back. There were big jungle leaves that had hit the sills of the train's open windows, every now and then, while en route. Panama City's night life was much more active than Colon's, I thought.

The starboard side of the Missouri was tied to a dock in Colon. Around noon, I ventured out onto the port side forward main deck area and peered down at the calm, smooth water. There, not far out and lying perfectly still was a barracuda, apparently sunning himself in the mirror calm light green salt water. He must have been at least four feet long. It had more time than I, however, and was still out there (asleep, perhaps) when I finally went below.

On the other side of the ship and up one deck (on the 01 level) was embedded a large circular bronze plaque marking where the signing of Japan's surrender at the end of WWII took place. As Midshipmen, we polished that plaque and "holy stoned" the teakwood deck surrounding it. First, the deck was wetted and then rubbed with bricks on the ends of broomsticks. A row of barefoot Middies would line up aside one another and keep time by singing a ditty over and over as they rubbed the teakwood with the cinder bricks, back and forth 16-20 times; then advance to the next plank (as the song ended; and was started again). Bricks were scooped out in the middle for the broom handles to fit into.

After leaving Colon and before reaching Rio, on June 19, 1953, we crossed the equator and changed our identities: from Pollywogs to Shellbacks. Everyone was issued a certificate and wallet size card to commemorate the event. Quite a ceremony!

Rio had not been visited by any U.S. military force since WWII, we were told. They were glad to see us, down there. I took a young lady out to dinner, one evening, and had to be chaperoned by her family's chauffeur the whole time. I don't recall having to buy dinner for him; but I might have. Class distinctions were definitely a part of Brazilian society.

From where the "Big Mo" was anchored in the harbor, I could see the top of Sugar Loaf Mountain. It had a famous and prominent statue on top, Corcovado. Later, on a trip up there by cable car, I found that when standing close to it, the statue with its outstretched arms seemed not as large as had been imagined from below. But, still, it was large enough to be detected from miles around and all directions.

Seen below and to the right of Sugar Loaf from the Big Mo, and just above sea level, were airport hangers and lots of twin-engine Douglas DC-3 aircraft parked close by. At night, overhead lights in the hangers reflected off shiny aluminum DC-3 wing and fuselage skins, as they were polished (and waxed, I presumed) with electric buffers. The buffers could also be heard, at times, depending on wind direction.

One day, I bought a round trip ticket to fly aboard a DC-3 to Sao Paulo. The pilot and copilot let me stand between them during the approach and landing at Sao Paulo. They made everything look easy. But I must admit that it took more than mere balancing on my part during the transition from descending to flaring for landing. I had to grab the backs of their seats to keep from falling over backwards, as the nose of the aircraft went from being down a bit to rising high enough for the tail wheel to land.

One memorable discovery in Sao Paulo came about in a small auto dealership that was not really open for service, only for car sales. In the back portion of the garage, under a light brown cover in an almost windowless space and crowded next to a white-washed wall with other covered cars also parked in front of, beside, and behind it, was an almost new 1951 light metallic gray Cadillac 4-door sedan. The cover was raised for me, enough to reveal its left front and left side. It was priced at around $13,500, as I recall, about 5-6 times what it had sold for new in the U.S.

Sao Paulo was a crowded city with many multi-story buildings jammed next to each other and filled with many cheerful people. Saying goodbye was only made easier by anticipating another DC-3 plane ride back to Rio.

As we sailed out of Rio and almost reached open waters, an AT-6 (WWII U.S. Army Air Force Trainer)appeared suddenly from astern and flew by us close aboard on the starboard side in a steep left banked turn at about bridge deck level, actually - and not far out from the ship's bridge. The pilot waved and smiled at us as he whizzed by, and made several more passes. We surmised that he was flying a war surplus airplane purchased from the U.S.

It was hot outside even at night as we rounded the eastern tip of South America and advanced north towards the equator. A lone white light of another vessel could be seen way up ahead of us and slightly to starboard, as we cruised along at about 15 knots. The unidentified vessel seemed to be maintaining a course and speed similar to our own. I picked up some scuttlebutt (gossip) that the light might be coming from one of the pirate ships suspected of plying the waters we were passing through. They looked for vulnerable pleasure yachts to board and vandalize, even taking some of them over and disposing of persons on board. Thus, we became aware that not even peaceful sailing yachts could always be considered safe in International Waters.

What I remember about "GITMO," Cuba, on that return passage was the mild heat, the base being well lighted at night, and a truck driving around spraying insect repellent into the air. It created a visible fog in the stillness of the night but eliminated mosquitoes and other pests.

What I had discovered about the Big Mo that troubled me was that its mechanical computers for aiming guns at incoming enemy aircraft were only capable of targeting planes flying at less than 600 knots. Even I, a Midshipman, could sense that aircraft in the future would be flying faster than that. So, eventually, I acquired the necessary schematics at the Academy and undertook, in my spare time, what became a lengthy project of preparing a modification proposal for submission to the appropriate Navy Bureau in Washington. Later, as I boarded my first ship after graduating and was preparing to drop my then-completed proposal off in the mail, I learned of a just-issued modification from Washington that consisted, essentially, of what I was about to propose. So I saved the postage and added what I had prepared to my files, which I still have. No regrets, either. The best learning experiences can evolve from pursuing improvement objectives, I discovered.

After the cruise, Midway Airport in Chicago was a welcomed sight; and so was home. Academy public relations personnel had forwarded news items about me, now and then, for publication by the local STAR newspaper. When I was again able to attend Sunday church services with my parents, many well wishers came up to congratulate me for just about anything and everything, it seemed.

At the conclusion of a Sunday morning service, an old boyhood Sunday School chum approached, as we stood outside in front of the church where the congregation gathered to socialize a bit before going their separate ways. Ronald MacAllister (that's a guess at correct last name spelling) was his name. Ron wanted to reveal something important that I can still recall today, some 50 years later. I remembered that Ron and his mother had been considered by many in the church as financially poor and a little slow. However, I had made efforts to befriend and be nice to Ronald so as to shield him from criticisms and others who didn't want to have much to do with him. My mother deserves the credit for encouraging that trait. What Ron came up and told me that Sunday morning after church came as a surprise.

"That Lucky Old Sun" was the title of a very popular song at that time. It was a hit on radios nationwide and sung by well-known entertainer Phil Harris. What Ron wanted to tell me was that he had written the words to that song and sent them to Phil Harris. Harris, according to Ron, had then changed one or two words in the lyrics and gone on to claim the song as his own. Ron had received absolutely nothing in return for his efforts.

My reaction, of course, was at first anger and then I suggested he take Harris to court. Ron then offered that he had two lawyers working on it. I don't recall ever seeing Ron again; and I never heard anything more about the reputed theft of his copyrights. I continue to hope, however, as I have all along, that everything turned out well for Ronald, somehow. It was (and still is) a good song.

Another incident involving patents came to mind after Ron and I had parted. I remembered a disclosure revealed at JENSON'S ONE STOP SERVICE station some years earlier.

A complete stranger had walked from his car at the gas pump island to the office to pay for his gas purchase. Before long, he and my father were conversing. That man, standing right there in front of us, identified himself as the inventor of the Vise Grip. He was likeable, to be sure, and he told us that he would much rather be back at his plant making Vise Grips and developing other new things than out traveling around the country looking for and finding Vise Grip imitations; patent infringements, which he then would alert his patent attorneys to so they could take the offenders to court. He was having to spend more time on the road looking for imitators, he told us, than what time he had devoted to inventing the Vise Grip in the first place.

Wish I could say the system works better, now, some sixty years later. But I can't. But I haven't given up on it, either. After all, it is a part of our Constitution.

One pledge I had to make upon entering the Navy as a Midshipman was to defend and uphold the Constitution of the United States against all enemies, foreign and domestic. We all have our obligations and duties to perform and cannot always drop everything and do what may need to be done at any given moment; but I pledged to try, as I could, to do my part in reading the Declaration of Independence, the Constitution, and the Constitution's Amendments, as many times as might be necessary to gain some familiarity with them. After all, I had sworn to uphold and defend them, with my life, if necessary. I should know about what I had sworn to uphold and defend. And I already sensed that, to a U.S. citizen, becoming familiar with those legal documents was somehow akin to comprehending and appreciating the Ten Commandments in the Bible.

Opportunities might arise in the future for me to do something to improve the patent system, but I would first have to serve in the Navy. And to serve in the Navy, I would first have to develop the Qualifications of a Naval Officer. John Paul Jones had described them in this way:

"It is by no means enough that an officer of the Navy should be a capable mariner. He must be that, of course, but also a great deal more. He should be as well a gentleman of liberal education, refined manners, punctilious courtesy, and the nicest sense of personal honor.

"He should be the soul of tact, patience, justice, firmness, and charity. No meritorious act of a subordinate should escape his attention or be left to pass without its reward, even if the reward is only a word of approval. Conversely, he should not be blind to a single fault in any subordinate, though, at the same time, he should be quick and unfailing to distinguish error from malice, thoughtlessness from incompetency, and well meant shortcoming from heedless or stupid blunder."

Plebes had to memorize those qualifications. There also were five short LAWS OF THE NAVY to memorize and practice:

"Now these are the laws of the Navy, unwritten and varied they be; And he that is wise will observe them, going down in his ship to the sea.

"As naught may outrun the destroyer, even so with the law and its grip, for the strength of the ship is the service, and the strength of the service the ship.

"Take heed what ye say of your seniors, be your words spoken softly or plain, lest a bird of the air tell the matter, And so ye shall hear it again.

"On the strength of one link in the cable, dependeth the might of the chain. Who knows when thou mayest be tested? So live that thou bearest the strain!

"Now these are the Laws of the Navy and many and mighty are they. But the hull and the deck and the keel and the truck of the law is – OBEY."

Youngster (sophomore) year allowed us some free time to catch our breath. First and Second classmen were in charge, so we had opportunities to expand our extracurricular horizons. One of my favorites, aside from marching Extra Duty a lot, was to become a disc jockey on the Brigade's radio station, WRNV. The signal was carried into every room via the electrical wires but it did not broadcast very far beyond Bancroft Hall. I became "GJ the DJ;" and continued working at the station in various capacities, including as station manager, until we graduated. One pointer I picked up by watching a professional DJ at a commercial station in Annapolis, one Saturday, was to smile when speaking into the mike. It can affect voice inflections - favorably. Works with telephones, too.

The summer of 1954 rewarded us with many training exercises that took place in several geographic areas.

A cruise to Halifax, Nova Scotia, taught us first hand about ocean tides. My ship, a small Destroyer Escort, came alongside a dock and tied up to it; but the lines were left dangling. They were tied to the ship and dock, but were dangling down almost into the water. Way too much slack in the mooring lines, I thought; until the next morning. When I walked out on deck, all I could see were vertical wood pilings that held back horizontal boards that were holding back the earth supporting the dock, above. I had to look up to see sky and the edge of the same dock that had been a few feet below our main deck when we had docked the previous evening. Tides averaged some 12 to 14 feet, I learned; and our mooring lines in the morning sure had the slack out of them. They sloped down from the dockside bollards, above, at low tide and had been slackened periodically all through the night.

Experienced naval aviators were also on hand, that summer, to demonstrate how flying was properly done.

Across the Severn from the Academy, a hanger full of old N3N biplanes equipped with floats allowed each one of us to be taken aloft in open cockpits and to cruise along at about 80 knots over the Chesapeake. What a view!

All but one member of our class had practiced the Dunker Drill, earlier in the year. The Dunker consisted of being strapped into a seat in an open airplane cockpit and riding it down on a pair of rails into a swimming pool where, after stopping, the cockpit flipped forward and over, turning the occupant and his seat upside down under water. It was a challenge not to become disoriented when getting unstrapped, out of the seat and back to the surface (in what seemed like the wrong direction).

The old N3Ns we flew that day had two front and two rear struts extending down from the fuselage to the main float below. As some of us were taxiing back to the ramp after landing, we passed one N3N that had suffered broken front struts on landing, which had allowed the propeller to drop down and slice into the front portion of the main float which had protruded a few feet out in front of the prop. As water entered the float, the nose of the plane gradually pitched downward. Eventually, the plane stood on its nose but seemed to want to remain in that position as rescue vessels sped towards it.

Cdr. John Haynie was piloting that N3N, I learned later: a good pilot and a man I respected. He was also the Commissioned Officer overseeing WRNV. The big surprise, however, was that the student with him was none other than the one and only classmate of ours who had not been available for the Dunker Drill, Richard "Buzz" Mann. Buzz had sustained a head injury playing football and had been in the hospital when it had been our turn at the Dunker. So, he then became our living example of what could happen if one of the LAWS OF THE NAVY is violated: "On the strength of one link in the cable, dependeth the might of the chain. Who knows when thou mayest be tested? So live that thou bearest the strain!" The N3N hadn't gone over all the way; but we had witnessed enough. We became true believers.

There also were twin-engine Grumman Albatross seaplanes across the Severn from the Academy, that took us aloft at over twice the speed of the N3Ns, in relative comfort and quiet.

The Patuxent River Naval Air Test Center was another summer cruise stop. The T-28 was there to be test flown for initial acceptance by the Navy. I had a chance to go up with a test pilot and fly one for awhile. With some 1,400 horsepower, it could really perform. Unbeknownst to me at the time, I later was among the first students to fly the new T-28 in Pensacola flight training. After using them for years as trainers, the old SNJs were phased out. (The Navy version of the AT-6 that buzzed us when we left Brazil). A final ceremonial SNJ formation flight was conducted over Pensacola on a Saturday morning. Every SNJ that could fly was put into the air. I was standing on a sidewalk in downtown Pensacola as formation after formation flew by overhead and can attest to feeling the ground shake under me for what seemed like (and may have been) a good half hour.

While in Virginia Beach, we also trained to come ashore in landing craft, off of Landing Ship Docks (LSDs) and Attack Transports (APAs). Those little (LCVP-Landing Craft Vehicle Personnel) vessels that we rode in bobbed around a lot in the waves and caused many to have to take off their helmets and use them as temporary containers. We were landing on friendly beaches, acting and equipped like Marines. We appreciated that it must have been extreme in WWII to have to maintain composure and ability to fight in those bobbing armored "boats" while under enemy fire.

The carrier, Valley Forge, also showed us how carrier landings and takeoffs were conducted - on a straight deck, too (vs. angled)! There were WWII Navy torpedo bombers, F4U Corsairs, F6F Hellcats, and more, to observe. And not a single accident!

Finally, before graduation, we made another cruise, this time to Europe.

From Barcelona, Spain, some of us rode a train across the desert and through 99 tunnels to Madrid. Every time we passed through a tunnel, black soot would enter the cars, landing on our khaki colored uniforms. The particles were usually large enough, though, to be easily brushed off.

The train had to stop for water about midway. Way out there in the desert came children carrying round woven baskets about 18 inches in diameter that were filled with fruit.

"Five cents," said the little girl standing on the ground under my open window and trying to hold up her basket.

"OK," I said in reply, thinking it was what she wanted for one piece of fruit. I got a nickel out of my pocket and reached down to her with it. She took it, there was genuine girlish delight in her eyes; then she quickly handed me the whole basket of fruit and started to run away. I called to her immediately and motioned her to come back. She did; and I motioned for her to give me back the nickel. She did. I then handed her a quarter, instead. My, my. The look on her face!

Before leaving Barcelona, visitors were allowed onboard for tours of a U.S Navy Destroyer. Two men, about my father's age at the time and wearing double-breasted suits and ties, were mine to escort through the ship's interior and thence out onto the fantail. As we stood out there in the open, I tried to describe the "inner workings and hidden mechanisms" of our depth charge gear; but those gentlemen were distracted and appeared to have something else in mind. Eventually, after looking all around several times, one of them drew to within a few inches of me, raised his hand and arm to cover his mouth, and almost whispered, "We're not free, here. Franco is a dictator." He then quickly pulled away, looking all around again; but came back and repeated once more, "We're not free, here. Franco is a dictator."

I smiled a little as I tried to look into the eyes of each of them and said, "I understand."

They looked again at the depth charges and launching racks as we moved along to the brow and said our good byes.

The Mediterranean was like a mirror in the morning when we sailed out of Barcelona. I had not seen open waters that undisturbed since 1939, nor did I again, after that.

Our port of entry into England was Plymouth. We not only saw a bit of London, but had the opportunity to fly to Paris as well. The Hall of Mirrors was an unusual sight; so was Paris from atop the 984-foot-high Eiffel Tower. I rode the elevator to the small observation platform at the top; and walked down using the stairs. Dizzying.

A humbling moment came unexpectedly at the airport while we were outside waiting for a plane to take us back to London. I was with a group of Midshipmen and there were just as many or more civilians sitting and standing around on one of the airport loading aprons out on the airfield. I was sitting on a simple wooden bench enjoying the stillness of the air and the bright, warm, morning sunshine when a well-dressed, middle aged woman, happened along, in the company of one or two other women. She sat down next to me and soon began talking. After I had confirmed her suspicions that we were from the U.S. Naval Academy, and as our plane was then seen for the first time coming to load us aboard, she revealed that she was from England originally and was married to a U.S. Navy Lt.Commander whom she had met during the war. She said she was very happily married, indeed.

"I know," she continued, "there are Englishmen and women who resent Americans. England, after all, has been the dominant nation in all the world for a long, long time. But, England is no longer the dominant nation in the world. You, the Americans, are. Despite what anyone may say to the contrary, Americans are the new world leaders, like it or not. I am proud of my husband from America and being married to him has taught me not to fear Americans." Then, she looked directly at me and said, "You are the next generation of Americans to come along. You are the new leaders of the world. Don't be afraid to accept that role. Take care to do it well."

Quite a salute! Memorable, too.

The "Father of Nuclear Submarines," Admiral Hyman G. Rickover, Class of 1922, was a short man, appearing almost frail, as he stood behind a portable podium a few feet in front of me, with a couple of aides standing behind him, in Bancroft Hall. He was addressing the Class of '56 and answering questions about the world's first nuclear powered submarine, the Nautilus. The Nautilus, itself, was anchored out in Chesapeake Bay so we could board and tour it, later. Its interior turned out to be spacious by old WWII submarine standards and central portions of the Nautilus looked much like a quality hotel lobby. I walked across the top of the reactor, for some reason, and about half way to the end, the thought occurred to me that

I could be inviting cancer of the groin in future years. So, I picked up the pace a little.

The date of Admiral Rickover's visit is only estimated, here, but it must have been in the Fall of '55, sometime, to be in time for recruiting submariners from our class; or else it could have been during the Winter, or as late as Spring 1956. The Nautilus had been accepted by the Navy on April 22, 1955, and, in May, it had made a thirteen hundred mile shakedown cruise to San Juan, Puerto Rico, in eighty four hours, mostly submerged. The passage to Annapolis would have taken place sometime after that and before June '56.

After bringing us up to speed on the Navy's newest submarine nuclear power plant development, a question and answer period followed. Several good questions were asked by my classmates - and properly answered by the Admiral.

When a pause came along, I raised my hand and the Admiral immediately gave me eye contact and a nod. My question went something like this: "Have you developed any ability for our submarines to replenish their torpedoes underwater from underwater storage facilities?" The Admiral looked a little puzzled. My classmates paused, then roared with laughter. "Why?," he asked, finally.

"Well," I responded, "lately you have been publicly criticizing the Strategic Air Command for the vulnerability of their bases to air bombardment. It seems to me that our submarine pens or torpedo replenishment facilities are just as vulnerable as SAC bases."

There was a pause. Silence from my classmates. I could see Admiral Rickover's eyes roll around for just a brief instant and then he answered me almost in a whisper, "No, we haven't." He then turned aside. One of his aides jerked forward raising his notebook pad as he neared the Admiral. "Make a note of that," instructed Rickover. He turned back, faced the front, again, paused momentarily, and continued: "Next question?"

Admiral Rickover passed away on July 8, 1986. But, a few months before his death, he made an evening appearance in the Hesburgh Auditorium at the University of Notre Dame, which I attended. After his presentation, a question and answer period followed. One memorable question from the audience was this: What do you consider humanity's most important responsibility? His answer: To reproduce.

When the question and answer period was over, I walked up and onto the stage, introduced myself and shook his small, frail, hand. (It was comparable to shaking Senator Everett Dirksen's hand.) I asked Admiral Rickover this question: "What's to become of nuclear waste?"

He seemed to have to think about it for a moment or two and then answered: "Some good people are working on that."

While I was digesting his answer, a heavy-set woman came out from behind a stage curtain and whisked him away. I had wanted to reveal to him that I had been the Midshipman First Class who had asked him about underwater submarine replenishment, in Bancroft Hall; but he was gone.

It may be useful to know that I vaguely recall hearing on two radio broadcasts sometime in the 1980s or 90s possible hints of a secret agreement between the President of the U.S. and the leader of the USSR to not store weapons under water anywhere in the world. Perhaps more definitive information will eventually become available; perhaps not.

As inviting, challenging and rewarding as signing up for the submarine service was, I chose two other options, instead: Destroyer duty for one year; to be followed by training to become a Naval Aviator after that.

Towards the end of 1ˢᵗ Class year, I and several other Midshipmen were unexpectedly summoned to the Superintendent's quarters and told we represented a sampling of Americans.

The President of Indonesia, Achmed Sukarno, soon appeared and shook hands with each of us. (His hand was as small and soft as Dirksen's and Rickover's.) When questions were invited, I asked, "Why don't you develop industries and use Indonesia's raw materials?"

"That's exactly what we want," Sukarno answered impulsively, his bright eyes and friendly smile flashing. The Admiral stepped in and politely ended our conversation.

A little TABLE SALT follows which we as plebes had to learn and be able to recite when called upon for it by upper classmen:

HOW'S THE COW, MR. JENSON?

Sir, she walks, she talks, she's full of chalk. The lacteal fluid extracted from the female of the bovine species is highly prolific to the (approximate number of glasses of milk remaining in pitcher) nth degree!

WHAT TIME IS IT, MR. JENSON?

Sir, I am greatly embarrassed and deeply humiliated that due to unforeseen circumstances beyond my control, the inner workings and hidden mechanisms of my chronometer are in such inaccord with the great sidereal movement with which time is generally reckoned that I cannot with any degree of accuracy state the correct time, sir. But without fear of being too greatly in error, I will state that it is about — minutes, — seconds, and — ticks past — bells.

HOW LONG HAVE YOU BEEN IN THE NAVY,
Mr. JENSON?

All me bloomin'life, sir! Me mother was a mermaid, me father was King Neptune. I was born on the crest of a wave and rocked in the cradle of the deep. Seaweed and barnacles are me clothes. Every tooth in me head is a marlinspike; the hair on me head is hemp. Every bone in me body is a spar, and when I spits, I spits tar! I'se hard, I is, I am, I are!

CHAPTER 7

DESTROYER DUTY

Fill 'er up! After driving on famous Route 66 to a crude log cabin filling station on the west side of Albuquerque, New Mexico, my practically new 1955 Olds 98 convertible needed fuel.

The car was a graduation present from Mom and Dad. Actually, per an agreement Dad and I had reached sometime before I entered the Academy: If I graduated, he would buy any car for me that I wanted. When it came time for that selection and purchase, I was easier on him than I could have been, by suggesting that we go to a used car auction instead of to a new car showroom. That was fine with him, so we wound up at an auction somewhere near 95th and Cottage Grove on the southeast side of Chicago. Before many more days passed in June '56, I had hand waxed that two-tone blue convertible with the dark blue top and scrubbed the leather seats with saddle soap as well. With some ivory colored upholstery thrown in, it was quite a car!

As the attendant was filling the tank, I walked around to the back of the station and happened upon a horse wearing a saddle with its reins tied to the northeast corner of the building. That horse looked really tired. I learned later the rider had come from San Diego on it; and was headed for New York City. Hmmm.

To the west, from whence that horse and rider had come, could be seen Route 66 stretching straight and slightly down then slightly up towards a clump of mountain ranges in the distance. There were about 900 miles more to go to Long Beach and San Diego. A classmate of mine from Joliet, Illinois, Dave Lloyd, was along, needing a ride to San Diego (and helping me with some of the driving). Dave had signed up for the submarine service; while my destination was the Gearing class destroyer, USS Rupertus (DD-851), in Long Beach. It was a most enjoyable road trip, made even more entertaining by radio stations across the country playing a new song, at that time: "Canadian Sunset."

While Ensign Jenson was fortunate to live on and to eventually be able to write this memoir; I regret that LCDR David B. Lloyd, USN was among 99 crewmen aboard the USS Scorpion (SSN-589) when it mysteriously sank in the Atlantic and was declared "presumed lost" on June 5, 1968, some 12 years after our graduation. Dave graduated #3 in our class.

The wreckage was found on the bottom of the Atlantic in 11,000 feet of water. The Scorpion was en route from Naples, Italy, to Norfolk, Virginia, when lost. Investigations continue; but according to authors Sontag and Drew in BLIND MAN'S BLUFF, a just recalled MK-46 battery in one of fourteen high-speed Mark 37 torpedoes aboard the Scorpion could have caught fire and precipitated an explosion. It seems the recall was conceived a mere day or two before Scorpion was to focus on her return travel. By the time necessary recall authorization was obtained, Scorpion was already Norfolk bound and conducting the usual exercising/testing of all her equipment to determine her next homeport overhaul and repair needs. Serving in the military even in peacetime can be dangerous, often requiring ultimate sacrifices, unfortunately. The loss of

LCDR Dave Lloyd, USN and his shipmates was and is sincerely regretted.

As I pulled into the USN portion of Terminal Island in Long Beach, I found it a busy place with dry docks and all the rest that a major port facility provides. What they did not have, however, was a decent place for me to park my car - except at the Officer's Club.

We went to sea on Monday mornings and usually returned on Friday afternoons. Then, every third weekend I would also have the weekend duty aboard ship, so my car could be left alone for almost a week at a time and every third week, for almost two weeks at a time. My car needed some long-term parking, preferably under a roof, since the gasses and fumes from ships in the area were hard on car finishes and particularly so on convertible tops. I have made suggestions about this car storage/parking problem to high-ranking classmates of mine in later years, but cannot say for sure if anything has been done to improve parking for unmarried officers and enlisted persons. Vehicles belonging to married persons, of course, are usually in family use during at-sea periods.

"Rusty Rupe," as she was sometimes called, was only her name in jest. I don't recall ever finding any serious unattended rust on board the RUPERTUS. After all, she had only been in commission since September 21, 1945. The ship was named to honor Marine Corps Major General William H. Rupertus, and was commanded by Cdr. Dan T. Drain, USN.

General Rupertus was second in command of the First Marine Division at the outbreak of WWII and opened the U.S. offensive in the Pacific by landing in the Solomons on August 7, '42. He organized and led the successful attacks on Tulagi, Gavutu, and Tanambogo. On July 10, '43, Maj. Gen. Rupertus succeeded to the command of the First Marine Division, which he led to further victories in Palau and New Britain. For his triumph at Cape Gloucester, New Britain, General Rupertus was personally thanked by General MacArthur, who awarded him the Army Distinguished Service Medal. His victory over an estimated 40,000 Japanese on Peleliu is considered outstanding in the Philippine Campaign, and he was awarded the Navy Distinguished Service Medal by Admiral Nimitz. Unfortunately, General Rupertus died on March 25, 1945, in the U.S., while Commandant of the Marine Corps School, at the age of 55.

ADMIRAL ARLEIGH BURKE, Naval Academy Class of 1923, was Chief of Naval Operations at that time and an old "tin can" (destroyer) sailor who gave us these words to live by: "WE ARE A DESTROYER! A big ship man would have trouble filling our shoes. We like to think we would have no trouble filing his. We have learned the lesson of self-reliance, of not being afraid of a little rough living or any tough assignment. We are real sailormen, the destroyer men of the fleet. When things are getting too hard for anyone else, they're getting just right for us."

After first being assigned to the Gunnery Department, I also had to be the defense counsel for sailors charged with offenses serious enough to warrant being court-martialed. It was a new experience for me, and, I would say, a profound one, thanks to two Naval Reserve Officers who happened to be aboard for their annual two-week cruise when my first case came up. They otherwise practiced law in the Denver area.

A sailor was accused of stealing some personal items from another sailor's footlocker. A myriad of defense tactics and questions came to mind; but I had the good fortune on a relatively calm and bright sunny morning while at sea to be able to share a cup of coffee in the otherwise empty wardroom with the two lawyers. What should I do?, I asked them, not being ashamed to let them know that this was to be my first case.

That's easy, one of them answered almost immediately. If there are any witnesses, simply ask, "Did you actually see the accused take the items?" The other agreed; for a second opinion.

That was far simpler than what I had planned to ask, and it worked. The defendant was found not guilty and I, unknowingly, had been placed up near the top as a desirable defense counsel, one to ask for when given a choice.

My initial 5 inch 38 caliber Gunnery assignment was soon changed to Sonar. But before I became the Fox Division Officer, I needed some Anti Submarine Warfare (ASW) training from a facility at the base of Point Loma in San Diego. My car came in handy.

ASW training was comprehensive. There were classroom sessions and then we went to sea aboard a Destroyer Escort to put into practice what we had learned in the classroom. Next, we went to sea aboard a submarine, dove and learned what it felt like to evade a sonar-equipped surface ship. Those instructors and ship's personnel were impressive. They knew what they were doing and I felt privileged to be one of their students.

Then, suddenly, there was a change of orders. Trouble was brewing in the Middle East and we were going to have to leave for WestPac as soon as possible. My orders were to return to the ship immediately; so I promptly left San Diego, heading for Long Beach. Once there, I tried calling around using the phone book Yellow Pages to find a place to park my car. The monthly rates were too high, so I wound up selling the car for about half of its value and arranging for the check to be sent to my father. I was ready to leave; but, as I recall now, we left about 4-5 days after that. Hmmm.

Anyway, the Fox Division Officer, Ensign Jenson, was ready to deploy and wrote about his Division in the later-to-be-published Far East Cruise book as follows:

"The Fox Division included (sic.) firecontrolmen, sonarmen and torpedomen. Our mission is to aim and fire the guns at surface and/or air targets, direct the ship in attacking submarines and to launch torpedoes when necessary.

"Aiming the guns includes use of directors and accurate radars and computer (sic.) solutions to problems involved with giving proper train and elevation to our gun batteries.

"Directing the ship for submarine attack includes, first finding the sub, then determining his movements, before guiding our ship into firing position for delivering our deadliest blows.

"Having two types of torpedoes aboard our ship, we are prepared to battle either surface or subsurface enemies. Our 'fish' are expensive, so we give constant attention to their maintenance and, in time of need, will do our best to launch them properly with intent to hit.

"The FOX DIVISION is the core of the Gunnery Department, in our eyes, and we, the men of FOX DIVISION, have been and will continue trying our utmost to make such a core the strongest possible."

Christmas Eve was spent at the O' Club in Yokosuka, Japan, a multi-story building with no windows. It had been built originally by the Japanese; as had all of the hidden tunnels and spaces for war materials production carved out of the rocky hills on the (yo kus' ka) base that partially surrounded the harbor. I had dinner with our ship's Executive Officer, LCDR "Bob" Burr, USN. I don't remember anyone else patronizing the pitched black ceilinged and walled dining room that was illuminated only by shaded lights on the tables that evening, except the two of us.

Bob was from Seymour, Iowa, originally and had enlisted in the Navy on November 15, 1938. He came up through the enlisted ranks during WWII and was commissioned an Ensign in April 1944. He often mimicked in jest someone from his early years in the Navy, a senior officer who had frequently boasted: "I'm the most even tempered S.O.B. in the whole United States Navy! – I'm ALWAYS mad!!"

Not much could scare Bob; except his attractive wife. I met her only once. Bob would hide enough money in his shoe for a bus ticket back to Long Beach when he went to see her in San Diego. She often emptied his wallet while he slept and would later stop the car out somewhere in the country and leave him standing by the road. More than once, I had to arrange transportation for him back to the ship from the Long Beach bus station, after he'd run out of money. A good man. He smoked a lot; but a good man nonetheless.

One night, we were patrolling the Formosa Straits, when my sonarmen picked up a target. It gradually developed into a BIG sonar contact as we steamed on. The unknown was north of us and west of where our track would carry us without a course change.

Prior to that time, we had been placed on extra alert status, arguably to look for any signs that might point towards an impending Chinese invasion of Formosa. So, when a big, BIG, sonar blip came along and we reported it to the bridge and then watched it slowly go by us and then begin to fall back behind us, and way behind us, and behind us still more, and begin fading, I left the sonar shack and found myself alone with Bob Burr in the ward room.

"Why did we not turn towards that target and investigate it?," I asked him.

No answer. Just another cigarette lighted, and he got up and poured two cups of coffee.

"If my men are going to stay sharp and find sonar contacts, what's the point of it, if we're not going to investigate what we find?," I asked him again.

Finally, he demurred saying that the Captain had been informed of the sonar contact and had ordered the ship to continue on course and speed.

"Well!," I responded somewhat surprised. "If that's what the Captain is going to do every time we find a sonar contact, I am going to have difficulty keeping the sonarmen at peak performance. What's the use of it? Let me talk to the Captain."

Bob shook his head: No.

We parted. He went somewhere and I went back down to the sonar shack. I said nothing to the men.

Then, the ship made a sharp left 180-degree turn and began heading back. The target had long since gone off the screen, but, eventually, it reappeared at long range and off to starboard.

The sonar operator began calling out ranges and bearings, while I informed the bridge we had regained sonar contact. The bridge then asked for continuous readings on the sound-powered phones of ranges and bearings to the target, something they had not requested the first time.

We were cruising along at about 10-12 knots, I think it was, and when the range had dropped to about 2-3 miles, the ship turned and began heading straight for the target.

It was dark outside, close to midnight, possibly. Down in the sonar shack, I was standing on the port side next to the ship's thin hull monitoring the sonar screen with a few others from the Fox Division.

The sonar contact was getting close to the screen's center when the engine order telegraph indicator attached to the overhead above us rang and arrows moved to Full Astern on the starboard engine and to Stop on the port engine. The rudder indicator also showed the rudder moving to starboard. The deck that I and 3 or 4 sonarmen were standing on began to shake from the ship's backing propeller. After some 30 seconds to a minute of it, the vibrations stopped and all seemed quiet and still.

We were wondering what was happening when I heard something rub against the hull beside me and felt the deck pitch up - enough to toss my feet an inch or two off the deck. The ship also jerked sideways and almost caused those of us who were standing in the sonar shack to topple over.

We had brushed up against something; something soft. What I learned later was that we had almost charged into a burned-out sunken hull of a Chinese junk. Very little of it was exposed above the surface so the ship's search light had difficulty finding it. In the last minutes, fortunately, it had been detected in time for us to slow and turn away, giving it only a glancing blow. No signs of life were detected; but a Notice to Mariners was sent out, declaring it a Hazard to Navigation.

Another port we anchored in was Sasebo, some 30 air miles from Nagasaki, where the U.S. dropped a second atomic bomb to end WWII. It also was near Korea. Not many Japanese citizens were seen driving their own cars anywhere in Japan at that time; but taxi fares were reasonable, at least to visiting American servicemen.

Early one Sunday afternoon, I ventured ashore and took a taxi ride around the area. That Toyota smelled like a new vehicle, though it wasn't. It had leather seats and was obviously given "tender loving care" by its driver. I remember thinking, "This would be a pretty good car in the U.S., except for it being so small." (What did I know about future oil shortages.) The driver began a winding road climb to the peak of what was a small mountain overlooking the harbor and City of Sasebo.

The view from the top was expansive, as I got out of the cab and strained to look around. Unnoticed, at first, but soon to become apparent, were two youngsters seated just below the parking lot rim: a girl and boy, sister and brother, most likely; ages around 7 and 8. The boy had one large wooden crate on his lap, while the girl seemed to favor something in her hand; seen later to be a pocket watch.

Hardly had the two children been noticed when both of them abruptly stood up. The boy lifted the wooden crate and began struggling with one end of it, eventually achieving his objective, to bystander approval. There had gathered several cars and persons to watch. The children's mission was revealed when, at what must have been a scheduled time, pigeons emerged from the crate and took flight. The boy and girl stood in awe looking up as their flock circled overhead, circled the mountain peak, and out before us, seeking direction.

A few more orbits and those pigeons did find their heading; "downhill" towards Sasebo. And just as quickly, the little boy and girl began their downhill hike, along a fairly straight path towards town.

A finale, of sorts, had been reached with the pigeon release, so I returned to the waiting cab, anticipating more touring. Approaching the Toyota, I noticed a white '50 Ford sedan parked alongside. A Chief Petty Officer was at the wheel, his nurse friend in the passenger seat beside him. With windows rolled down, they easily caught my ear, and invited me to abandon my cab and join them in their car. I begged off; but they insisted. So, next, I found myself seated in their front seat next to the door.

We started down the winding road, soon noticing the two youngsters moving along their path. It crossed our road every now and then. Once ahead of them, we stopped and waited as they came down the hill towards us.

The nurse spoke Japanese to them as they came and stood beside the car and me. They hesitated, at first, while the nurse continued speaking to them in Japanese. Finally, the tenor of voices and the children's body language suggested an agreement had been reached. I did not know what the agreement was, only that the youngsters just stood there, staring at the right rear car door.

The nurse finally asked me in English to please reach around and open the rear door for the children. "We're going to give them a ride back to town," she added.

After the children had climbed in and seated themselves, empty pigeon crate and all, they sat erect and looked straight ahead - while the rear door remained wide open. I reached around again and closed it.

Not much was said as we drove the short distance to Sasebo. We were close to the city limits. As we entered Sasebo and passed a grouping of storefronts, the children unexpectedly turned around - in unison - uttered a few words to each other in Japanese and began looking ahead, then back, then ahead again, and back, every few seconds.

Two blocks further and the children said something aloud in Japanese. This time, the car pulled over and stopped. The children stared expectantly at the right rear door again. I reached around and opened it. They got out and stood on the street like statues looking back at the rear seat. The boy was carrying the crate, but the little girl had seemed capable and unburdened enough to have closed the door behind them, I thought. But, no, I had to reach around for it once more and close it. As we drove off, I looked back. Those two children remained standing on the street at curbside and continued looking at us as we faded into the distance. The nurse then explained to me what had happened - in English:

Those children had never ridden in a car before! They simply had not known about door handles, nor how to work them. The storefronts were near where they lived. But, since it was their first ride in a car, they chose to ride as far as possible - thus, the extra two blocks and the looking back and forth, before asking to be let out.

Memorable. So was entering and visiting Hong Kong for the first time. I include entering because the stem on my Omega wristwatch broke off that very morning, as we were headed for the anchorage. I was going to reset the watch to the new time zone. So, what better opportunity could there have been for buying a replacement wristwatch than to be able to shop for one in Hong Kong?

Eventually, I purchased a Rolex (with a cap that sealed the stem from salt water corrosion) for $65.00. It was an Oyster Perpetual with a self-winding movement that lasted some 40 years. Towards the end of its useful life, the Rolex (factory) cleaning charge was about $100 each time and needed to be done about once a year. That watch had successfully withstood many pressure changes, especially when I flew unpressurized planes to lofty altitudes.

High atop a hill overlooking Hong Kong and Kowloon was an old two-story red brick mansion with gray stone window sills and a slate roof. It had been converted into the International

Press Club Headquarters. There were spectacular views and interesting people to lunch with, one day. How or why another ship's officer and I were there, I don't recall; but I do remember sitting at a fairly large table with four or five others from Hong Kong and being treated to lunch. The dining room walls and all of the other walls in the downstairs rooms and hallways were mahogany paneled. What I also remember was the luncheon group's swiftness and ability to put together a fund raiser of some kind in just 20 minutes or so, while we ate. One man worked for a newspaper; another for a radio station; another for a magazine, I think; and yet another had ticket printing capability. They welcomed me to lunch and then proceeded with their short debates back and forth, followed by agreements to do this and that, and assembled a fund raiser with all of its details taken care of in less time than it took to eat lunch. After that, one of them offered us (and we accepted) a ride in his chauffeur-driven Jaguar sedan down to the boat landing, or anywhere else we wanted to go. "Just tell my chauffeur where you want to go, and he'll take you there," he said. He rode off with someone else, while we enjoyed a ride down to the boat landing and returned to the ship. It was almost time to leave Hong Kong and return to CONUS (Continental United States) via one more replenishment stop in Yokosuka, Japan.

An Air Force transport plane was reported lost at sea. It was carrying dependents of U.S. servicemen and had gone down somewhere between Japan and the U.S. This unfortunate event almost coincided with our preparations for returning to Long Beach, so our return track was laid out, ostensibly, to follow the estimated flight path of that transport. We were to look for and report anything we could find adrift in the Pacific Ocean that might relate to that plane, its passengers, its cargo.

Besides the RUPERTUS, there were three other destroyers in Destroyer Division 32 (DESDIV 32): George K. MACKENZIE (DD836), Leonard F. MASON (DD852), and the Henry W. TUCKER (DDR 875). Commanding DESDIV 32 from onboard the RUPERTUS was CDR. Richard H. Woodfin, USN, a Naval Academy graduate, Class of 1938.

The plan was for our four ships to proceed eastward side by side with about two miles of separation between ships. Theoretically, at least, that would create an 8-mile wide search sweep leading back to Long Beach. Our lookouts were to be extra vigilant.

Also determined on our return passage would be a fuel economy winner. All four ships were sailing together, so we would have to monitor even the small stuff to win.

Ensign Jenson had been the Fox Division Officer and had been the OOD (Officer of the Deck) on the bridge only a few times. He was ready, willing and able, however, to say "I have the conn" at any time.

Ensign Jenson had grown to sense, nonetheless, that his Commanding Officer did not want to let him "have the conn" very much. Just a feeling he had. But Ensign Jenson didn't let it bother him. After all, he would be automatically receiving orders to Flight Training, after exactly one year of duty aboard the RUPERTUS. Whatever credits he might miss out on by not becoming a "Qualified OOD Underway" he could easily make up for later by flying fighters and attack planes on and off carriers, he reasoned.

It was 11:45 AM on a sunny day, somewhere near the middle of the Pacific in relatively calm ocean waters when, after a briefing from the off-going Officer of the Deck, Ensign Jenson saluted him and announced, "I relieve you, Sir."

The off-going OOD then declared to all persons on the bridge, "I stand relieved. Mr. Jenson has the conn."

Mr. Jenson then announced to everyone on the bridge, "I have the conn." I also had acknowledged our being the formation guide ship and that I had tactical command of all four destroyers in DESDIV 32.

The ship's Captain and the DESDIV 32 Commodore looked around and wandered around the bridge for a while. The Commodore could see the other three destroyers in the distance off to port. We were on the starboard end of a four-ship line-abreast formation, with about 2 miles of separation between ships. That placed the farthest ship 6 miles out; and on an imaginary line between us could be seen the other two ships. Since we were the guide ship, the others used the RUPERTUS to position themselves in the formation. The guide could be shifted to any of the other ships, usually decided by the Commodore, and usually done by radio or signal flags. The ocean was exceptionally calm.

After they were satisfied that not much could go wrong, the Commodore and Captain proceeded to the wardroom, below, for lunch. The only ladder down was on the port side of the pilot house and was an inside ladder with no view to the outside. So, the Commodore lingered a moment or two at the top, gazed straight out to port at the neat line of three destroyers in his division, and finally descended to the wardroom with the captain following close behind.

The clock on the bulkhead in the back of the pilot house was near the ship's PA (Public Address) mike and the radio mike for communicating with the other ships in the formation. It had almost reached 12 noon when one of the bridge lookouts called out that he saw something floating in the water up ahead and off slightly to port. I walked out of the pilot house and over to the port side lookout who was standing on the forward outdoor walkway at the front of the bridge. He pointed the object out to me and, through the binoculars, I saw that it looked like one of those glass balls wrapped in rope: sometimes used as a decoration; sometimes used by fishermen to hold or mark something. I decided to retrieve it just in case it had been part of someone's baggage on that lost Air Force transport.

The ships were all doing about 15 knots, in a line-abreast formation. The glass ball was still some distance away but gradually drifting closer. My estimate became that it would pass down our port side as we went by it. It was far enough out, though, so we could later turn the ship around and just about have it on the bow for a grappling hook pickup.

Since we were also participating in a fuel economy contest with three other ships, I quickly thought of a way to preserve our standings. Maintaining a constant speed was vital to achieving good fuel economy; and we had been at the right speed for maximum economy, 15 knots, most of the time. I knew what to do.

After ordering the bos'n mate to notify the engine and boiler rooms to stand by to stop all engines; I radioed a 180° left turn together signal to the formation and executed it. "Left full rudder," was my next command to the helmsman. While the other ships were using only left standard rudder, their turning radii would be wider than ours and it would take a bit longer for them to complete their turns. I then shifted the designated guide from RUPERTUS over to the ship that was outboard on the other side of the formation.

The bos'n was instructed to call away the boat hook party on the ship's intercom, as our ship began to lean outward and away from the hull's sharp left turn. I gave the new reciprocal course for the helmsman to steady up on; and, as we came around in the turn, I saw the boat hook party assembling on the forward main deck; and our approach to the glass bulb wrapped in rope was such that I ordered "All engines stop!" We were set to coast right up to it.

The other ships in the formation, meanwhile, were still moving along nicely at 15 knots, but headed back to Japan. Just as soon as the grappling hook party had retrieved that bulb, I was going to radio another formation left turn together signal; order our own engines back up to 15 knots; order "Hard left rudder" and a steadying up on our original course and speed; and as the rest of the formation then caught up to us, I would redesignate RUPERTUS the guide ship. We'd be back in formation and on course and speed as before. Meanwhile, the other ships in the formation would have maintained a relatively constant speed for achieving fuel economies; and the RUPERTUS may have saved a little fuel in the process of stopping, but would have consumed more, again, accelerating back up to 15 knots. That was my plan. But only part of it, the most important part, fortunately, the pickup, was carried out.

What you've just read was never allowed to be revealed by Ensign Jenson. His superiors never asked him to explain his actions. What follows, adds to this.

The ship's lean in the turn got the attention of the captain and his luncheon guests, below. The pilot house phone soon rang and I found myself speaking calmly to the Captain, explaining we had sighted an object in the water and were going to retrieve it. "Very good," I thought he said.

We had completed our 180-degree left turn and were coasting up to the glass bulb. I observed the boat hook party on the port side and slightly aft from the bow reaching down to make a retrieval, when things became a little disorganized on the bridge. Unraveled might be more accurate.

Recall that before turning left 180 degrees, the other destroyers in the division were seen by the Commodore off to port, just as he descended the ladder. Now, after that 180 degree turn, those ships were shifted around to being off to starboard. And further, as we had slowed and stopped to make a retrieval, those other ships had continued on and were positioned somewhere forward of our starboard beam. That's when the Commodore charged up the ladder, looked out to the left, more to the left, back around to the right, then in all directions with the pilot house blocking his view of the other destroyers, and he YELLED, "MR. JENSON! WHAT HAVE YOU DONE WITH MY SHIPS??"

The captain was right behind him and didn't see them either, apparently. "I HAVE THE CONN," he shouted. "Where are we? What's our course and speed?" (We were still almost stopped dead in the water making the retrieval.)

The boat hook party hand signaled up to the bridge that they had retrieved the object and held it up for us to see. (As far as I was concerned, my mission was accomplished. I would not argue about having to stand aside.) But the Commodore still did not have the picture of what was going on when he grabbed the radio mike and ordered his division of destroyers to, "Resume base course and speed!"

There were three ships out there, on the same course, and two miles apart. After some hesitation, the ship on the right turned right. The one on the left turned left. The one in the middle waited to see which way the others were turning before making its turn.

The RUPERTUS eventually got under way again and turned around. But, by then, the other three had joined up, gone by us, and were almost over the horizon in the dark as the sun went down behind us. It took us half the night to catch up; and it seemed the commodore had conveniently forgotten about the fuel economy contest.

We pulled into Midway Island for fuel, and an overnight stay. It was a chance to look over an island made famous during WWII. Next to the channel entrance was some rusting wreckage left behind after the war. There was a lot more of it to see when entering Pearl Harbor. Makes an impression no matter where you find it.

After tying up to a dock, we had a chance to wander around the island for awhile. The sand was soft, the gentle breezes comfortable, and gooney birds had buried nests almost everywhere in the sand.

A paved runway was found; but it stood alone without any planes or hangers. Later, we learned the gooney birds were protected by an animal rights society in the U.S. and were "Off Limits" to everyone. And they had been declared sufficiently hazardous to flight operations for the field to have been officially closed, except for emergencies.

Four-engine prop planes had experienced gooney birds flying into their propellers, windshields and wing leading edges. We were told the last users of Midway's airstrip were four National Guard jet fighters based in Hawaii. They had landed successfully, refueled, and attempted take-offs for returns to Hawaii; but only one of them made it. Two planes caught gooney birds in the intakes before lift off but were able to abort successfully. Another was able to take off, but ingested a bird after turning down wind and had to land immediately.

Those three aircraft had to be barged back to Hawaii and were the last planes to use the airfield at Midway, we were told. Those gooney birds were thought by researchers to have no other place to reside.

In the morning, I went out on deck and discovered another surprise. A fresh water barge had tied up next to us during the night. It was painted Navy gray and, except for metal vent pipes, cast iron twin bollards and mooring line fairleads that became visible to me in an instant, the barge was made entirely of concrete. The sides and stern looked to be about 1-2 feet thick. I could hear pumps operating that were transferring fresh water to the RUPERTUS. It was another useful item left over from WWII.

Soon, we were under way again and, before long, my first WestPac cruise was over. And then one more surprise: My mother and a friend of hers from Chicago Heights, Mrs. Judith Samuelson, came aboard in Long Beach to greet me. I gave them a tour of the ship. After all, I was the OOD (in port).

Long Beach citizens were complaining. Their city was slowly sinking, they said. If the oil companies pumping oil from Signal Hill and elsewhere around the city didn't do something soon, Long Beach would gradually sink into the ocean. A solution was finally proposed: For every barrel of crude oil pumped out of the ground in Long Beach, the oil companies would have to pump a barrel of sea water back in.

They were arguing about that when I finally left the area. Years later, I learned that the oil companies had been forced to comply with that new resolution - and that it eventually benefited them. Seems the underground oil supplies had been running low and wells were having to be abandoned. Then, the new regulation came along and ultimately it was discovered that by pumping water into the wells, the crude oils floated to the top, and into the well heads again. Wells that were thought to have run dry were flowing again.

Destroyer Duty, for me, then advanced to a dry dock period; followed by being tied to a dock and overhauling everything aboard that needed it. All of those work orders written up while at sea, months earlier, for fixing this pump and that motor, etc., had been forwarded on and made the shipyard ready for us. Experiments had determined that stopping work about a half hour early each day for conducting a "Clean Sweepdown fore and aft" led to much earlier completions and better equipment performances afterwards.

One full year of duty aboard a destroyer had been interesting; even entertaining, at times. Quite a learning experience. Several months before leaving for Pensacola, I was allowed a weekend away from the ship to return to Chicago Heights and marry my first wife, Margaret Orr, the blue-eyed, blonde daughter of a wealthy contractor.

Living in a one-room poolside apartment in Long Beach took some adjusting, but it was only for about four months. I had Shore Patrol Duty on a carnival-like strip about a block south of Ocean Boulevard a few times. And I applied for the services of a patent attorney in a high rise also on Ocean Boulevard.

My new wife and I had discovered that there was nothing available on the market for carrying shoes from place to place. So, I designed a shoe case that could accommodate one pair of a woman's or man's shoes; and the cases could also be stacked and latched together to form one suitcase-like unit. A firm in Pasadena made a sample from my drawings, and I had visions of getting a patent and making a deal with a company like Samsonite to produce them; the first few, of course, would go to the Jensons, who needed them.

That patent attorney was as pleasant and accommodating as he could be; but the average patent pendency time of 36 months that he reported the U.S. Patent & Trademark Office (PTO) would require for processing gave me a rude awakening.

That was too long to do me any good, certainly. But, even more, I wondered how the U.S. Government could find that acceptable in fulfilling its Constitutional obligations. The time would eventually come when I would reluctantly have to declare: "If the USN were managed by patent attorneys, our warships would still have sails!" Really!

CHAPTER 8

MACH ONE

My mother's cousin, Mildred, was married to a United Airlines DC-3 pilot, Wallace Fagen. He was based at Midway Airport in Chicago, where United also had its modern Art Deco style headquarters offices running along the east side of Cicero Avenue and its hangers across the street. There seemed to be an increasing flow of DC-3s and other propeller-driven aircraft in and out of Midway after WWII, eventually making it the world's busiest airport.

Wallace and Mildred lived in Oak Lawn, near Midway, and would visit us in Chicago Heights from time to time. On one of those visits, I was profoundly influenced.

It was around 1946, or thereabouts, when Wallace gave me something. He did not appear to want to make a big deal of it, but handed me a small box and said, "Here's a present for you. I want you to have this."

It took a few moments to get the box opened, but, inside, I discovered a pair of silver wings with the United Airlines red, white, and blue logo design in the center. Later in life, I surmised that I, too, had received what United Airlines stewardesses had handed out routinely to passengers on every flight in what we, today, would refer to as a promotional/advertising effort. But, at that time, the gift from Wallace of those silver wings to me was electrifying. I had been surprised and the wings looked real. They stimulated a new kind of confidence in myself that I had not had before. My whole perspective seemed to change from thinking of myself as just a passenger to actually believing that I could someday become a pilot.

Some fifty years later, I had the good fortune to visit Wallace again in Sun City, AZ, before he passed away. I was able to thank him for the silver wings he had given me when I was growing up; but he didn't remember it. Mildred, his wife, did, however. She's 93 as I write this and still lives in her favorite Sun City desert environment. More power to you, Mildred! And thanks again.

The entrance to the Naval Air Station at Pensacola was impressive, with the red brick and white trimmed buildings, expansive manicured lawns, and with trees, shrubs and flower beds scattered about; it was beautifully landscaped.

Saufley Field is one of the nearby auxiliary airfields and the one I landed a T-34 on for my first (Navy) solo landing. That happened after a lot of ground school preparations and some dual flights with my assigned instructor, Lieutenant "Ole" Olson.

When instructors take their new students up for the first time, they usually return with airsick students - who have either filled a paper bag or a kid leather flight glove, making it appear like a cow's udder. The only question those crafty instructors might be mulling over in their minds as they walk with you out to an airplane for that first flight is how long and how many aerobatic maneuvers might it take before you show your hand. The good news? That will probably be the last time you'll get airsick.

Being promoted from Ensign Jenson to Lieutenant Junior Grade Jenson towards the end of 1957 was nice; but, person-ally, I did not attach much importance to it. There was a small pay increase, of course; but my promotion seemed to affect more the people I came in contact with. What I sensed about it later in life, however, was that I had outranked most of the other students going through flight training with me and had probably benefited from that, here and there, without ever realizing it.

Flying had many definitions that were bandied about from "Hours and Hours of Boredom Interrupted by Moments of Stark Terror," mostly applicable to those pilots who are the least prepared for emergencies, I think; to the more legitimate, "Flying is a constant series of corrections to average out where you want to go." That was truer before auto pilots came along, however.

One day, I was called to the Squadron Commander's office. Not knowing why, I was a little apprehensive on entering. In short order, my flight instructor, Lt. Olson, appeared and stood next to the Commander when I became the recipient of a yellow plastic T-34 model airplane and a certificate declaring me the "Student of the Week." My picture was taken - several times, including for publication in the base newspaper.

Perhaps it was a picture of me in that paper, I never knew, for sure; but, one day soon after that, a young ensign student aviator approached me and asked for help. We were brown bagging lunch, so I invited him to lunch with me in my car. I may have driven somewhere else on the base to get away from the hangers. He was the first black naval officer I had come across, and there he was, trying to become a Naval Aviator.

"They're going to drop me from the flight training program," he insisted. "On my next check ride, I'm going to fail."

"Just concentrate on flying the best you can," I advised him. "Don't let anything interfere with that and you'll be OK. Do your best in the air and the rest will take care of itself."

He was still apprehensive and convinced that, because he was black, there was resentment and a plan to remove him from the flight training program.

To help calm his nerves, I said that I would appeal to my instructor for assistance on his behalf (which I did and eventually was told there was nothing that could be done).

Still wanting to help him as much as possible, I invited him and his wife to have dinner and to take in a movie with me and my wife in Pensacola on the following Saturday. He agreed to it.

We met at a restaurant somewhere on the near west side of Pensacola, as I recall, and I was truly impressed by how attractive he and his wife were. An outstanding couple, I thought. As we ate in that crowded and busy restaurant, no one seemed to pay any extra attention to us. We enjoyed ourselves and I became even more favorably impressed by the young black couple's intelligence, manners and courteous behavior. After dinner, we left and drove in each of our cars to a movie theater in downtown Pensacola.

The movie shorts were about to start as we walked down the aisle in that crowded and noisy theater, found four empty seats, approximately in the middle of the center section, and sat down. As the movie previews started the crowd calmed down and attentions turned to the screen.

Later, after the feature movie had been running for about 15 minutes, for some reason, I distinctly sensed that the audience had become totally silent. I turned my attentions away from the movie, looked around and immediately noticed that people had gotten up and moved from their seats, leaving the four of us in the middle of a huge circle of empty seats. People were crowded in the back rows. Some were even standing behind the last row of seats and looking down at us. There were no persons sitting within 10-12 rows or 10-12 seats of us in any direction. Empty seats extended back behind us to beyond the balcony overhang.

"What should we do?" I remember being asked, apprehensively.

I thought about it for a second, or two, and replied, "Let's just enjoy the rest of the movie. We don't have a problem; they do." And so we did.

Afterwards, I don't recall seeing anyone else as we left the theater. We parted and walked to our separate cars. I lost contact with that ensign and his wife. Never saw him or her again. What I can state for the benefit of this memoir is that I did try to defend that ensign's rights to be treated fairly. I appealed up my chain of command to Lt. Olson several times; and he made my concerns known to his higher authority each time, as far as I could tell. Eventually, I was told there was nothing more that I could do for the ensign. For all I knew, he may have gone on and completed the program. Quite possibly he wasn't a good enough pilot. I had no way of knowing.

My wife and I needed a bit more furniture, being newly-weds. Thinking there were others in the Navy with similar needs, we eventually opened an unfurnished furniture store close to the base and named it, "Sand and Stain." I thought it would give my wife something productive to do while I was away; and we intended to open more stores to serve more Navy families near some of the other Naval Air Training facilities, if that first one worked out.

Another flight student, Sam Purvis (USNA Class of '57), and I enjoyed making a few "Bob & Ray" type radio ads. One ad had us bailing out of an airplane holding on to a piece of unfinished furniture that we then had sanded and stained by the time we hit the ground. Unfortunately, sales were too slow and eventually each of the other more established furniture stores in the area began to carry one or two unfinished furniture items at rock bottom prices. Once I had figured that out, I was reminded that our lease would soon expire. What to do with a store practically full of unfinished furniture? We had a sale. $5.00 bought any single unfinished furniture piece that we had in the store. It didn't take long to liquidate that inventory. No doubt people in need of basic furniture were helped in the few days that it took to empty the building. If there were to be more unfinished furniture stores near other Naval Air Training bases, however, someone else would have to provide them.

All of us were busy, in those days, and having to learn new things took more energy out of us and a little longer to accomplish. What we seemed to be stuck on were touch-and-go landings. We did nothing but touch-and-go's, it seemed, in the mornings and then again in the afternoons, with other activities sandwiched in between.

From the beginning, Lt. Olson made it clear that he could chop the power at any time after starting a take-off roll and I would have to handle it. The result, of course, was having to begin looking for an emergency landing site immediately after lift-off, if not before.

The engine was usually not turned off during such maneuvers, just throttled back to near idle. If power was pulled back at altitude where it was cool or cold, the instructor would warm the engine up by occasionally adding throttle and then taking it back off during the descent.

While quickly trying to take observed surface winds into account, a landing area would have to be selected and a glide to it established. After extending the landing gear, in the last moments before touchdown, the instructor would usually take control, add power and pull up (provided the engine had been kept reasonably warm during the descent). After raising the landing gear and regaining a safe altitude, the student would be given control again and the instruction flight would continue.

There was one accident often mentioned in connection with those power-off emergency landings that had happened to a student and his instructor in a T-34. With landing gear extended, they had unknowingly descended between two high tension line towers. Their flight path was perpendicular to a high tension line that they didn't see. As they landed on and snagged the line with both main gear struts, that line was the usual very long high tension line, so, as the plane nosed over from having caught the line, the line moved out and upward and sort of held on to the plane a bit longer, stopping its forward motion, and then released it as the plane did an outside loop and fell to the ground. The plane then landed on the main and nose gear with such force that the struts were driven straight up through the wings. Fortunately, both pilots survived.

One lesson learned was to be wary of electric and telephone lines when having to make a forced landing. They can be more difficult to detect from above than from below.

Barron was another auxiliary airfield, located north of Pensacola, and where we were introduced to the T-28. Take-offs in it, with the canopy open, reminded me of my Ford hot rod, except that the T-28 was considerably faster – and smoother.

During some early morning takeoffs, when dew drops were still on the vegetation, adding full power in a T-28 would cause vapor trails to form on the propeller tips and soon there would also be vapor trails streaming off the wing tips on lift-off.

One afternoon, I took one up to altitude and began a gentle descent as I added full power and monitored the prop pitch to avoid overspeeding it. It didn't take long to get up to about 360 knots, which was at or near the plane's red line speed limit. The flight control stick at that airspeed was rigid. I could not move it without possibly bending or breaking it, I thought. So, I used the trim wheel to roll in some nose up attitude and eventually it slowed enough so I could use the stick to fly it again. Later I would fly F9F-8 Couger jets with hydraulic boosted elevators in the tail and I understood completely the need for such hydraulic assistance at high airspeeds.

Basic instrument flying was also taught in T-28s at Barron Field in addition to night flying. On my last check ride, I had control of the plane in the back seat with the hood up (covering my head) and was following the approach to landing instructions given over the intercom by the check-ride instructor in the front seat. He was playing the part of a ground control approach operator. "Slow your rate of descent to 300 feet per minute. Come left two degrees to heading 240. Stand by." KLUNK! On deck. "I have it. Pop your hood."

It's a rare, great feeling when you can see the runway you've just landed on using instruments only. Credits belong also to the instructor in the front seat!

The Navy took pride in its ability to adapt to new needs and conditions. So, by June 1958, I was transferred to an old Naval Air Station near Memphis, TN, for the next phase: Cross country air navigation.

While the T-28s had been faster than the little T-34s, what I came to Millington, TN, to fly would be faster yet. The Lockheed T2V-1 jet was new to everyone, at that time, and had become our new cross country instrument trainer. It could take us from point to point to point, swiftly.

Elvis Presley had recently become famous by that time. An unusual and attractive gate guarded the entrance to his

Graceland estate. A two-story white brick house could be seen up on a hill not very far from the gate. Well done, I thought. While waiting for service in a Memphis Oldsmobile garage, one day, I ventured back into the service area and asked the mechanics if they knew Elvis. "Sure," they said. "He used to come in here all the time. He drove a delivery truck and carried a guitar with him in the cab. If he had to wait for any length of time, he'd take out his guitar and play it while he waited." Everyone that I came in contact with in Memphis was proud of Elvis Presley.

Our syllabus in Memphis was relatively short, so, we were soon ready for our final check rides. Weather, however, turned inclement, and for a while we had to try to make the most of our time on the ground in classroom sessions. I had not been made aware of it until then, but a Naval Academy classmate of mine was reportedly interested in becoming the first to complete the new T2V-1 instrument training program. His father, I also learned, was a rear admiral. It didn't take me long to realize how proud that father could become if his son did, in fact, become the very first student to complete the program.

During some of that "grounded due to inclement weather" time, an instructor had clued me in on this and at the same time had said that the instructors had agreed that I should become the first completion. That was the first I had heard of any of this, and I was flattered, to be sure. But, after digesting that compliment, I turned to him and asked that Pete be allowed to finish first, once the weather cleared. "Think of how proud his father will be," I offered. Nothing more was said about it, and inclement weather seemed to hold for a few more days; then it cleared.

After the check ride with a pilot I had never seen before, but who looked a lot like comedian George Goebel, we were taxiing back to the hanger area. I had popped the hood and my eyes were adjusting to the bright sunlight, while the instructor raised the hydraulically operated canopy. We moved along rather swiftly, I thought. There, up ahead, was a raised wooden platform that I didn't remember ever seeing before. We turned a little towards it and I instinctively felt we were getting ready for MY becoming that first completion. Yep.

Rear Admiral Peter B. Booth, USN (Ret.) and I are good friends; have been all along. Pete had command of the aircraft carrier USS Forrestal during the 1970s, and also was the Chief of Naval Air Training for awhile. In 2002, he authored a book, "Humble in Victory," that he dedicated to the seagoing sailors of the U.S. Navy, past, present, and future, and to those left behind on the homefronts. While we were in Memphis, Pete found his wife, Carolyn, and they have been together ever since.

"Do you still want to fly?," I was asked by a commander I had never seen before who was standing alone in our hanger office in Kingsville, TX, as I was passing through.

"You bet I do," I answered, "but I'll do better in the morning after a good night's rest."

He smiled and waved, as I walked on. He was hard to miss in dress blues, when everyone else changed back into khakis from their flight suits.

Kingsville, Texas, was where I had been sent for Advanced Naval Air Training; and the swept-wing F9F-8 Grumman Cougar jet was what I was flying. But we were still practicing those touch-and-go landings and takeoffs. One difference, though, was the mirror at the approach end of a runway.

A horizontal row of yellow lights aimed at a concave mirror could be seen by approaching pilots as a round yellow light called the "meatball." When that "meatball" was centered between the top and bottom of that slightly tilted mirror, the pilot was on a proper glide slope for landing. If the "meatball" was at the top of the mirror, the pilot knew he was flying too high. A low "meatball" meant he needed to come up. Just keep that "meatball" centered, the airspeed very, very slow (just above stalling), get lined up with the runway centerline, and KLUNK, you'd complete another FCLP (field carrier landing practice - some called it a controlled crash landing). It was all in preparation for our first actual carrier landings, required before we could graduate and qualify to wear those gold Naval Aviator wings.

That commander's question arose after I had been out shooting touch-and-goes and had experienced an engine problem.

After touching down, we would let the plane roll on the runway a short distance as the engine came back up to full power. Then, as airspeed increased and reached what was needed for takeoff, a lift-off would be followed by a slight climbing turn to the right (called a clearing turn), followed by another slight climbing turn back to the left and a leveling off so as to fly beside the runway at about 50 feet altitude for awhile, gaining enough airspeed to then climb back up and re-enter the landing pattern.

A clearing turn refers to carrier operations. After having been catapulted off a carrier's bow, a clearing turn away from where the carrier will soon pass is prudent. Sometimes, for one reason or another, planes are forced to land immediately in the waters ahead and carriers cannot maneuver to avoid them.

The F9F-8T was the newest version of the Grumman Cougar and had tandem seats: one in front, another in back. On a sunny afternoon, I had been alone in an 8T with the canopy opened shooting touch-and-goes. The open canopy was also for carrier operations so that if one had to land in the water, the canopy would already be opened. An open canopy, besides being drafty, did cause slight lift reductions; therefore, we opened canopies when simulating carrier approaches over land as well.

There were some four or five other Cougars in the oval landing pattern with me as I touched down on about my fourth or fifth landing and commenced another takeoff. The roll and turn to the right were uneventful, but a surprise loomed ahead as I made that left climbing turn. The wind blowing around in the cockpit was pretty noisy. What I heard in the next few seconds was even louder. It sounded like a drum roll coming from under the cockpit on my left side that changed to a loud WHACK followed immediately by a persistent WHISHHHHHH sound. The fire warning light came on.

Instinctively, I had pulled the throttle back and done several other things at the same time. Again, it takes longer to tell about them than to do them. In my left rear-view mirror an expanding ball of fire was glimpsed as it quickly dropped back and went out leaving an irregular pattern of black smoke around where flames had been.

I was about half way down the 8,000 foot long runway. An arresting cable was stretched across the runway some 1,500 feet from the end with ship's anchor chains tied to each end. The plane had a Martin Baker ejection seat; I could safely eject; the plane would crash in an open area between runways; but I elected not to eject. I could make it, I told myself; and pushed the nose down and banked left towards the runway with the power still at idle and the fire warning light still on.

The Landing Signal Officer, from beside the runway back by the mirror, radioed that he had seen a ball of fire come out of my tail pipe during the last clearing turn.

I maneuvered over the runway and banked right to get lined up with it. KLUNK! Throttle was moved around the horn to shut off fuel to the engine. Fire warning light still on. I reached down with my right hand, grabbed the tailhook handle and pulled it, and pulled it, and pulled it some more, until it finally locked. I had raised the nose for some aerodynamic braking but was still approaching the wire at a good clip. I had not been able to reach the middle of the runway, so I would catch the wire off center to the right. Brakes applied; then released.

Center or not, I didn't care because the end of the runway was coming up fast and the grass and gravel piles off the end didn't look good. Hope the hook catches that wire. It CAUGHT. It pulled the hook to one side so the nose of the plane (and the plane, itself) went up in the air and pointed left. It felt like I was trying to bust a bronco for a few seconds as I kicked the rudders to try to straighten it out. The plane quickly came back down a little sideways onto the runway, left wheel first, then straightened, then to the right and back. The left tire blew, but the wire then really began to do its job. In about 1,000 feet, the 8T was stopped. Dust flew from the dragged anchor chains, mostly on the right.

The fire warning light was still on. I turned off the electrical switches, twisted and punched my seat harness collective to release the parachute harness and seat belt. I did not know for sure what was happening in the engine compartment or anywhere else, so I thought it wise to assume the plane had a fire going somewhere and that I needed to get out of it as soon as possible. I was alone out there; no fire trucks or other vehicles were to be seen.

As I tried to stand up on the seat, I discovered that I still was hooked to this, then that, and when I had climbed out and hung over the side, I still had to unhook something else. When I was finally free to let go, I dropped some 3 feet to the runway and ran from the plane towards the middle of the runway. Whew!

The plane looked OK from a distance. No smoke. No fire. No apparent damage, except for a blown tire.

Eventually, the crash crews arrived, I was picked up, and the plane was towed back to the hanger area. I had filled out the necessary aircraft maintenance report and was leaving when I walked by that commander who asked me if I wanted to fly again.

There is a little more to this story.

About a week or two later, I was walking alone across an empty hanger headed for the Flight Line Office when one of the more senior maintenance chiefs came alongside and spoke: "Mr. Jenson, I'm really not supposed to be doing this, but I thought you should know about something." We stopped in the middle of the hanger. We were alone, and he proceeded to inform me about what had happened to the airplane after I had used the arresting wire to stop it.

Night maintenance had taken the plane practically apart but could not find anything wrong with it. They were about to tow it back out onto the flight line when one of the chiefs asked in the last minute: "Who was flying it?"

They found the yellow sheet and announced, "Mr. Jenson."

"Are you sure?"

"Yes!"

The Chief then ordered: "Take it apart again. If Mr. Jenson says there's something wrong with this airplane, there's something wrong with this airplane and we've got to find it!"

He had my full attention as he then led me to one of the maintenance rooms located just off the hanger floor.

He picked up a metal casting about the size of my fist. In the middle of it was a ripped sliver of the casting that stuck up about 1/2 inch and was about 1/4 inch wide. It was from one of the burner cans on the centrifugal flow jet engine I had had trouble with, one of the cans nearest the bottom of the engine. He showed me where that small sliver of metal had broken and bent downward in exactly the right position to sever the fire warning light wire, a wire that looked much like solder wire. The maintenance crew had taken all night to find it; but they did find it. Otherwise, thinking it had been accidentally cut during the tail section removal, the wire might have been spliced or replaced and the plane towed back out onto the flight line and pronounced "UP" and ready for flight. The next time it was started, it likely would have caught fire amidst other planes and who knows what may have happened after that.

Thank you, Chief, for letting me know.

The King Ranch was enormous. Ranch property obtained for the Naval Air Station represented a very small dot, almost, on a map of the Ranch. I drove onto the ranch property just to look things over, one day around noon. While not seeing one single person anywhere, I did happen upon a resting bull. He was lying down on the other side of a barbed wire fence. His head and shoulders were upright, but his rear quarter twisted around to flat on the ground. I say he was a bull because there was no mistaking what had the shape and size almost of a loaf of bread, extra large size. I'd seen enough, turned my car around and departed.

The King Ranch also had desert roads on it that were used by a tire testing company. Driving the heavier Cadillacs, Chryslers and Lincolns, the rubber hit the hot King Ranch roads for hundreds of thousands of test miles every year.

On the way north to Corpus Christi, one would also drive by property named the Chapman Ranch. What a story it had behind it, as published one Sunday by a Corpus Christi newspaper:

Seems the heirs to the King Ranch were beginning to run short of money, so they were advised to sell a portion of the ranch. The portion they put up for sale was priced at $750,000.

One Friday morning, a man named Chapman from Oklahoma came along and looked it over. Later, he was in the bank that was handling the property sale and the time was after 4 and moving towards 5 on a Friday afternoon just before banks everywhere in the U.S. closed for the weekend. The bank did not want to offend Mr. Chapman, whom they had never seen before, but who had just agreed to purchase the property and wanted the papers all signed so he could return immediately to Oklahoma. Finally, they found the courage to ask him, "How would you like to pay for the property, Mr. Chapman?"

"By check, of course," he answered.

Again, they wanted not to offend, so they agreed and Mr. Chapman wrote out a check for $750,000 to be drawn from his bank in Oklahoma.

Chapman's check was taken into another room, and behind closed doors a telephone call was made in the last minutes of business hours to Chapman's bank in Oklahoma.

"A Mr. Chapman has just written a check for $750,000. to be drawn from your bank. Is he good for it?," the banker was asked.

Chapman's banker in Oklahoma burst into laughter and after finally settling down said, "Hell, Yes! And seven more like it!"

Mr. Chapman had been a farmer in Oklahoma, had discovered oil and had passed along his Oklahoma properties to his sons. He wanted to start another big (ideal) farm, there, in Texas. He did that and then also discovered oil on that property, too. Hmmm.

Later, the King Ranch also discovered oil. Someday, it might be of interest to learn if as much oil would be pumped from the King Ranch as from the Chapman Ranch.

Looking down on the King and Chapman Ranches from the air, one could note how dry and how little green vegetation there could be. After a few days of rain, however, those same areas could sprout green vegetation everywhere, almost overnight. It was said that when Texas was dry, 10 acres of it could be required to feed one cow. But when it was wet, one acre could support 10 cattle.

On one of those rainy days when we didn't fly, we were visited in the Ready Room by two Catholic priests who had participated in WWII.

"Should I say a prayer when I'm in the air and a problem develops with my airplane?," asked one of the student pilots.

"No," answered one of the priests. "You can pray to your heart's content when you're on the ground, but not when you're flying. Give the plane your full attention and you can pray later, after you've landed, or before you go up."

One priest had volunteered to fly on the Burma Run in WWII as a morale booster and for his own experience. After some delay, permission was finally granted and he boarded a C-47 for the daytime jungle crossing in his priest attire, white collar and all.

At about the half-way point, they were on top of clouds that obscured the jungle below. The plane's engines were failing and the pilot ordered everyone to parachute out, the priest first!

He jumped, the chute opened, and he landed beside a huge boulder near a pond of water in the only clearing he could see anywhere around him.

Animals came and went to the pond for water, including elephants, mostly at night. The priest kept his cool - and even his white collar on for almost a week, expecting to be rescued at any time, and not wanting to be unpresentable when that happened.

Finally, on the seventh day, he couldn't stand it any longer. He stripped to naked, washed everything in the pond and laid out all of his garments on the boulder to dry. It was around noon and a clear day. A small observation plane then suddenly cleared the nearby treetops. The priest felt that he had to wave at the two observers he could see aboard the plane in order to be noticed. He did; and they noticed. A rescue party arrived about a week later and returned him to civilization.

According to my Aviators Flight Log Book, on March 3, 1959, I made six carrier landings but was catapulted only 3 times. Hmmm. Believe that should read 6 and 6.

We flew south from Pensacola to the carrier some 85 miles out, in the Gulf of Mexico. It had the last of the hydraulic catapults and arresting gear systems. After hydraulics came steam. Steam catapults offered a gradual, steady acceleration all the way up to flying speed; while the old hydraulic cats jerked the plane to flying speed almost immediately during the first 10% or so of travel. Likewise, the old hydraulic arresting gear did not bring a plane to as smooth a stop as the new steam system did.

The old WWII carriers had a Landing Signal Officer (LSO) standing on a platform at the rear of the flight deck holding paddles, slightly larger than tennis rackets, we'll say. He could be seen by the planes landing because those planes flew slower and their shorter turning radii kept them much closer to the carrier. When jets came along, however, they had to fly much faster to stay in the air and so their turning radii expanded, so far out that the LSO became only a dot. The position of his paddles to indicate whether a plane was too high, too low, or just right could not be seen from that distance. Therefore, the mirror was developed; a gyro stabilized mirror, at that, to accommodate ships' pitch and roll.

The first of anything can be challenging, of course; but coming across the ramp and trying to fly so the "meatball" passes out the side of the mirror as you go by it that first time, gave credence to the values already instilled by LSOs that getting set up properly in the approach makes all the difference. Indeed. After six landings, I was getting slightly accustomed.

"Bingo," radioed to me from the carrier's tower as I waited for a cat shot meant I was instructed to return to Pensacola once airborne. Getting six landings and cat shots for the first time was exhilarating, so much so that I applied slightly too much brake pressure on the left brake too soon (and perhaps the runway had a little sand on it) and I popped the left main gear tire on landing. With power brakes, that was very easy to do. I shouldn't have done it; but I did. The plane rolled to a complete stop, eventually, without further incident; but had to be towed back to the hanger area.

That tire was soon changed (not as fast as they can do it at the Indy 500, but close), and back we flew to Kingsville.

The next day, three of us were ushered into the Squadron Commander's office along with each of our three instructors who stood behind us as we waited for the Squadron Commander. Jim Ellis, the Marine student aviator in our group, whispered to me, "Do you know why we're here?"

"I have no idea," I answered. "Do you know anything?," I whispered to Gene Conner.

He shook his head: Negative.

Finally, the Commander came in and explained that we had just become qualified Naval Aviators by virtue of having completed our carrier landings successfully; but would we be willing to hold off on receiving our wings and become the first students to fly the supersonic F11F Grumman Tiger jet, before receiving our wings?

Yes! Sir!

F11Fs had been introduced into the fleet some two years earlier, in March 1957. The Blue Angels also received F11s and had given their very first performance in them at Barron Field, just north of Pensacola, on March 23, 1957. The "Blues" would continue flying F11s through 1968.

The F11 was the Navy's first supersonic fighter. Aside from an afterburning axial flow (more slender) engine, it had what became known as a "coke bottle" fuselage, a design using the new "area rule" concept.

Dr. Richard Whitcomb, in the early 1950s discovered that supersonic airflow was not the problem. It was when airflow slowed back down from supersonic to subsonic speed over a plane's skin surface that a smooth laminar airflow disappeared into disruption. That disruption usually continued rearward and could affect the trailing edges of wings and rudder elevators, rendering them ineffective. It became as if those control surfaces were moving up and down in areas without air pressure on them.Whitcomb had seen the same wind tunnel projectile movie produced by Shell Oil Co. as thousands of other engineers, but his take on it had been different from everyone else's.

As the cross sectional areas of the swept-wing F11 were plotted on a graph, from front to back a curve could be drawn that gradually rose and then turned downward. Whitcomb had determined that each lateral cross section measurement should include the wings and fuselage totals as one number. The curve representing fuselage and wing area totals would peak and then begin to drop at approximately above the wing root. It was aft of that peak where supersonic air flows would slow to subsonic speeds and change from laminar to non-laminar disrupted air, and remove (or greatly reduce) air pressure from skin surfaces, usually from the ailerons.

By slenderizing the fuselage shape (into what resembled a coke bottle) the peak of the area curve could be flattened a little at the top and the beginning of its decline moved aft. That shifted the disrupted air to the rear and to behind the wing control surfaces where it could do no harm. From then on, smooth, laminar air-flows continued over all of the wing surfaces and no loss of control was experienced at any speed from subsonic, through transonic and into supersonic speeds.

On April 18, 1958, in the United States, Lieutenant Commander George C. Watkins, USN, flew a F11F-1 to a new world altitude record of 76,932 feet (23,449m). Two weeks later, however, Watkins' record was exceeded in France by 2,520 feet by R. Carpentier in a Sud-Quest S0.9050 TRIDENT. The F11 could have benefited from a more powerful engine.

On March 5, 1959, two days after our first carrier landings, according to my Log Book, we became the first student aviators in the Advanced Naval Air Training Command to fly supersonic.

Flls had single-seats, so instructors flew with us in their own planes. My chase pilot for that first flight was Cdr. Vince Kelley, who was introducing the F11s. Later, as CO of an F8 training squadron at Moffett Field he moved them to what became known as Fightertown at Miramar NAS near San Diego. "Top Gun" came later in 1971 via my classmate Cdr. Roger Box. Still later, Kelley would take command of the aircraft carrier INTREPID and be much involved with it becoming the Air, Sea, and Space Museum in New York City.

Years later, Captain Kelley reflected in his 80th Birthday leaflet: "Best thing that ever happened to me is that I lasted this long." (He died in La Jolla, California on September 30, 1999 at age 81.) "My happiest moments were when I was having my way," he went on. "My successes are all God given"; "Women deserve more respect than we give them"; "You can't learn anything when you're talking"; "I never believed anyone was any better than me"; "I didn't know how to tell a lie"; "Worry is useless, senseless, worthless. Someone has said that worry is like a rocking chair … you do a lot of rocking, but it gets you nowhere"; "Voluntarism has always had a big effect on my life"; "The things that will destroy America are (these): Prosperity at any price, safety first instead of duty first, the 'get rich quick' theory of life and the love of soft living." Kelley is easily remembered. His only regret about his career in the Navy, he once told me, was not going to Annapolis.

With three students and three instructors, there were six very loud F11s parked in a row facing some very large hanger doors. The sounds from five F11s reflected off of those doors as I endeavored to find a plane that was OK to fly. I downed the first one, after strapping in and getting it started; and an instructor downed the second. Each time, I tried with hand signals to Cdr. Kelley to let the others go ahead without me, but, each time, Kelley moved his head from side to side, so everybody waited. My concern was over having been briefed that the F11 needed to be passing through air in order to cool off its internal parts. Just sitting there at idle for a long time could damage some of those internal parts, I thought. But, finally, the third plane was OK to fly and we taxied out for takeoff.

That afterburner was enjoyable: not quite as much acceleration as a catapult shot, but it lasted longer. We took off on a westerly heading, and immediately commenced a right climbing turn. In only minutes, we were passing over Corpus Christi and heading out over the Gulf of Mexico while climbing to 45 thousand feet. Gradually, Mach 1.05 was achieved in level flight.

After seven more F11 flights, the last one on March 12, 1959, we had completed our Flight Training and were awarded our Navy wings of gold.

Five days later, one of my Naval Academy roommates was killed in an F9F-5 Panther jet landing accident right there at Kingsville. I had not even known that Phil Brainerd was there, much less that he had been training to become a Naval Aviator, after serving for one year aboard the destroyer USS Moale (DD-693). I regretfully attended his memorial service at the base chapel before heading west for Moffett Field, California.

Phil had been a bachelor and left no wife or children. At the Academy, he was an undefeated wrestler, 1st Class year. He had been pictured in uniform with five classmates (all very handsome, my wife says) on the cover of SEVENTEEN magazine in November 1954. Years later, I determined from reading his accident report that pilot error had caused his accident. His plane stalled and crashed in the landing pattern at the 90.

Some people can adapt more easily to flying than others. Phil's record shows that he handled academics well but not the actual flying. It can be difficult and challenging for instructors to have to washout students. But there are times when doing so can prolong human life. There should be solace in that. Phil's record reveals that he had ample warnings and flying opportunities. And he could have easily asked to be returned to the surface navy – and been welcomed.

Godspeed.

CHAPTER 9

1000 MPH

WELCOME TO SAN FRANCISCO! At the Fairmont Hotel atop Nob Hill in 1960 a new song was introduced by Tony Bennett: "I Left My Heart in San Francisco." He sang it on stage with an orchestra and a talented bongo player behind him. (I wonder whatever happened to that bongo player.) The audience applauded, while Bennett seemed humble and almost uncertain, yet appreciative of the unanimous good response.

After finding a home in Sunnyvale in 1959, approaching Moffett Field, California, from the south, on Highway 101, on a bright and sunny workday morning, I saw several F8U-1 Crusaders waiting in line for takeoffs. They were the Navy's newest and fastest fighters, with afterburners, and were capable of doing 1,000 miles per hour, and more. A rotating red beacon could be seen on the fuselage of one F8 at the head of the line as it approached almost head-on, turned, then taxied out onto the left runway for takeoff.

In the distance were three huge airship hangers, a cluster of tan-colored barracks and some tree-shaded administration buildings. As I returned the Marine guard's salute and was allowed to pass through the Main Entrance Gate, off to the left was a large structure enclosing the world's largest wind tunnel. It belonged to the Ames Aeronautical Research Facility there. Later, I learned that an average-sized WWII fighter plane could be mounted and actually flown inside that wind tunnel. It was that large.

When I had first glimpsed those F8s waiting in line to take off, thoughts crossed my mind as to how fortunate those pilots were and how professional they must be. Almost as quickly, I realized that I would soon become one of them.

Fighter Squadron 124 was a Replacement Air Group (RAG) for checking out pilots in the F8 Chance Vought Crusader. It was also the Navy's largest squadron at the time and was commanded by Capt. William D. Houser, USNA Class of '42. (Houser eventually became a Vice Admiral and is still alive as I write this in '03.) VF-124 was also an instrument refresher squadron with a number of F9F-8T Grumman Cougars, the same as what I had flown in Kingsville and made my first carrier landings and takeoffs in.

Initial assignment was to the instrument refresher program. For me, it was more of an introductory course to jet airways. Jet airliners were just coming off the production lines and their higher airspeeds and higher altitude requirements (for fuel economies) had prompted new Federal Aviation Administration (FAA) rules: for separations, mostly. Altitude separations were essentially doubled above 29K feet in what had been named Continental Airspace. That was done as a safety measure mainly because altimeters were thought to become less accurate in thinner air at the higher altitudes.

Today, it is famous worldwide as Silicon Valley, but, back then, there were mostly orchards and farmers tending them in the areas around San Jose, Mountain View and Sunnyvale. Two parallel runways at Moffett (in Mountain View) and their taxiways ran between a single airship hanger to the west, where VF-124 was located, and the other twin airship hangers, across on the other (east) side of the field, near a Lockheed Aerospace facility. Usually, winds blew down the middle of both runways from the northwest.

Highway 101 passed near the south end of the runways. A farmer who tended his orchard lived a little further to the south. After I had been around awhile, I learned more about that farmer. Every plane that landed at Moffett had to pass over his orchard. There was no other way. That farmer, in turn, telephoned to register a complaint every time a plane passed over his property. A Duty Officer had to be assigned just to receive and log his frequent calls, 24/7. That farmer even had an outside phone installed, so he could avoid having to run back into his house to make a call whenever a plane passed overhead.

Ultimately, I was assigned to VF-191, based in one of the twin hangers on the east side of the field. Air Group 19 would be the last with pure jet aircraft to be deployed overseas aboard a carrier from Moffett Field. We left in April 1961 for San Diego and a WestPac cruise aboard the Attack Carrier, USS Bon Homme Richard (CVA-31), and never returned. I expect that farmer had had something to do with it.

Takeoffs from Moffett were in the other direction (away from that farmer), to the northwest; but we had to turn left about 160 degrees almost immediately after taking off and then turn right about 90 degrees when abeam the tower. While staying under the airways and above the little mountains below, we flew out past the coastline and then for what seemed like miles and miles to sea. Once far enough out over the Pacific to be clear of the airways running along the coastline, we made a climbing left turn and headed for the omni radio at Monterey while climbing to 20K feet. Once there, we reported to Air Traffic Controllers who then released us to fly our missions, whatever they were.

Those departures still come to mind whenever I happen onto a televised golf tournament from Pebble Beach. In turn, that also brings to mind a meeting I had had with two of the VF-124 instrument instructors, one day, about a week to ten days before they disappeared.

It seems that, in the course of making that departure from Moffett in an F9F-8T, they never reported over Monterey and were never heard from after they "Rogered" clearance for take-off at Moffett. Some six months later, however, their two little rafts were found tied together and washed up on a beach on one of the islands south of the Santa Barbara Channel. There was a skeleton in one of the rafts. The other raft was empty. That's the unofficial story I heard, later, but from someone I considered a reliable source.

The F9 had a row of batteries somewhere under the cockpit on the starboard side that needed to be at least partially charged, or they could explode when exposed to cold air while being recharged from a low state. That kind of event was suspected to have caused the loss of that Couger while it climbed to 20K feet and headed for Monterey. Both pilots probably ejected and landed safely in the waters off Pebble Beach. Search parties looked for them for nearly a week, unsuccessfully. They could have drifted along the coast with the shoreline in sight, all the way down to San Miguel, Santa Rosa or Santa Cruz Island on the Santa Barbara Channel. And, for as long as they had their senses, they probably yelled, now and then, "Jenson! Get that idea of yours moving!" - Oh, the irony!

Let me add, here, that I had flown with each of those two instrument instructors on separate occasions in the past, so I knew them. Before this happened, however, I had also been transferred across the field to VF-191 on the other side to pre- pare for going on a WestPac cruise. It also can be mentioned that, in the interim and to my surprise, Commander Vince

Kelley, my "Kingsville, TX, wingman" had arrived and taken command of VF-124.

Sometime earlier while still in VF-124, I had submitted another improvement "idea" to one of the Navy Bureaus in Washington but had not received a response. So I had arranged to return across the field to VF-124 to ask the Commanding Officer, who turned out to be Cdr. Kelley, to check on it for me. That was about a week or two before the two instrument instructors were reported missing. As I was leaving Cdr. Kelley's office, I happened to accidentally run into them.

Kelley's office was on the second deck and at the south end of the lone hanger on the west side of the field. There were two entrances to his office. I was using what may have been his private exit. The hanger doors were open and a bright afternoon sun was shining down onto a platform with a railing outside his office that overlooked the hanger floor. As I left and closed the door behind me, I turned and there were the two instructors.

"How do you get your ideas?," one of them asked me, as if he knew what I had just discussed with Cdr. Kelley.

"I just imagine a problem realistically and try to conceive of a better or the best way to resolve it," I answered. They seemed awe struck and I felt truly respected as we talked briefly and parted. That would be the last time I would ever see them; but the memory of them facing me on that platform with the sun shining down on their heads and on the backs of their leather flight jackets lingers.

My "lost" proposal involved a solution to the problem of how to find aviators lost at sea. Helmets or life preservers or even rafts could be coated with a particular colored material that, in turn, could be the only image picked up on photo reconnaissance aircraft film used for Search & Rescue, I had suggested. Time and navigation coordinates could also appear on each photo, so that when a downed pilot was spotted on film, his location could be traced.

Depending on weather conditions, different search patterns could be flown and maybe thousands of pictures developed as soon as possible after reconnaissance aircraft had returned; but, on the ground, any number of persons could then share in carefully scrutinizing the photos. Once a pilot was found, the exact location of where that picture was taken could be determined and the time established when it was taken. Winds and currents could be accounted for and, eventually, a rescue made.

As they drifted south along the California Coast, probably within sight of it, those two instrument instructor lieutenants probably used my name in vain for not acting sooner. I read about the search for them in the SAN FRANCISCO CHRONICLE and hoped and prayed for their eventual rescue; but it didn't happen.

Today, from what I have observed, pilots can use radios and even cell phones to assist in their rescues, if they are conscious and able to communicate, that is. Some thirty years later, as a civilian, I tried to reintroduce my concept via a direct appeal to Kodak. They were interested and developments looked promising for awhile; but, then, suddenly it was as if our communications had been severed. Nothing more was heard from them.

There was better luck with another, different improvement idea, however. Single engine Navy jet pilots are motivated to handle any emergency that might come along - including having to deal with a complete engine flame-out. Not good, of course; but not necessarily a bail-out situation, either.

The prescribed doctrine for handling single engine jet flame-outs was to maneuver clear of populated areas and eject; or, if high enough and conditions permitted, to glide over an intended landing runway at 10k feet and begin a (dead stick) descending 360 degree gliding left turn, adjusting it closer or farther out, on the way down, so as to land safely on the runway. We practiced flame-out approaches with reduced power settings and speed brakes extended and were confident we could handle any such emergency.

However, as confident as we were, I, at least, recognized that extenuating circumstances could arise that might contribute to a pilot getting off an optimum flight path and cause him to either land short or land long. If that happened in a populated area, the pilot could probably eject safely, but his plane stood to inflict damage.

Adjustments could easily be made during descents by moving closer or further away from the runway. I imagined as a solution to the problem being able to look down and being able to see a yellow light shining up from near the middle of an airport when I was where I should be. If I drifted out and too far away from the runway, a red light could warn of setting up to land short. If I were too close, a green light could alert that I would land fast and/or too far down the runway. A plausible guide would offer a yellow light path to pick up and follow from about half way around to near touchdown.

The light source on the ground could adjust itself automatically for various wind speeds and directions; and it could maintain settings for standard jet glide ratios, which I found to be quite similar; or be adjusted to accommodate specific aircraft types and weights, if radio contact with pilots approaching for dead stick landings could avail tower operators of that information.

After submitting that proposal to Washington, I was offered a suggestion by a former Patuxent River Navy test pilot who was in VF-124 at the time, Bill Russell. While wondering again how my proposal could have been revealed, I became quite interested when he mentioned that a space vehicle landing system was being considered by the new space agency, NASA; but, as far as he knew, a straight-in type guidance system had been favored. He suggested that I might consider it, too. I did, and reasoned that a circular approach was better. It would allow for more flight path corrections. If you're making a straight-in dead-stick approach and you're too low, then what?

After resigning from the Navy in 1962 and living in Flossmoor, Illinois, for awhile, I happened to pick up a copy of "AVIATION WEEK" magazine, which I subscribed to but seldom had time enough to actually study. While thumbing through it, I happened upon a black and white picture of a huge ball that was sitting on a flatbed trailer. My guess: judging by the size of the trailer, the ball measured about 8 feet in diameter. Reading the caption: the ball was covered with adjustable long-range pin-point lights that were to be used by pilots making emergency landings. Wow! "They built it!!," I yelled to my wife. "They finally built it!" I should add here that our Space Shuttles also make 180 degree turns on landing approaches in Florida. I can only assume the same type of turning approach is used for power-off (dead stick) landings in California. Computers, radar and GPS are necessary to do the work of human eyes in the Shuttle system. Like the change from prop planes to jets making carrier landings, those Shuttle landing approach speeds and turning radii, relatively speaking, are awesome!

There still remains a place for visual straight-in glide slope assistance equipment, however: at municipal airports today where planes approach and land with engines running. Called the Visual Approach Slope Indicator (VASI) System, you may have seen it from an airliner passenger seat or from a car when driving past an airport. A pilot sees a red light if he's too low; a white light if he's too high; and a (blended) pinkish light if his glide slope is OK.

Patience may be a virtue, but I discovered I had little of it when sitting in an F8 on stand-by and waiting for launch to intercept incoming aircraft. The real thing might be something else again; but an exercise with the U.S. Air Force comes to mind when two of us were finally sent out from Moffett Field to intercept an incoming B-52.

Commander James Heffernan was our VF-191 Executive Officer and my flight leader on this exercise. We sat in our planes, strapped in and ready to start-up and go. It rained a little, then stayed just cloudy and gray.

When radar finally detected an incoming bogey, we were ordered to scramble. The ground crews first had to wind up their air impingement starters before Jim and I could wind up the engines on our F8s (like 4 sirens slowly revving up one after the other). There was no having to wait on anyone. We were immediately cleared by the tower to the runway and then for takeoff. Another plus was not having to fly that eternal standard departure pattern out of Moffett and out to Monterey. We just took off, contacted the radar operators and gladly followed their instructions to head west while climbing to altitude.

Normally, we spent as much time briefing for a hop as we did flying it. Then, there would be more de-briefing time required

afterwards. On this particular day, I cannot recall much briefing, before or after the flight. But one question I had held in
my mind for a long time was soon to be answered. I knew how
to get behind a bomber, listen for the heat-seeking missile tone
indicating that the missile, if released, would then fly to the target it was locked onto. The F8 had air-to-air Sidewinder mis-
siles, but it also had four 20 millimeter guns (some would call
them 0.78 inch diameter cannons). What if the Sidewinders
had been expended and all I had left were the 20mm's. Could
I avoid being hit by the tail guns of a Soviet bomber and hit the
bomber with the 20mm's? That was my question.

We were about 350 miles west of San Francisco and still
heading west. I was flying loose on Jim's right wing. We were
doing about 0.8 Mach at about 35K feet. We could climb or
we could dive from that altitude. A few clouds were here and
there at altitude, but there was mostly overcast down close to
the ocean, below.

Radar controllers were heard loud and clear when they finally directed us to a target. It turned out to be an incoming
B-52 flying at about 30K and approaching us almost head-on
but slightly off to our left. Jim and I must have seen it in the
same instant. I began to follow his gentle left turn and sensed
quickly that he was setting up to swing around behind the B-52
for an easy missile shot.

Instinctively, I then ceased maintaining the wingman's
position and pulled into a hard descending turn inside Jim's
turning radius and looked to the B-52's tail guns as defining a
vertical plane that I could not fall behind. For to do so would
theoretically allow the tail guns to shoot me down.

That B-52 was moving. I remained ahead of the imagined plane by diving into the turn and dropping well below the
bomber. Finally, I was under it, headed in the same direction

and was still slightly ahead of the imaginary plane running through its tail guns as I lit the afterburner and gradually was able to start climbing. At first, I could only maintain a steady altitude in order to keep up with the B-52, but, then, finally, the F8 began to gain on the bomber. I picked the nose up gradually and maintained a steady bearing on the B-52 as our closing rates began to increase. I was still ahead of that imaginary plane and as I got closer, I could also see that there were no belly guns to have to contend with. I was well ahead of the tail guns.

Judgment comes into play a lot when flying for the USN and I finally judged it was time to roll over, pull on the nose to reduce and stop the closing rate and then roll back into about a 45-degree right bank while still ahead of the tail section and within a few yards of the B-52's fuselage and starboard wing, raking the wing and engines with simulated 20mm gunfire from slightly below, as I gradually turned to starboard. I had come out of afterburner, reached the "bogey's" altitude, and was slowly drifting away from it and falling slightly behind when Jim came on the radio and asked the B-52 pilot, "How's it feel to get shot down?"

There was a pause. Then the pilot answered for all to hear, including the radar operators ashore, "In a big operation like this, a few losses can be expected."

Not a bad comeback. Little did I know then, but that expression would be repeated often in the squadron. It became one of several favorite squadron slogans, in fact: IN A BIG OPERATION LIKE THIS, A FEW LOSSES CAN BE EXPECTED.

A new carrier, the Kitty Hawk, was about to undergo sea trials and enter the Fleet. Our Air Group 19 was rumored to be awaiting orders to fly to the East Coast, go aboard and ride it to the West Coast; then, perhaps, make a WestPac cruise on it. That would have been great; but that big, big, carrier seemed never to be completed and an alternative eventually would have to be sought.

Our training flights continued, of course, but I came face to face with having to make a career decision: Whether to stay in or get out of the USN.

A San Francisco patent attorney a few years older than I and who had also been raised in Chicago Heights, almost within sight of my parents' back porch, in fact, had extended an invitation for me to play golf with him, on a weekend. He lived on the side of a hill overlooking San Francisco Bay and the airport in fashionable Burlingame. It was south of San Francisco and north of Palo Alto, where Stanford University was constructing an accelerometer atop a hill overlooking the campus, visible to us pilots when we approached to land at Moffett Field. The interesting hilly course we played on was somewhere near his home. It was the first golf course I'd seen with so many greens that were just over the next hill. He was familiar with the course; but I had to walk up to the top of a hill, find the green, and then try to remember the correct bearing and estimate the distance to the green after returning to my ball. Challenging. And, since we were almost the same age and from the same hometown, after we had played a few holes, I ventured to question him about his profession.

"What's the average patent pendency time?," I asked.

"About 36 months right now. Depending upon whether it's a simple patent or a complicated one, the pendency time can range anywhere from about 24 months to 48 months, or to as long as 10 years for a more complicated application," he answered.

"Why is the Patent Office so slow in making searches and awarding patents?," I then asked. "Can't something be done to speed-up the process?"

He looked a little puzzled. The gist of his answer was that he did not see the need for, nor expect much change to Patent Office operations and time requirements. I was disappointed, of course. Here was a man from my own home town who thought the U.S. Patent System was acceptable and even un-changeable. I would have to add this information to the rest that was accumulating in the back of my mind concerning the U.S. Patent Office. I already knew the process was too slow; but I would have to await future opportunities to try to do any-thing about it.

The Kitty Hawk was a huge carrier, by previous standards, and worth waiting for, we thought. But it never seemed to get ready. One report we heard was that final inspectors had found a compartment that could not be entered due to there being no doors (or hatches) for entering it. After cutting out an entry with acetylene torches, a fully equipped compartment was dis-covered. So, then, entry doors (hatches) had to be added. We were beginning to understand some of the reasons for delays. We also suspected there could be more delays ahead.

Meanwhile, my wife's parents and a couple who were their close friends and neighbors in Chicago Heights decided to fly out for about a week's visit with us. The man was very interested when I helped him climb up to have a look at an F8 cockpit while it was being worked on in one of the double hangers. My father-in-law, however, seemed uninterested.

"You don't have to do this. What do you want to do this for?," he declared, a little louder than just under his breath.

I just glanced at him and turned my attentions to the neigh-bor who was needing help to climb down.

After a tour of the Squadron Ready Room and locker spaces, we drove across the field and parked near the Officer's Club. It was on a clear, bright Sunday, close to noon. We were going to take our wives to lunch or brunch at the O'Club. What happened next would ultimately change my career.

We walked along and then stopped on an open patch of concrete under an elevated water tank. My father-in-law, around 72 years of age at the time, grabbed me gently by one arm so we would face each other. "I've talked it over with the nephews ... They said it's OK with them ... if you come and work for the company," he said. "They'd be glad to have you. You're not gonna make any money here," he added. "Come with us. You'll make some REAL money! We've got a good thing."

"Thank you very much, Bill," I answered slowly. "I'd like to think about it. Can I let you know?"

"Sure," he said. "Think it over." We walked to the O'Club and met the ladies for lunch. When I told my wife about her father's invitation, to her credit, she begged off: "Do what you want; but I want no part in this decision."

Ever since I had been a commissioned officer, I had felt it best to perform as if I intended to make the Navy a career. A "short timer's attitude" left too many things undone or not done correctly, I reasoned. So, when it came to deciding whether or not to resign, regardless of my decision, I intended to carry on with my duties as if I were going to stay in the Navy.

At that time, I was the Personnel Officer of VF-191 and had some very competent enlisted persons to depend on. They ran things and only called on me for document signatures, mostly. I enjoyed flying, of course. And then, somehow, another enlisted man who was stationed at Moffett got a hold of my name and I was assigned as his defense counsel in a court-martial on the Base.

The accused enlisted man was living in one of the barracks located near the fence bordering Highway 101. He was accused of stealing and/or having a pistol in the locker under his bunk that belonged to another sailor in the same compartment, as I recall. If I don't remember all of the details about this case it's because I tried to forget it, to get over it, as some would say, now, in this, the 21st Century.

Once again, as the defense counsel, I only reverted to asking simple questions: "Did you see him take it?"

"No."

"Could someone else have put the pistol into the accused's locker?"

"Well, yes, I suppose..."

Case dismissed!

What troubled me afterwards about that particular defense "duty" which I was pledged to carry out with as much ability as I could muster was that I suspected, at the time, that the man I defended was actually guilty as charged. He denied guilt when I asked him point blank about it before the trial, but his demeanor during my questioning suggested I had a guilty man sitting before me. Nevertheless, it was not for me to decide his guilt or innocence; that was for the Court to do. Nor was it my duty or obligation to force him to confess. I can sympathize with lawyers who find themselves having to defend criminals. But, somebody's got to do it, or the innocence of persons charged with violating laws in a free society could not be determined with any reasonable expectation of objectivity being applied.

It had been my understanding upon graduating from the Naval Academy that I was obligated to serve a minimum of four years on Active Duty. As that limit approached in 1960 and as there seemed to be no forthcoming carrier cruise in sight, I decided to submit my resignation from the Navy. Also, I sensed a greater need developing for my services in the private (civilian) sector than in the Navy.

My father-in-law was glad, as far as I could tell; and my wife seemed non-committal about it. I was transferred back to VF-124 and became an instrument instructor in F9s.

Naval Aviators were scheduled for two weeks of instrument refresher courses and flying each year, provided they were stationed somewhere in the U.S. So, there was a constant flow of Naval Aviators passing through.

As it turned out, however, some changes were made back in Washington that resulted in extending my service obligation 1.5 years, ostensibly because I had spent about 18 months going through flight training. With my duty status extended, I was happy to return to "Satan's Kittens," a name and logo the Walt Disney organization had developed for VF-191.

The squadron "Skipper" at the time was Cdr. Dick Linnekin, a U.S. Naval Academy graduate from the Class of 1944. I flew on his wing, one afternoon, on an unusual, but useful mission. And it became memorable!

We took off in formation from Moffett Field and headed southeast, climbing to altitude over San Jose and beyond. We were recording fuel quantities on our kneepads after completing the departure, so we could calculate, later, how much fuel had been expended for each segment of the flight. I was flying a loose right wing position as we climbed so I could look away, now and then, to read fuel quantities and write the numbers down without fear of bumping into the skipper's F8. It was useful to learn, later, how much fuel had been expended for this flight activity and that one; and to compare numbers that, more or less, reinforced our confidence in what we'd just observed.

After the de-briefing, the skipper and I had walked to our cars and were about to go our separate ways, when I decided to ask him, "Did you happen to see that airliner?"

"What airliner?," he quickly asked.

So I told him: As we were climbing out over San Jose, I had just finished writing on my kneepad and looked up to see his plane just miss a pure white (4-engine) Lockheed Electra turboprop with Western Airlines written in burgundy on it that was descending in the opposite direction and passed so close on the other side of him that I saw the pilot and co-pilot through their windshield in their white shirts, ties, caps and sun glasses looking down at their instruments in the cockpit. They never saw us.

Close, but no cigar. But the skipper enjoyed a cigar anyway. He chewed them all the time. It had been another day at the office for us. Again, we had cheated death (we liked to say); so we went home to our wives for cocktails and dinner.

John Paul Jones was born in 1747 and some 32 years later was given charge of an old merchantman named "Duras." In deference to Benjamin Franklin who had always been his close friend, Jones renamed his wooden sailing ship the "Bonhomme Richard," honoring Franklin's famous nickname: "Poor Richard." In due course, the contemporary Attack Carrier USS Bon Homme Richard (CVA-31) was assigned to take us on a WestPac cruise, in place of the Kitty Hawk.

Launched in 1944, the "Bonnie Dick" had set sail in June 1945 for the Pacific and as part of Task Force 38, her air group participated in the Okinawa campaign and conducted succes-sive strikes over the Japanese islands of Hokkaido, Honshu,

Kyushu and Shikoku. On 16 September, 1945, the "31 Boat" entered triumphantly into Tokyo Bay as a member of the US Pacific Fleet, just 14 days after the formal Japanese surrender on the decks of the USS MISSOURI.

Again, in 1951, the "31 Boat" was called into action in the Korean War. During two tours there, due to the nature of the war, her squadrons flew mostly close ground support and CAP (Combat Air Patrol) missions, resulting in an impressive record of ground targets being destroyed.

In 1955, the 872 foot long, 27,100 ton, Essex Class "Bonnie Dick" underwent major conversions, acquiring a hurricane bow and an angle flight deck. In October 1960, it arrived in San Diego with a crew of 3,400+ to prepare for another WestPac cruise with our Air Group 19 aboard. By comparison, the Kitty Hawk was 1,063 feet long, displaced some 83,960 tons and was manned by 5,400+ personnel. The flight deck on the Kitty Hawk was 1,046 feet long and 252 feet wide vs. 819 feet by 106 feet on the 31 Boat.

Air Group 19 had to begin practicing those FCLPs again, eastward over the next ridge of mountains from Moffett, at an airstrip on the edge of the San Joaquin Valley named Crow's Landing. One of the more colorful LSOs who was known throughout the Pacific Fleet was there to preside over our landings: Darl "ACE" Jewell. Ace would know if you were too fast, too slow, too high or too low, almost without looking. It didn't matter what type of aircraft you were flying, either. And even if you were a high ranking senior officer, your carrier landing approach had better be within Ace's limits, or you'd catch h... even on the radio.

Ace and I could talk, informally. We respected each other. He was in VF-124 while I had been reassigned to VF-191, in the twin hangers across the field. In the mean time, a semi-trailer had been dropped next to our hanger and I had had an opportunity to fly the F8 simulator that had been installed inside that trailer. It was one of the first simulators, one of many to come, and a big improvement over the old (Edwin A.) Link Trainers we had "flown" previously.

One day shortly after my simulator "flight," I was called from across the field by Cdr. Vince Kelley and asked a favor. He knew about the F8 simulator and had been trying without success to get Ace to use it. Finally, Ace had agreed to come over to the VF-191 hanger area to "fly" the simulator if I would go with him. "Sure," I said. "Send him over."

The simulator had the front-end of an F8 mounted on hydraulic pistons in the front two-thirds of the trailer; the rear third was given to an enlisted man's station for observing duplicates of all of the dials in the cockpit plus a few more for operating the simulator. The operator could also induce various emergencies from there for pilots to have to cope with.

Ace climbed aboard and took off. I went outside and waited for about 30 minutes while he flew instruments and dealt with various "induced" emergencies. Finally, when I felt his simulator time was about up, I climbed the stairs to the "back room" and entered. The door on my left to the F8 cockpit suddenly opened and there was Ace. As he walked through it, behind him, the lights were on and I could see the F8's raised canopy. Then, all h... started breaking loose, as the saying goes.

Ace and I looked at the operator and he looked back at us with alarm and uncertainty. Through the door, I could see the F8 fuselage (what there was of it) jerking up and down, from side to side, and tilting back and forth. The operator looked back at his panel of gauges and saw dials spinning and lights flashing. A few horns may even have been blowing amidst the confusion. The F8 was hitting many of its hydraulic stops, as could be heard and felt through the floor decking.

Moments before the end finally came, Ace realized what had happened. The operator was still trying to figure it out when Ace told him, "By mistake, I landed and climbed out of the cockpit at 10K feet."

Everyone smiled, including Ace. A mystery solved.

After Ace had monitored and coached us through more FCLPs at Crows Landing, we flew to San Diego and practiced a few more actual carrier landings and catapult shots aboard the 31 Boat a few miles offshore. I made a really dumb move after one of those landings.

The gear handle was on the left side of the instrument panel, while the handle for lowering and raising the hook was on the right. After I had landed, been stopped by the arresting wire and the plane had rolled backwards a few inches, the flight deck signalman gave me a "raise hook" sign and I momentarily grabbed the gear handle instead of the hook, raised it, realized instantly what I'd done, and lowered it just as quickly (but not in time). A moment after I had returned it, the left rear wheel moved forward and pivoted over center; stopped; then tried to go back to where it had been; but the hydraulic pump pressure just wasn't enough to push it back over the pivot point. So, the wheel gradually swung forward and beyond its previous stopping point, causing the left wing tip to gracefully settle onto the flight deck. The other wheels remained OK.

There was a safety switch designed to prevent being able to raise the landing gear when the weight of the aircraft was on the gear and it "ground checked OK" before and afterwards; but it had not worked for me. My self-inflicted remorse over damaging an F8 may have been overdone, as I realized later that that wing was designed to withstand a lot more weight than had been placed on it in that incident. What I did need to remember in the future, however, was to pay closer attention to what apparently was becoming routine. In other words: Stay focused!

CHAPTER 10

THANK YOU, MY SON

On April 26, 1961, we left San Diego for WestPac aboard the USS Bon Homme Richard (CVA-31). Most, but not all of us, would return.

After a brief stop in Hawaii, we sailed for Subic Bay in the Philippines. It was about a month after our departure from San Diego (and 43 days since my last carrier landing) when I was flying wing on another VF-191 pilot, Lt. Dick Richardson, high over the South China Sea. We had departed from Cubi Point (at Subic Bay) around noontime and were headed for the 31 Boat that was cruising around an imaginary geographic reference point that was new to me, called Yankee Station, located some 650 nautical miles away and off the coast of Vietnam. We were high (above 50K feet) trying not to waste any fuel.

As we passed the estimated half-way point, I looked down to check the fuel gauges and noticed the wing tank gauge begin to unwind. It gradually dropped all the way to zero. I looked out to see if the wingtip fuel dumping valves had opened somehow. I needed the fuel in those wing tanks. Nope. No sign of fuel streaming. While I had experienced a variety of F8 equipment failures, this was a new one. But, seeing no leakage, I told myself the gauge had failed. Even if a fuel shortage had developed, we had passed the midpoint and there was no turning back.

Eventually, we approached the carrier and the lush, green, serene, sun kissed, gentle, fertile hills of Vietnam came into view. Why would anyone living there ever want to fight? I have wondered. We descended and approached for landing.

Our fuel states were low. I don't remember the exact quantities, but we did not want to have to go around again after somehow missing being trapped on the first try. Dick was the flight leader and landed first. I was right behind him and observed that he landed a little short, catching the #1 wire. He promptly taxied clear; then I came in - and also caught the #1 wire. Talk about being anxious to get aboard! (I had been trying for #3.) The only thing closer to the stern than the #1 wire was the ramp that formed the contoured end of the flight deck.

Mention of these landings is prompted by my wanting to reveal a tendency that developed during those landings. There were four arresting gear wires that were raised and stretched across the deck. Ideally, the #3 wire would be the one to catch for what the Landing Signal Officer (LSO) would grade as "good" or "O.K." But, somehow, after once landing short and grabbing the #1 wire, it could become awfully difficult to fly higher and farther on future landings to catch that #3. The LSO would try to warn about coming too close to hitting the ramp in his evaluation of your landing in the Ready Room afterwards; but it still took a determined effort to "get it back up there" a few more times, before grabbing the #3 would seem normal again. At least that was my experience. And if something unusual were to arise, a pilot could easily return to his old "rote" habits, if distracted or not sufficiently on guard.

That may have been what happened to Richardson several years later. I considered him an excellent Naval Aviator. Nevertheless, I learned from friends that when he was attempting to land an F8 aboard a carrier at night, he came in too low, hit the ramp, broke his plane in half and was killed. Perhaps he may have wanted to get aboard too much. Godspeed. My sympathies to his family.

Hong Kong was as busy as ever, it seemed. A trip on a water taxi to the Kowloon Peninsula (now Jiulong) and a look at their airport proved inspiring, one afternoon. Those water taxis may not look very impressive from a distance, nor sound like much when aboard one of them; but it's hard not to admire their smiling captains who also proudly polish some of the brass parts atop their openly exposed little diesel engines. The clean, varnished wood benches on board were also inviting, but not always comfortable.

At the airport, I happened to find a Boeing 707 parked next to the world's first commercial jet airliner, an English De Havilland Comet. They were facing me on an apron below the sidewalk on which I stood. From high up, it was interesting to observe that each plane had one mechanic working on an engine. The Comet had four engines mounted in the wing roots, two on each side. The 707 had four engines that were suspended independently under its wings, two under each wing.

The British Comet mechanic was under one wing, almost at the wing root, where the wing connects to the fuselage. He could be seen bending and twisting while trying to look up and work on one of the engines. Panels that he had had to remove in order to gain access to the engine from below were scattered about on the concrete apron around him. A strong wind gust could have blown them away, I thought.

The 707 mechanic, on the other hand, was seen calmly standing beside one of the 707 engines that he was working on. It was waist high and had a hinged hood-type cover raised and locked in the up position, exposing the top half of one side of the entire engine; a design resembling the raised hood of an older model car. With only a toolbox on the concrete beside him, he was working with the greatest of apparent ease. What a difference; what a credit to Boeing's design.

Later, I returned aboard the Bonnie Dick after a day and night out in Hong Kong. There were no aircraft left on the flight deck. They had all been moved to the hanger deck, below. I sensed it might be my last visit to Hong Kong. The ship was anchored in the middle of the harbor. Under the many stars, I walked around on the flight deck and could see in almost every direction the many attractive signs and lights that were a part of Hong Kong. The weather was clear and balmy. What sights! What a privilege to be here, I thought. A memorable experience.

Asphalt covered roads and streets are better now, but they used to become very slippery after a rainfall, often resulting in car accidents. I learned about asphalt runways that also could become slick and dangerous in the rain after we left Hong Kong.

The sun was setting as I catapulted off to head back alone to Cubi Point, at Subic Bay. A brief glimpse at the southern part of Formosa (Taiwan) from a climbing F8 reminded me of my Destroyer duty days. Kaohsiung had to be down there along that southern coastline; but I needed to turn away and head south into the darkness. Hugging the western shoreline of Luzon seemed appropriate, in case of having to eject for some reason. Reportedly, there were head hunters still living in the jungle down there.

The F8 had no landing lights, so we used runway lights to guide us. We had heard that Admiral Arthur W. Radford, Class of 1916, a Chairman of the Joint Chiefs of Staff, had argued for and obtained the 8,000 foot long runway I was headed for at

Cubi Point. During what little use I had made of it until then, I had noticed the runway had 1,500 feet of concrete at each end, and 5,000 of humpback asphalt in the middle. Built on the side of a hill, the runway was higher in the middle and sloped slightly downward each way from there.

It was raining and a dark night when I arrived and was cleared to land. Not suspecting anything out of the ordinary, I approached slow enough to have been able to land aboard ship. After touching down in the center and near the start of the front concrete portion of the runway, I raised the nose for aerodynamic braking before transitioning onto the blacktop. I then became wary of the asphalt's smoothness. It could mean it offered little to no traction for braking.

A plan quickly came to mind: After slowing enough to lower the nose, I tapped the brakes and nothing happened. Really slick. The runway was wide enough to turn slightly to the left by using air pressure on the rudder, which I did. Then, there was still enough airspeed for the rudder to start a turn back to the right from the left-hand side of the runway, as I started downhill from atop that midpoint ridge.

Brakes were applied when the main gear crossed onto the concrete near the runway's end. The nose went down immediately. Good traction. I was still moving fast and wanting to turn a little more to the right in an effort to head for the concrete turn off ramp, which had been built closer than at the very end of the runway. More turning was hard to accomplish, but I did manage to reach the turn off ramp at a slight angle off the runway while applying all the brakes I felt the pavement and tires could stand. It slowed dramatically, but I had to let up and turn more (which then had become barely possible without tipping onto the left wingtip) to avoid going off the side of the turn off ramp. On the far edge of that turn off, that F8 and

I finally stopped - and sat there for a few moments in the rain at idle, before asking the tower for clearance to taxi.

The next night, there was more rain, and another F8 came in; but it wasn't as lucky. It ran off the side of the runway and into a ditch. The night after that, it rained again and yet another F8 went almost onto its side in another ditch. (In a big operation like this, a few losses can be expected.)

General Douglas MacArthur made his last return to the Philippines while we were there. It had been publicized that he would address the Philippine nation from an outdoor auditorium in Manila on July 4, (1961), at a specified time. My wingman that afternoon, Sam Purvis, will likely have to read this in order to learn that we honored General MacArthur on that particular occasion. At the time when I had estimated MacArthur would be about half way through his speech, Purvis and I made a pass in loose formation near downtown Manila, engaged our afterburners and climbed noisily up and away into the overcast. A salute.

Another salute which I made alone went to the folks manning the Sangley Point Naval Air Station, located less than ten miles southwest of Manila. After completing a test hop in an F8 that I had flown off the carrier, I needed to reduce the fuel load before landing back aboard. Rather than just dump the fuel, I sought to be more productive.

Sangley Point was one of the alternate airports listed for us to be able to use in an emergency, and I had never seen it. So I thought I'd give them a fly-by while looking their facility over in the process. Dropping down over Manila Bay from the north and gradually picking up speed as I endeavored to find the field visually, I called the tower and was granted permission to make a low pass.

Eventually, the field was spotted as I approached with the afterburner on and speed advancing to Mach 1. (Leading edge droops were up, for you F8 drivers monitoring this.) In a wide right turn at about 100 feet above the water, I was too low to be seen by the tower operator and so I called to him on the radio when I was 5 miles out, 3 miles out, and 1 mile. Consistently, the tower operator reported not to have me in sight.

Barely enough trees had been cleared in the jungle to make room for the runway, with just a little extra clearance on each side. As I quickly approached, I saw the runway was about 25 feet above the water. Aligned and with wings level, I radioed the tower on reaching the end of the runway. The bottom of the fuselage was only a few feet above the runway; pushing Mach 1. About a third of the way along, I caught a glimpse of the tower through a clearing to my left. Directly ahead were tall trees standing at the end of the clearing just beyond the end of the runway. I passed the tower in an instant and then applied a little back pressure on the stick to begin a gentle climb over the tree tops without scraping the tail section on the runway; followed by solid stick pressure into a 4g climb. Heading up towards the vertical, I called the tower: "Thank you very much."

"Thank YOU!!" was the tower's instant response.

Half way to the top, I came out of burner and let the F8 continue easily at 4g's to what would be the start of the Continental Airways in the U.S., 24K feet. Some ride. But it wasn't over yet.

While headed back to the 31 Boat and descending, I just happened to fall behind one of our Air Group's propeller-driven Douglas attack planes also headed back to the ship. He was way ahead, but I was closing on him fast. Those AD pilots were way above average and next to impossible to catch like I was catching this one.

To remain undetected: Don't move; but if you must, make only limited movements gradually. I was closing on this AD from slightly above and nearly behind him. He apparently didn't know I was coming. Then, he commenced easing into a left turn and caught sight of me coming at him from his upper left quarter. He immediately tried turning inside my turning radius, but it was too late. I followed him in my gun sight the whole way and, in the last second, pulled up and away.

Later, the door opened at the front of our Ready Room aboard the carrier and one of the AD pilots came charging in to look at the board listing aircraft numbers and pilots. He appeared to find what he had been looking for and then turned around for a scan of the VF-191 pilots present. We looked eye to eye for a few moments, then he looked down and left.

On another occasion, the tables were turned. I was descending and looked down, aft and to my right and saw a Philippine Air Force jet fighter with two pilots aboard flying almost on my wing. They had caught me by complete surprise.

Another surprise had come just before my first catapult launch at the beginning of the cruise. Out there on the flight deck giving me hand signals to turn up the engine to full power for launch was the Catapult Officer whom I also recognized almost immediately as one of my old Kingsville F11F instructors, Lt. Charles Klusmann.

Some 3 years later, on June 6, 1964, while flying an unarmed photo version of the F8 Crusader, Chuck would gain world recognition by becoming the first to be shot down and taken prisoner in what was officially called the Vietnam "conflict."

Then, almost three months later, on September 1, he would establish another admirable and remarkable "first" by becoming the first POW in the Southeastern Asian "conflict" to successfully escape from captivity. He and another Laotian captive trudged some 30-35 miles the way the crow flies through hilly, enemy-infested jungle to safety behind U.S. lines. Unfortunately, five other Laotians who had attempted to escape with them were caught and killed en route.

The Russian Cosmonaut, Yuri A. Gagarin, had completed the first manned Earth orbital flight on April 12, 1961, two weeks before our departure from San Diego. Some five months later, the 31 Boat arrived at Kobe, Japan. As we entered the harbor channel and steamed slowly towards our assigned pier, I had a chance to try out newly purchased 7x50 binoculars. One of the Admiral's aides had advised me that a 7x50 lens admits more light than can be picked up by the naked eye; better to see with in poor light conditions; and one reason for the Navy's OODs having 7x50s available on the bridges of most, if not all, USN ships.

There were many ships to be observed tied to docks and facing towards the shoreline as the Bonnie Dick eased along slowly behind them. I scanned ahead and discovered something amazing. A rusty, multi colored, small- to medium-sized cargo ship had part of its pilot house freshly painted white. Painters were working to expand the painted area in all directions from one apparent starting point, a new sign identifying the name of the ship. No prepping; they just painted over the rust. As we drew a little closer, all of the crew members suddenly withdrew into the ship's interior.

A freshly painted sign atop the pilot house identified that ship in large gold letters on a black background as the "YURI A. GAGARIN." We slowly passed by its stern and I looked back at the other side and saw another Gagarin sign and more fresh white paint that also seemed to have originated at the sign.

Kobe was famous for its prime steaks. They were as good as any I had tasted, including those I'd had at the Stockyard Inn in Chicago. We would have enjoyed staying longer, but Typhoon Nancy was headed in our direction. We were forced back out to sea to prepare for it.

Eventually, the waves became high enough to reach over the bow and break the uplocks on one side of the forward elevator used for lifting aircraft up and down. Water then poured down and into the well area under that elevator on the hanger deck, creating something akin to a giant sized swimming pool. As the 31 Boat then pitched and rolled, that pool of water became like a tidal wave and loosened some oxygen and acetylene tanks that had been strapped and tied to the sides. They were tossed back and forth and around until a few brave and capable ship's personnel jumped in, captured and removed them, one at a time, and, fortunately, without injuries.

The carrier's speed was down to around 4-5 knots, I was told, just enough for the rudder to be effective. It rained and the wind blew. The "Little Boys" (destroyers) escorting us could be seen with their bows rising completely out of the water, from time to time.

Had we been called into action, I doubt that any planes could have been launched. For sure, none could have landed. A carrier the size of the Kitty Hawk, on the other hand, with three times the flight deck area and more hull length and width, would likely have been able to launch AND recover aircraft during that typhoon. What could President Jimmy Carter, a Naval Academy graduate, Class of 1947, have been thinking when he argued so strenuously for small carriers and against big ones! Fortunately, the Pentagon won that one.

As the carrier approached Yokosuka, Japan, one evening, the Maintenance Officer, LCdr. Bob Aumack, and I, his

Maintenance Planning Officer, were catapulted off to land ashore as advance men to arrange for the squadron's use of facilities at Atsugi. The sight of Mt. Fuji up ahead and a little to the left remains in my memory. What a mountain! Several VF-191 aviators left as young men to climb it; and returned looking and acting a bit older. The carrier docked the next morning. (Bob Aumack would later command the Blue Angels, from 1964-66; flying F11F Grumman Tigers.)

The Japanese were excellent gardeners. The air station at Atsugi had an 18-hole golf course available to military personnel that was maintained by the Japanese. Although I never played there, what I found most interesting was that extra "Winter" putting greens, used only for about 30 days in Winter, were planted and groomed near the Summer putting greens. Winters were mild and golf was played year around.

In Tokyo, across a huge open park expanse from the high up and very visible Imperial Palace, the famous earthquake-proof Imperial Hotel stood, afloat on quicksand as designed by Frank Lloyd Wright. It had a courtyard garden surrounded on all four sides by the old 2-story brick hotel. The yellow bricks were no doubt darkened by fires in WWII. That little "world of its own" had rocks, water ponds with goldfish, small trees, bushes, grass, plants and flowers that were carefully manicured by white uniformed female Japanese gardeners under the watchful eyes of patrons in the dining and hotel rooms above.

Atsugi also had an overhaul and repair facility. They had a number of F8s sitting around, and they begged us to fly them just to keep them operational. So we did. I can claim to have spent more time over Japan than the Emperor.

A lesson in air pollution became obvious one day on one of those "boring holes in the sky" flights in an F8U-2. Tokyo was covered by haze, as heavy as could be found over Los Angeles. One could see the ground only by looking straight down. Otherwise, there was just thick haze that also prevented being able to detect other aircraft.

After passing over Tokyo and leveling off at about 40K feet, I turned left about 45 degrees and headed away from Tokyo Bay and into the Japanese countryside. It was flat and green below, around 10 AM. There were no clouds, just haze, or was it? The hazy area seemed to be shrinking. Far off to the left and right, I could see more of the ground.

About an hour after taking off, I came to what appeared to be the end of green flatlands and the beginning of a low ridge of mountains. Built into the foot of that mountain range was a beige-colored building with a tall smokestack. Thick, light gray to beige-colored smoke was pouring out of that stack and was being carried by the wind towards Tokyo in an ever widening cloud. That one, single, stack was polluting all of Tokyo and its surrounding communities. I wondered what people in Tokyo would do if they could see what I was seeing.

Having your name and rank painted on the side of an F8 was somebody else's idea, not mine. Planes were often "down" for maintenance and not flyable, so pilots with missions flew the planes that were "up" and available. It was unreasonable to expect to be able to fly the plane with your name on it every time you went up. Having the name of the Plane Captain who took care of only one plane painted on the side, however, seemed to make sense.

Anyhow, the plane with my name on it, #108, was ejected from and it crashed somewhere during an approach to Atsugi. The pilot flying it landed safely, but the location of the wreckage was unknown.

Lt. Richardson had another Naval Aviator friend who was stationed at Atsugi. That friend was in charge of the portable radar unit for landings (called GCA: Ground Control Approach), and he had to look for flying opportunities to fulfill his minimum flight time requirements. He had access to a twin-engine Grumman seaplane and, one morning, told Richardson he would take anyone along who might want to help look for #108.

Richardson arrived in the coffee shop, as we were finishing breakfast and getting ready to take up whatever duties we had before us. His offer was tempting. #108, after all, had my name on it, and I had even flown it a few times. Why not join in the search for it? But I thought of some work I needed to do and decided I should stay and do that, instead. But, thanks, anyhow, I offered.

Anyone else?

Another 191 pilot, Ltjg. Fred Gray, spoke up. "I'd like to go," he said. Then, after a slight pause, "But I don't have my flight jacket with me."

"You can borrow mine," offered Jon McBride.

"Anyone else want to go?," Richardson asked again.

McBride murmured something about wanting to go, but, now that he had lent his jacket to Fred, he was glad to let Fred use it and he (Jon) preferred not to go. Fred offered it back, but Jon refused it.

Whatever had possessed me to stay and finish up the work I needed to do saved my life, that day. We learned, later, that the twin-engine seaplane was struggling to make it over the top of a mountain ridge when it hit the ridge and careened down the other side. Fred had been standing between the pilot and co-pilot, apparently. Enlisted men were in the rear passenger compartment looking out the windows for signs of the wreckage.

After several days, ground crews were finally able to reach the seaplane's wreckage. Three or four enlisted men riding in the tail section were the only survivors.

The 31 Boat returned to sea and I was reminded once more of that phrase learned at the Naval Academy: "On the strength of each link in the cable, dependeth the might of the chain...."

We had a former Patuxent River test pilot in our squadron, LCdr. Bill Brooks, a very capable aviator and person; but he needed glasses to see well. Once in the cockpit, he would put them on and lower the sun visor on his helmet. I was his wingman, one clear day, not far off the Japanese coast from Atsugi, as he pulled up behind an A4D to refuel. The sun was almost directly above us. We had just rendezvoused at 20K feet with the tanker. I was flying below on his left side and looking up at him and the tanker; a sparkling sun positioned slightly above both of them.

The F8 refueling probe would swing out and move forward on the left side of the cockpit until it was within a few feet of and beside the canopy. Standard procedure was to approach the basket that was being dragged at the end of the tanker's fuel line, stop, get lined up, boresight on some part of the tanker and then carefully move ahead so as to drive the F8 probe into the basket and then securely into the tanker's refueling nozzle in the middle of the basket.

The basket was intended to make a bigger bulls eye, so to speak. But, if the F8 probe were to land on the basket's 9 o'clock rim position and push on it enough to bend the refueling hose, the basket could slip off and slam into the cockpit canopy and shatter it. That is what happened, as I looked up and saw broken pieces of canopy reflected by the sun blown outward and away into the airstream.

After quickly descending into warmer air, Brooks, without benefit of a pressurized cockpit, elected to land back aboard the closer 31 Boat.

In the Ready Room, afterwards, he showed me where half of his helmet's sun visor had also been broken off by the rim of the refueling basket and blown away into the airstream; but his black, horn rimmed, glasses had just barely been missed. They had stayed on the whole time.

After another flight as Brooks' wingman, on returning back aboard the Bonnie Dick, I made it to the Ready Room before he did. As I sat in one of the back rows waiting to de-brief, I noticed the squadron skipper and a few others stirring about in the front area of the Ready Room as if they were preparing a surprise of some kind. Then, it dawned on me. It was my birthday.

Not wanting to spoil any "best made surprise plans," I kept silent and appeared not to notice anything. Suddenly, my flight leader, the Pax River guy, LCdr. Bill Brooks, entered at the front of the Ready Room and sounds of "Happy Birthday to you" went up. A little cake was even brought in, as I recall. Good thing I kept my mouth shut, I thought. Wouldn't want anyone to be embarrassed.

That was the first birthday celebration I could remember witnessing in the squadron Ready Room while at sea. But, if one was just recognized, who could have overlooked mine on the same date, I wondered. The Personnel Officer, that's who. And who was that dumb Personnel Officer who had overlooked setting up procedures for automatically recognizing birthdays on time in VF-191? Hmmm. Seems I had only myself to blame if anyone were to be blamed. I was no longer the squadron personnel officer; but I had been its personnel officer back at Moffett and had had plenty of time to set up such a system. That is one event I can remember with a little remorse.

After Typhoon Nancy had pushed the 31 Boat way out into the Pacific, to where there were no landing facilities available other than the carrier, itself, my flight leader, LCdr. Tom Wilson, landed ahead of me and broke a nose wheel. I noticed it almost immediately as the fuselage of his F8 went tail up and the red wave-off lights astride the mirror flashed on.

A late afternoon sun was barely visible through the low clouds directly ahead. It was not a good weather day. Just then, the carrier disappeared into a bank of low clouds ahead that also extended as far to the right and left as I could see. My radio had failed at the end of the hop, so I could not communicate (not unusual). The ship's low frequency homing beacon had been turned off to observe radio silence.

At about 200 feet with the carrier disappearing ahead and seeing clouds fast approaching, I advanced the throttle, moved the gear handle up, the wing handle down, and eased back on the stick as airspeed increased and commenced a climbing 90-degree right turn. The carrier was still obscured in clouds from above and it would take awhile to remove Wilson's plane from the flight deck landing area, so I endeavored to climb and conserve for as long as possible.

After leveling off at 20K feet, I noted the time, flew a few minutes and made a left 180-degree turn to head back. After the same number of minutes elapsed, I powered back and commenced about a 3,500 foot per minute rate of descent while maintaining 350 knots. The carrier was nowhere in sight. In fact, the ocean had become totally overcast. The low fuel warning light came on, indicating 1,250 pounds of fuel remaining.

Turbulent air jostled the plane as I punched through little cumulus buildups and kept a lookout through intensifying haze. Passing through 5K feet, I reached and began penetrating a lower stratus cloud layer that offered no turbulence. (Although it wasn't apparent to me at the time, I realize, now, that its effect was akin to becoming as relaxed as one becomes immediately after turning off a vibrating bed.) In a strange way, I was being lulled to sleep, while descending rapidly on instruments through 3K feet.

The fuel gauge dropped to less than 1,000 pounds. If I should experience a hook-skip on landing, I knew that about 850 pounds of fuel were needed for one go-around.

Where was that carrier?!

The radio direction finder needle had been slowly spinning around without the 31 Boat's beacon being turned on, but unexpectedly it stopped and held a steady bearing directly ahead. My dead reckoning estimate was right on. The carrier was somewhere directly ahead. But how far? I would just have to continue on until I reached it.

The altimeter seemed to be unwinding at a pretty fast rate and was dropping below 1,000 feet as I also noted a high rate of descent on the indicator. In a flash, the following raced through my mind: "Nobody needs you: not the Navy, not your wife, your parents, your in-laws. They all have plenty of money." A short pause followed, then, "But, wait! Your little son needs you. He REALLY needs you! – PULL UP!!"

Still in the soup and on instruments, I pulled hard on the stick, caught sight of the altimeter still unwinding through 300 feet, just as quickly it seemed to whip through 150 feet, but begin to slow. The little plane on the attitude gyro came up through the horizon bar as I broke out under the hazy cloud bottom and instantly realized the fuselage was rotating only a few feet above lapping ocean waves.

Instantly, I eased stick pressure to avoid rotating the plane's tail into the water, while allowing enough rotation to begin a slow climb. I saw lapping ocean waves making gentle white-caps and one water spout standing on end, the wind blowing spray off its top just to the left, as I swiftly passed it. The wind was blowing from right to left. The water was green. My tailhook might have dipped into the ocean, just then. I wasn't sure. I was low. Too low! Just as quickly, I was headed back up into the overcast.

Thank you, my son!, eventually flashed through my mind.

Where was that carrier? Still directly ahead, according to the ADF needle. Glad I hadn't rammed it! I'd been LOW enough to hit it below the flight deck!

After climbing up to 500 feet, the reduced throttle glide was over. Airspeed had slowed to 250, so I added a little power. I was still in solid overcast. A glance at the fuel gauge: 800 pounds; not even enough for one go-around! Where was that carrier?!

What follows may sound too convenient to be true; but it is the truth as I lived it and is told to the best of my ability.

Abruptly, I emerged from what looked to me like a solid vertical wall of clouds extending right and left and all the way down to the water. There, directly ahead about a quarter mile or so, was the 31 Boat, cruising as before, from left to right, still headed into the wind. I was slightly ahead of its starboard beam and soon flew over its bow; throttled back, lowered the gear, raised the wing (I don't remember ever checking the hook), and began flying around in a modified pattern for landing. A circle had opened in the clouds, just large enough for me to fly around inside of while keeping the 31 Boat in sight. As I flew around, penetrated some ragged cloud edges here and there and passed through the 90 with the ship and meatball coming into view despite the low angle sunlit haze, this thought came to mind: someday, you'll have to write about this hop.

Through the haze, I easily saw the bright yellow "meatball" and observed that the flight deck had been cleared of all aircraft. I landed without difficulty.

The weather had already deteriorated to a low ceiling in drizzle, by the time I climbed out of the cockpit. The fuel gauge read 650 pounds on engine shut-down.

That opening in the clouds had been just the right size and had been at just the right place. Had I arrived minutes sooner or later, the carrier would not have been visible to me.

It would take a bit more fuel to fill this F8, I thought, as I walked away from it and headed for the Ready Room. And the tailhook shoe (the part on the very end of the tailhook, that snares the wire) could probably stand a fresh coat of grease. Water, after all, has a tendency to dissolve grease; especially salt water ... at 350 knots.

CHAPTER 11

NORTH ISLAND

My letter to President John F. Kennedy on 13 September 1961 asking to be allowed to resign and leave the USN included something like the following: "It is my hope to be as effective in civilian life as serving the nation at the pleasure of the President has allowed me to be." One more year, and I could return to being a civilian, again.

Meanwhile, instead of Moffett Field, we flew off the 31 Boat and landed at Miramar Naval Air Station near San Diego, at the end of our WestPac cruise, on December 12, 1961. Miramar was a new facility. I stayed with VF-191 for about two months before being transferred to VU-7 at nearby North Island Naval Air Station in Coronado to complete active duty obligations.

North Island was first developed in December 1910 as the Glenn H. Curtiss Aviation Camp. Curtiss leased the land from the Spreckels company for less than $100 a year. On December 23, 1910, Lieutenant Theodore Gordon Ellyson, a husky redhead who had graduated from the Naval Academy in 1905 and had had two commands in the submarine service, was ordered to North Island. He later became the Navy's first pilot. After WWII, North Island was advertised as having the largest expanse of runway in the world. It had concrete north/south and east/west runways. A large area between those runways was also paved with asphalt to allow propeller planes to take off and land into the wind in any direction.

While still at Miramar with VF-191, I and others could view the main east-west runway from a second floor balcony outside our Ready Room. From time to time, an F8 would take off and hug the runway while the wheels came up followed by the wing coming down and the fuselage having to rotate nose up to compensate for it. The tail could then swing down to within 0-12 inches of the runway during that rotation, but, as airspeed then increased, the nose could be lowered to keep the F8 on the deck with reduced chances of the tail scraping the runway. On approaching the runway's end, above average airspeed made climbout easy; but over La Jolla, we had to maneuver to avoid residential areas and remain slow and under the airways until well out to sea. There was something habit forming about making that runway-hugging takeoff. Once I had done it a few times, it was difficult to revert back to standard takeoffs. Perhaps it was the challenge, the danger, the dare (or the audience).

VF-191 was scheduled for another WestPac cruise, so they soon commenced FCLPs and awaited the carrier for some actual landings and catapult launches. My old flight leader from Moffett days, Cdr. Jim Heffernan, was still the Commanding Officer, having moved up to C.O. from X.O. during the cruise.

Meanwhile, my transfer to Utility Squadron VU-7 in February 1962 offered new opportunities to prepare and submit another improvement proposal for the folks back in Washington to consider. It would be my last "extra" for the Navy.

As an F8 Driver, I had had my fill of airborne radio and other electronic malfunctions, not to mention hydraulic leaks, pump failures, etc., etc. There had to be some better way to avoid having them occur repeatedly in flight.

It sounds simple enough now, but I finally came around to devising a system intended to replace parts just before records would project that they were about to fail.

Already, there were hour limits on engines before they had to be inspected, overhauled and/or replaced. The same was true for airframes and a few other major parts and systems, but more and better foresight was needed. Unnecessary repairs and parts replacements, of course, also were to be avoided.

Computers were in their infancy and rumored to consist mostly of expensive centralized mainframe units. I could imagine data being sent to them and results returned. Still to come were the small, inexpensive, personal computers we now enjoy and that can do more than many mainframes could even be imagined able to do back then. I could sense what some computer inputs would have to be; and what some outputs could become. What I had in mind in 1962 should be adaptable onto computer systems that I imagined would be forthcoming in the not-too-distant future. And, whatever I devised, it had to be simple.

VU-7 had several types of aircraft and more F8s than two or three fighter squadrons. They were older and used mostly for towing banners over the desert near Yuma, Arizona, for aerial gunnery practice. When you're sitting there towing a banner attached to the end of a long cable behind you and other planes are rolling in for straffing runs, often with Naval Reserve pilots in their cockpits, you get the picture of what's happening more clearly than do some of the pilots making the gunnery runs, I think. A few of those towing flights came my way; but I was busy mostly with creating and starting up a recorder tag system.

Whenever a part failed, a new part would be installed and a yellow tag identifying it and the date would be affixed to

that new part or near it on the airplane to alert the next maintenance person. A bottom portion of the same tag also was
filled out and routed into Maintenance Logs. The next time
that part failed, the maintenance man would be alerted by the
tag. Operations could then tabulate and inform how many
flight hours had been logged by that part since it was installed.
Patterns and trends might then be discovered, over time, leading ultimately to replacing parts due to fail before they failed
in flight. Simple.

After submitting this proposal up the chain of command,
my wife and I were having lunch somewhere in the San Diego
area. It was just after I had signed out of the Navy and was
getting ready to drive back to Chicago. It may have been at the
Mexican Village in Coronado, often frequented by Navy personnel. The restaurant was nearly empty except for a group of
officers seated together at a table on the other side of the room.
I vaguely recognized one of them as being on someone's staff,
when he unexpectedly called out in my direction: "Should data
be sent to one place, or should each squadron keep its own
records?"

What a question! What a surprise! The other officers
laughed, then became silent. I quickly reviewed the concept
in my mind and tried to estimate what the future might hold.
I also realized that my answer was likely to be repeated and
could end or give support to the proposal. "Each squadron
should keep its own records," I declared, finally. As I recall,
they got up and left shortly after that, not one of them saying
anything more or even looking in my direction. That choice
has surely proven correct after the development of personal
computers that followed.

When taking off from North Island on runway 27 (heading
west), we had to be careful not to fly over Point Loma, straight

ahead. We had to keep an F8's wing up (and flaps down and leading edge droops down) for an immediate 90-degree left turn in slow flight over the entrance channel after lift-off, then we could proceed to clean up, move out and climb to altitude out over the ocean.

A surprise came my way, one day, after I had landed and taxied to the approach end of runway 27, while heading back to the hanger. Before I could cross the runway, I was instructed by the tower to hold my position. Then, a little Air Force jet (a T-38, I learned later) came taxiing along towards me on the other side and was cleared for takeoff on 27, right in front of me. It appeared to have two little engines and two pilots sitting in tandem on board. As it started its take off roll, I was cleared to cross 27 behind it. I had a bird's eye view from behind of a new way to avoid flying over Point Loma. After lifting off and raising its gear and flaps, that T-38 climbed straight up, over the channel. Wow! I don't know about the Air Force, but NASA still has T-38s for astronauts to fly. Quite a plane.

Unexpectedly, on another day, I learned that Cdr. Heffernan had been lost at sea. After making a few traps (arrested carrier landings), he was directed to launch and head back to Miramar. The ceiling, reportedly, was down to around 1,200 feet with tops at 20K. Jim was climbing up through the overcast, but never made it to the top. "I'm having instrument trouble," were the only and last words heard from him. No wreckage was ever found.

Jim's son, Robert, was 4-5 years old, about the same age as my son. I was asked to take care of them both during Jim's memorial service at Miramar. So I took them to Disneyland in Anaheim. We had a great time. Walt Disney, himself, was there.

The boys and I were leaving one attraction and heading towards a mountain. It was some distance away, but we had a straight sidewalk to follow. Off on the right, about 20 feet ahead of us, was a wide but low bush. As one of the boys approached it, a man gradually stood up from behind it wearing a very big smile under a pair of happy eyes. It was Walt Disney. He stepped onto the concrete sidewalk and was obviously prepared to say a few words to some of his happy visitors, but the boys ran passed him and on ahead towards that mountain. I couldn't stop to exchange even a few words for fear of losing track of my young charges, so Walt Disney and I traded smiles and waves.

The loss of Cdr. Heffernan to an instrument failure was unexpected. He was a green card pilot (most qualified to fly instruments).

Flying partial panel in an F8 was next to impossible. After you banked to the left, for example, the turn needle would show a right turn for awhile before finally moving to the left; but, by then, you could have initiated a turn to the right, knowingly or unknowingly, and the turn needle couldn't be counted on to reveal it. Without a functioning gyro horizon indicator, the F8 was dangerous to fly in instrument conditions. True, I had not heard of many F8 gyro horizon indicator malfunctions, nor had I experienced one myself, but as a result of Jim's accident I became even more motivated to develop and submit my parts replacement concept to Washington.

Unexpectedly, the Chief of Naval Personnel, Vice Admiral William R. Smedberg III, Class of 1926, came to North Island to speak to any officer wanting to attend his presentation. I was in the audience with just a few others, numbering perhaps 15-20. The Admiral became Superintendent at the Naval

Academy some 2.5 months before I graduated, and had a son in the Class of '58 who I remembered.

In addition to citing a few statistics, the Admiral went on to carefully review how President John F. Kennedy, in office for little more than a year, had changed USN Flag Rank promotions. "It used to be," said the Admiral, "that a billet requiring certain qualifications and capabilities could only be filled by someone having those qualifications and capabilities. That used to be why and how one was promoted to Flag Rank in the U.S. Navy. There was no other reason to promote an officer to the rank of Commodore or Rear Admiral unless the Navy needed a Commodore or Rear Admiral to perform certain functions," asserted the Chief of Naval Personnel.

In the short time that Kennedy had been president, he continued, so many Rear Admirals had been "created" that they could even be found acting as aides in the halls of the White House wearing gold ropes over one shoulder, white gloves, and standing around like ushers, with nothing meaningful to do. Knowingly or unknowingly, President Kennedy was destroying a traditional flag rank promotion system by arbitrarily promoting officers needlessly and en masse. The Chief of Naval Personnel was visibly disturbed.

Based on the facts and figures in his presentation, I couldn't blame him. It was becoming an extra expense to taxpayers that was unnecessary; and it likely would reduce the quality of officers promoted to Flag Rank. In turn, the effectiveness of the entire U.S. Navy would be adversely affected. If I ever had an opportunity to restore the old system of need before promotion, I intended to do my part.

Night flying, now and then, was a proficiency requirement. Easiest for me were over-water flights up and down the coast from San Diego to Los Angeles and back. It took a decade or more after I had left the Navy to finally figure out what I had occasionally seen at night coming from somewhere near Pasadena.

Once in a while a bright light would appear in that area. It was about as bright as a carbon arch search light, but this light was not focused into a beam. Too bright to look at directly, even from 40K feet, it was just a bright light that lit the sky in all directions. It took awhile before I saw it for the first time, but then it seemed to begin appearing more frequently. At times, it stayed on, while I eventually would turn around and head back to San Diego with it still on behind me. One night it offered a different clue: it went out as I was trying to watch it. Disappeared completely. On a subsequent night, the light went out but, later, it came back on again. I left the Navy without ever knowing what I had seen. In future years, however, I deduced that it had probably been a space rocket engine being tested on a stand in some hidden valley in the Pasadena area. For it to be turned on and off like that, it was probably a liquid-fueled rocket engine.

John Glenn became the first American to orbit the Earth on February 20, 1962. I remember driving down the bumpy ramp timbers onto a ferry on the San Diego side, that morning, to go across to Coronado, as Glenn lifted off. In those days, a ferry was the main connection between Coronado and San Diego.

The father of a classmate of mine, Navy Captain Dick Tarbuck (Retired), was a retired Rear Admiral, Class of '21. Living with his wife in Coronado, he became one of the civic leaders who helped develop the bridge that now spans San Diego Bay.

When I first came to San Diego, in 1956, there were huge twin engine Martin P5M Marlin anti-submarine flying boats taking off from and landing on San Diego Bay, day and night. They were engaged in offshore submarine search patrols. That no collisions occurred between ferries and P5Ms suggests there must have been a reliable system of communications between them.

As for John Glenn, many described his flight in a capsule, at the time, as equivalent to going over Niagara Falls in a barrel. That was before a better understanding of space flight was generally attained.

My last flight in an F8 was on September 18, 1962, in Navy Jet 142412. Palm Springs had become my R&R destination of choice, for it seemed to have the warmest and best California weather. So, on my last hop, I went up that way via Santa Barbara, and then dropped down to near sea level along the western edge of the Salton Sea. Down on the deck, I found short piers (some of them tall) built a few feet out onto the waters of the Salton Sea, here and there, but there was not a single person to be seen. All pretty barren, desolate, and brown! The water: green.

An instrument approach to North Island required one to fly a racetrack holding pattern at 20K feet above the ocean, a few miles south of the Mexican border and a few miles out over the water from the coast of Mexico. It was interesting to be able to distinguish Mexico from the U.S. even from up there. Mexico appeared almost undeveloped, mostly dirt brown with little clumps of vegetation here and there; while, up north, the sun reflected off of car windshields intermittently where also some green vegetation, buildings and roads could be seen.

After shooting a penetration down and around towards North Island, one flew close to the Hotel Del Coronado and its outdoor beach area and facilities. Often I wished I didn't have to fly so close to it and scatter exhaust fumes over it, but the approach end of runway 27 was just ahead.

The F8 I flew that day is on display at the Smiley High School in Houston, Texas, as I write this. The school has an NROTC unit. Hope they can learn something from that F8. Aviation progress often develops in mysterious ways.

A few days before departing from North Island, I learned of intentions to assign me to the Naval Reserve. I had nothing against the Naval Reserves, but I knew that I would probably give the Navy too much of my time. If I had no other choice, OK, but if I didn't have to serve, I would prefer arriving at the construction company with no additional obligations outstanding or forthcoming. After checking into it, the Personnel Officer at VU-7 assured me as follows:

LT JENSON was interviewed and apprised of his opportunities in the Naval Reserve. Since he has completed his total military obligation, LT JENSON elected not to accept an appointment as a Reserve Officer in the United States Navy.

LT JENSON's performance of all duties while assigned to this command has been outstanding. Should he at some later date reconsider this decision, it is recommended that the Reserve Commission be again proferred.

There is a lot of brown beige and beige brown in California. It mostly stays that way year around. In fact, I began to miss the seasonal changes such as those enjoyed in the Midwest, after living in California for several years. I signed out of the USN at 0930 on 9/22/62.

California had become a nice place to visit.

CHAPTER 12

ORR CONSTRUCTION COMPANY

It was fascinating to think one could crush limestone into fine powder, add sand and gravel for bulk, plus a few chemicals and water, then mix all of it and pour it over raised reinforcing steel bars on the ground and have it gradually return to rock but as street or highway pavement.

Also inspiring was how trees could be felled, trimmed into boards, dried in huge ovens, and cut again into building materials, furniture, floors, cabinets, pianos, guitars, lots of things.

In northern Minnesota and elsewhere in the world, iron ore was dug out of the ground and eventually delivered to melting pots in Gary, Indiana, for example, where ingots and slabs of metal were formed to eventually be made into parts for engines, bridge and building structures, and into pipes, concrete reinforcing steel rods, and many other useful items.

Mostly, however, I admired being able to convert solid rock, boulders and stones into smooth concrete roads. A retired State of Indiana civil engineer once visited one of our jobsites in southern Indiana and wanted me to know how building roads made of concrete had started.

The only man around the town in southern Indiana (that he named, but that I can't remember now) who owned a concrete mixer was a burial vault maker. So he was asked to get a crew together and build a concrete road, which was to be the first of many to come. The vault maker ordered his foreman to get a crew together and go out there to the site and lay as much concrete as the mixer could mix in a day. On completion of that first day's effort, the vault maker came out to see the approximate 12 foot length of pavement that had been laid. Happy with the result, he then instructed his foreman to call that amount of pavement "a day's work," and that he could call it a day whenever that much pavement had been laid. Soon, "a day's work" had been accomplished by noon. A far cry from current operations; but THAT is how it all started in Indiana, said that engineer.

When I thought of construction, in my early years, to build meant one could be creating something new, useful, interesting. I often reminded myself of such idealistic thoughts when the going got a little rough.

One morning, our seven brand new twin-engine diesel Euclid scrapers filled the countryside with their usual humming sounds as they loaded, traveled at speeds up to 30 mph at gross weights in excess of 180K pounds, and dumped their damp 24 cubic yard sand loads onto a rising embankment designed to carry Interstate 80 over several railroad tracks near Gary, Indiana. On completion, it would be the intersection of I-80 and I-65. The firm, J.C. O'Conner, had obtained the contract for what was the largest job of its kind ever let by the State of Indiana, and Orr Construction had obtained a subcontract from O'Conner to excavate and backfill the intersection where the Interstates would meet.

We had purchased 80 acres of floodplain land adjacent to the intersection. I had hired an artist to paint a water color picture of what the 80 acres would look like after we completed the project, and used it while seeking a mining permit from Lake County officials to dig. After stripping off the topsoil and leaving two peninsulas for NIPSCO (Northern Indiana Public Service Company) high tension line towers, we wanted to remove about 1 million cubic yards of sand, if possible. The water table was close to the surface, so we had to run pumps during months of excavation and a lake would be left behind, on job completion.

Obtaining that permit took some time. What finally seemed to turn the tide in our favor was our offer to give title to that 80 acres to the County when we had finished. My hopes and dreams of developing a company-owned lake and fishing pond were forfeited.

Until stepping outside, I didn't notice from inside the office trailer what was happening. The twin-engine Euc's were pulling in and parking, one by one; and the background sound of humming engines was gradually diminishing. The work day had barely begun. I was a time keeper plus anything else useful as a supervisor that I could be, when the operators, one by one, drove their machines in, parked them, and, without wanting to look me in the eye, took to their automobiles and left. Some of them were big, burly, WWII veterans who had shown me how to operate the big rigs and were somewhat disappointed when I moved a TS-24 only a few feet, stopped, jumped down and turned it back over to them.

As I stood in front of the office trailer in wonder, a clean, new, black, Cadillac sedan drove up and stopped a few feet away. A short, middle-aged man, well dressed, got out of the driver's seat. He was alone. He stood beside his car for a moment, then looked towards me and announced, "I've just put your [heavy equipment] operators On Strike in sympathy with the local bridge deck iron workers." Then, he looked at me from the corner of his eye and added, "We have the same lawyers as President Kennedy; so what are you gonna do about it?" After a brief pause, as quickly as he had arrived, he got back into his car and drove off.

Our contract involved removing a top layer of about 12-14 feet of unsuitable peat material and replacing it with good sand. Two of our 100-ton cranes with 100-foot booms and dragline buckets kept themselves on huge timber mats and worked 24/7 to cast unsuitable materials off to the sides of what would become new road and bridge approaches. We could build the approaches to the overhead bridges higher by simply adding more sand after digging down to good sand. But we did not have a contract or subcontact to build any bridges in the area, certainly not on this jobsite. Any bridge under construction here and there on that jobsite was contracted for by some other firm, whose identity I was not apprised of. What seemed to add insult to injury was that a bridge under construction in the middle of our jobsite and within sight of my office trailer was not struck but continued to be worked on, with no sign of a strike in progress, by ironworkers, or any other trade; while our expensive new scrapers stood parked.

The Business Agent of Operating Engineers Local 150 was the man who had come calling, I learned. What he wanted and eventually got was money; not for the union and its members; but for himself (and it was tax free, unless he declared it as income, which was possible.)

As for me, when you have over a million dollars worth of equipment sitting around in good weather and a job to complete on time, one can conclude after several days of idleness that losing thousands of dollars a day for the sake of a few hundred dollar payoff can seriously challenge the affordability of honesty and good ethics. And since only cash becomes acceptable in such transactions, mere denials are about all one can expect, should one attempt to pursue "justice," at some future time.

All men may be created equal, but, by their own actions, they won't stay that way.

When the job started, we retained lawyers Al Gavit and Son to represent us in local matters, should they be needed. I remember meeting them for the first time in their Gary office and asking, "How did Gary get this way?," meaning so lawless.

Mr. Gavit Senior answered easily: "Elbert Gary was the Chairman of U.S. Steel and founded the City of Gary. He ran things his own way, and the City seems not to have changed much from the examples he personally set."

Workers have had to endure many abuses. Federal Laws have finally provided for secret union balloting. Before unions, industrialists had to deal for the first time with masses of workers, and they didn't always have much interest in individuals, either. Americans have moved ahead on many fronts; but labor relations improvements seem to arrive at a slow and careful pace. A question that arises in the back of my mind as I write this is this: "Can future generations of Americans be wise enough to remain civil and free if they have not shared some of the hardships of previous generations? Or must they also endure hardships, hardships they may not be able to recover from?" I do wonder.

Orr Construction Company in Chicago Heights, Illinois, had been founded by two brothers, Joe and Bill Orr. "Joe Orr was a gentleman's gentleman," said a man in the State House in Springfield, Illinois, as he handed me a new set of highway plans that I had flown down in the company Beech Bonanza to pick up, one day. But, years prior to my joining the company, Joe Orr had been killed in a car wreck: hit by a train at a railroad crossing. He left two sons, Donald and William C. Orr, whom we called WC. Donald was the head bookkeeper;

WC ran the company, with the advice and consent of my father-in-law, William J. Orr, who owned half of the company and whom we called WJ.

"Everybody likes Bill," my father-in-law, WJ, would often declare. Perhaps WC had taken up where his late father had left off.

WC had been a Naval Aviator in WWII, trained to fly sea plane scouting missions after being catapulted from the deck of a cruiser. He had been flying the Bonanza for over a year when I came along. On our first flight together, WC piloted and all four souls on board rode silently over the tree tops and windmills from the Lansing airport, near Chicago, to Springfield, Illinois. As we deplaned, WC handed me the keys and said, "You've got it. From now on, you're the pilot," and he never flew it again.

My first flight, later, became one from Springfield to Effingham, about 65 air miles to the southeast, where we had a job in progress. Having been a jet jockey, I took off and climbed to 8K feet (which took quite a while). On an airways map, I had located Effingham. Then, from 8K feet, I saw it and immediately had to commence a descent (almost diving) in order not to fly past Effingham. The runway was paved and long, for a reassuring first landing in the company Bonanza. WC said nothing then, nor during the many flights we made together after that, except in answer to a question of mine when we returned that evening to Lansing at dusk. Trying to land on that short, grass runway, for some reason, seemed unsafe to me. I would approach at a slow enough airspeed, clear the fence, touch down and roll along for a short distance and then feel it necessary to add full power and go around for another approach. I was used to landing jets at much higher airspeeds and consuming prodigious amounts of runway before slowing down enough to be able to apply the brakes and not blow tires; and this just seemed like too short a runway.

Finally, after about the third try, I told WC that I thought we didn't have enough runway to make it. He gently replied, "There's plenty there. You can make it. Just let it roll out." So, on the next touchdown, I pulled the power off against my better judgment and the plane seemed to stop almost immediately, about half way down the runway. I had to add power to taxi and turn off at the end.

That became my introduction to Bonanza 4251D with passengers, a good, reliable little airplane that never crashed nor was it ever involved in any kind of ground incident, except one.

One Sunday morning, I had flown about 60 miles west to Starved Rock State Park, beside the Illinois River, with my young son along. We had had lunch in the Park Service Hotel Dining Room and returned to the plane. I started it up and began taxiing slowly in the grass towards the runway for take off when suddenly the nose dropped and the propeller bit into the ground blade by blade, throwing dirt and grass everywhere. I immediately shut off fuel to the engine and later got out and looked things over. The nose wheel had fallen into a hidden gopher or ground hog hole in the tall grass, allowing the propeller, in turn, to drop down and bite into the grass and dirt. Standing off to one side and looking at the propeller, I could see the blade tips were bent slightly forward and would not to be able to grab as much air as they had done previously; but both blades seemed to be bent equally. If no vibrations developed after restarting the engine and running it up to full RPM for take-off, we would still have sufficient power to fly back to home base, I concluded.

Later, after that repair was ostensibly completed at Wings Field, where we then kept the plane, I again looked at the prop from the side and saw that nothing had changed. The prop tips were still bent forward; so I called it to the attention of the repair men involved. Eventually, that prop was replaced.

The Navy had developed something called the "Critical Path" method. It involved sketching lines on a long sheet of paper showing step-by-step procedures for building ships, repairing ships, or for whatever else that might need to be organized before getting started doing it. A major purpose was to be able to foresee and then reduce or avoid potential bottlenecks. I had heard about it and seen a few examples when Cook County, Illinois, let a bridge contract for a new bridge to be constructed in Blue Island, Illinois. For the very first time, it required the winning contractor to prepare, submit and implement a Critical Path plan.

Orr Construction won that contract, quite possibly because we were the only bidder who understood how to prepare a Critical Path schematic for the County Engineers. It was to be a long, time consuming, expensive job mainly because there were few opportunities for doing what we called production work. The job was filled with a little of this, a little of that, here and there this and that. What is preferred is to be able to set up and then continue an activity for awhile before having to change to doing something else, again. But, Eddie Abroe, our bridge superintendent, and I were able to produce a visible Critical Path portrayal within about a month after winning the contract. As far as we knew, that was Cook County's very first use of the Critical Path method.

Eddie and I even went one better than the Navy version: along the bottom of the presentation we showed calendar dates. As each step in building the river bridge was described above, a horizontal line was extended to represent the time that was expected to be required for completing each step.

With jobs scattered far and wide in Illinois and Indiana, there were dozers, dozer blades, graders, water trucks, scoops, cranes, back hoes, buckets of all kinds and many odds and ends lying around that needed to be better accounted for. So, one day, I came up with a solution.

With the help of a carpenter, an equipment panel board system was created and mounted on a wall in the office opposite WC's desk and his right hand man, John Mooney's desk. Each vertical panel had pre-drilled holes into which different colored and labeled wooden blocks representing cranes, scrapers, dozers, trucks, and what have you, could be inserted for viewing. At the top of each panel was a large clip for holding a 7x5 inch hard paper card with a job site printed on it. Only Pete Myteka drove the low boy truck trailer around and it became his responsibility to update the equipment board each night after moving equipment from jobsite to jobsite during the day.

Before I came along, the company had built a section of the Calumet Expressway in the 1950s that ran north to Chicago, south to a little town called Goodenow, and was located east of East Chicago Heights, now called Ford Heights. The Expressway has also been renamed the Bishop Ford Memorial Expressway. In time, it may run south to a new Peotone Airport.

On the southeast corner of that Expressway and Route 30 (Lincoln Highway), the company had purchased about 160 acres of land for use in building the expressway. Not much was thought of nor said about that parcel, but I gradually learned that the top soil had been stripped off and about 2-3 feet of material removed to provide fill for the adjacent Expressway. Then, the top soil had been replaced, leaving the property a bit lower than the surrounding area, but still useable as farmland. This quarter section of land was located out in the country;

but I came to view it as a potential mobile home site. Jobs in nearby communities seemed available and convenient. At that time, however, I learned from Mobile Home Association representatives in Chicago that, in order to sell mobile homes, one had to be able to provide a place to park them after the sale; and obtaining permits for building and operating mobile home parks was usually difficult or impossible. (We could sell homes, too, I imagined.)

So, why did communities consider mobile home parks so undesirable? They were in disfavor, I learned, mainly because typical mobile home owners had no children living with them and, in turn, they did not want to have to pay property taxes to support schools. Also, I learned that it was not unusual for parks to be designed to site as many as 10 or more mobile homes per acre, including allowances for yards and roads. Typically, at that time, mobile home parks could charge $150 monthly parking fees, or more.

"Western Town" was the name I came up with for that mobile home community. By creating a lake, the material removed for the lake could be used to raise the rest of the land areas back up to where they had been originally. The construction company could park equipment out there, only several miles from the home office, and work at digging the lake and creating the roads and parking pads a little at a time, as opportunities arose. Eventually, the park could contain its own grocery store, filling station and whatever else some 3,000 or more persons living in some 1,500 mobile homes there might need.

My father had been a supporter and friend of Maurino Richton, a one-time mayor of Chicago Heights. Richton had also been my dad's attorney. I called him and presented my drawings and intentions for developing Western Town. Would he help me obtain the necessary permits?

"Why, of course. I'll be more than happy to help," he replied.

Together, we appeared before the necessary officials and, without much effort, we soon obtained the necessary permits to proceed - and we didn't have to pay anyone off, either! "Wow!," I thought. "This could be as good or better financially as the construction business!"

Unfortunately, WJ vetoed it. "What do you want to do that for?," he asked.

"To make money," I answered.

He walked away and absolutely refused to talk about it any more, after that. Richton couldn't believe it, after all we had done - so successfully! But WJ had a reputation. When he was good, he could be very good; but when he was bad, look out! I was never afraid of him; but I was also aware of how difficult he could be to reason with when his mind had been made up and, essentially, closed.

By then, IBM had developed a Model 360 computer that seemed capable of simplifying many corporate operations. I managed to see one in a climate-controlled room, in downtown Chicago one day, across the river from the Wrigley Building. It was round and had layers of discs spinning at very high speed: 57K RPMs, as I recall. There were finger-like arms between the discs that moved in and out to retrieve data bytes. It took a specialist to start it up and to keep it from vibrating apart while it accelerated to operating speed. Too large and expensive for us; but we did eventually employ another company with access to one for doing our weekly payrolls. Donald Orr drove off with time cards and later picked up payroll checks that only needed to be signed.

What I had in mind was more inclusive. At some future time, I hoped we could set ourselves up to retrieve data from previous jobs well enough to be able to bid more accurately and with greater ease on new work.

Also, I wanted the capacity to keep track of the jobs other contractors had been awarded with dates when they had received their awards so as to be able to estimate their interests in bidding on jobs we might also be interested in at any given letting. The State kept track of contractor workloads, why couldn't we?

Preparing and submitting bids could be challenging. It required all night stands, usually, in Springfield, Illinois or Indianapolis, Indiana, depending on where the jobs were that we were bidding on. Those bids were usually due at 10 o'clock in the morning. We would prepare as much as possible in advance before flying to those capital cities. Once there, we would rent a suite of rooms and have almost a steady stream of sales representatives and subcontractors coming and going with prices for various job items, late into the night and early morning hours. Sometimes, we had to run with our bid proposal in order to submit it in time.

By 11 AM, the bids were usually announced and we could either celebrate and go home; or wonder why we missed out, on our way home.

Since I flew the plane that brought all but one of us back to the office (Ralph drove and ferried our very heavy office machines), and since I had been made fully aware while in the Navy of how dangerous those final landings at the end of a long trip could be, I made special efforts after being up for some 36 hours or more to stay alert during those many final landings at Wings Field, west of Park Forest, Illinois.

WJ and Mrs. Orr usually spent January through April in their home on the western edge of Biscayne Bay, with an expansive view of Miami Beach off in the distance, across the Bay.

Leaving a morning snowfall in Chicago and stepping off an airliner onto sun-drenched concrete in Miami a few hours later, one day, left me just standing there. I wanted to soak up those relaxing rays and warmth. What a country!

The Doral was a brand new hotel on the Beach in the 1960s. I don't think it had officially opened, yet, with construction crews still working around it. From across Collins Avenue, I was drawn to noticing its many chandelier lights that hung inside, over the entrance foyer. Because those lights were on, I reasoned, they might be open for business. I turned the car around and drove up the entrance ramp to inquire about checking in.

Yes, they were open; and my young son could be cared for in our very large room by a responsible baby sitter.

There were two more pleasant surprises in store: In the cocktail lounge that evening, my wife and I were the only persons in attendance, I think, to hear Count Basie and His Orchestra perform right there in front of us. No stage. They were just seated in chairs on the same floor as we were on. What music! The best! Loud, too.

The second surprise was that the Doral Hotel in which we were staying also had a golf course in Miami - at which a tournament was about to begin - and we would receive free passes as guests of the hotel.

After one afternoon of walking around that course, I gave our tickets to a friend visiting from Flossmoor and his wife, Charlie and Vera Thompson.

Charlie, a contractor in Chicago, was over 80 and still played golf. He had sponsored me for membership at the Flossmoor Country Club. His tee shots weren't long, but they were persistently straight. His putting: exceptional! Charlie enjoyed life. He and his wife took us out to dinner at the LaGorce (of course) Country Club in Miami Beach a few times and they truly appreciated the Tournament passes.

Eventually, I was unintentionally clued-in to something I considered very important, while playing a round of golf with Charlie at the Flossmoor Country Club.

Orr Construction had just won a contract for work some-where (I don't remember where) and Charlie, I believe, merely wanted to offer congratulations, as we walked downhill on the 17th hole fairway beside Western Avenue, the road my hot rod and I had used while escaping from the Flossmoor Police some 15 years earlier. As we walked together towards a little bridge that crossed over a small stream, Charlie asked me, "Was it set?"

Hmmm. Having been around for a comparatively short time, I had developed a few suspicions, but none that I was sure about. But Charlie's question came from an old hand, I reasoned. After pausing and thinking it over, I answered truthfully: "I don't know."

Nothing more was said about it. But the question seemed to fit in with something WJ often murmured to me almost un-der his breath when we were alone: "It only takes one." To do what?, I wondered, never really stopping to ask him, directly. Perhaps, in deference to my father-in-law, I did not want to hear the answer.

"Who's the Boss?," was another question WJ would often ask my little son when I was standing around with them in a threesome. When WJ and I were alone, he occasionally would ask me, "Who are you?"

Usually, I would choose to ignore it and walk away; but, one day, I answered, "I'm Gunnar Jenson and don't you ever forget it!" I can't remember him asking me who I was again, after that.

Driving back and forth between North Miami and Miami Beach can be pleasant. There are little bridges to cross and many attractive buildings along Collins Avenue to see and enjoy. The bright-colored hotels on Miami Beach with palm trees and tropical flowers assure visitors that all is well. But, I remember one incident while driving north on Collins Avenue with WJ along, when I realized that all was not so well.

As I pulled to a stop for a red traffic light, WJ, who had been quiet, suddenly offered to forgive me for having had the equipment location boards installed in the office. "It's not important," he said. "A mistake like that can be overlooked."

I said nothing. I was surprised and disappointed. I was not looking for praise, but, if anything, I thought a little gratitude would have been more appropriate. If an improvement as simple and necessary as that equipment panel board was not wanted or appreciated, I thought, what other contributions of mine to Orr Construction will he try to avoid, deny or terminate?

When summer arrived, WC decided we could use a few new experiences. So, off we went in the Bonanza to Rapid City, South Dakota. It was about as long a trip in the Bonanza without a pit stop as we could make. On approaching the Badlands, east of Rapid City, I descended to almost ground level and turned south. We saw, close up, how dry and uneven the ground under us was, with boulders of all sizes and shapes scattered around. Off on the right was an almost sheer cliff that would have prevented any wagon train from even wanting to approach it. Those early pioneers had had their work cut out for them, as they moved across America.

Once we had landed and found motel rooms in Rapid City, after dinner, we ventured into a cocktail lounge for an after-dinner drink and a little entertainment. One of the musicians came over to our table for some conversation and, to our amazement, told us he was from Chicago Heights! Small world.

WC took his assistant, John Mooney, along; and we also brought Bob Nelson, one of our Dirt Bosses, with us. We headed for a job site where a contractor was using scrapers that he had modified himself, to move dirt. And how!

While we had 24 cubic yard scrapers with engines on the front and back, that contractor had attached another 24-yard scraper with a rear engine to the back of a twin engine scraper, making each unit into 3 engines, two scrapers, and one operator. With 3 engines, those scrapers did not need a pusher tractor to get loaded, either. They just dropped the pan on one scraper at a time and slowly moved along (saving the costs of a pusher dozer and an operator). Obviously, that contractor knew what he was doing. Caterpillar, GM and Allis-Chalmers could learn from him. So could R. G. LeTourneau.

Unbeknownst to me at the time, I would one day bid against that contractor to build an earth filled dam near Des Moines, Iowa. I remember having to fly over some reported tornadoes in order to reach Des Moines with my bid. I say "my bid," because that was what it was, my bid. I had been encouraged to prepare and submit it, more or less, as an exercise, since WC and, therefore, WJ, did not think much of our chances to beat those dirt movers who would be coming down from the South Dakota hills with their "customized" equipment.

WC and WJ were right. The job went for what I had determined to be our cost. In other words, had we been awarded that contract at the low bidder's price, we would have spent as much as we received, and consumed more than a year doing it. However, with those 3 engined, twin scoop, single operator units, the job was likely profitable; provided more jobs were won and sufficient volume was handled to ultimately pay for that equipment.

The figures carved into Mount Rushmore looked smaller from about 1,500 feet above them than had been imagined. We flew over them and headed back to Chicago Heights.

WC was so well liked he was elected president of the Illinois Road Builders Association. Over six feet tall, you might say he stood tall over his peers.

Occasionally, when we were together in a cocktail lounge on an evening prior to a state letting, he would say to other contractors who would approach us for conversation, "He thinks we're whores!," indicating with body language, yours truly. I would smile and try just to ignore it. I never answered that one.

The contractors I met were all friendly. One told me he wanted to invent a new construction tool, patent it, and live on the royalties for the rest of his life instead of contracting. Another had just bought a small plane and was taking flying lessons. Every time he saw me, he'd come over and want to sit down and talk about flying. Unfortunately, he didn't last long after we had met.

One of my frequent "instructions" was to not make appointments that couldn't be broken when traveling to them by plane. Weather was changeable and staying on the ground could easily become necessary unexpectedly. My new pilot friend had no instrument training yet, and I tried to discourage him from flying up through what we used to call in the Navy "sucker holes" in the overcast. For, once up there, that sucker hole was sure to close.

Not long after what turned out to be our last meeting, I had flown to Rockford, Illinois. Returning that afternoon, I encountered strong winds behind me from the northwest and narrow but elongated cloud formations that were perpendicular to my flight path and that also had extended clear areas between them. I was able to fly under those clouds after leaving Rockford, but they gradually descended and I was forced to climb up through a "sucker hole" to "on top" when I was approximately abeam Chicago's Midway Airport. Over Wings Field, later, I had to orbit once to allow the clouds to pass by before landing. A few of my thoughts had been about that Bridge Builder with the new airplane, that afternoon. The way those clouds had gradually descended would have forced a pilot attempting to maintain visual flight to fly too close to the ground, or go up above the clouds, or to turn around.

The word I received was that he, too, had been flying that day, headed southeast near Bloomington, Illinois, and had descended into a farmer's windmill and been killed. Damn!

On another occasion, WC and I were seated in Chicago's City Hall, somewhere, with a large room full of contractors. A City (or Cook County) Councilman, I think, approached the podium to address the audience. "Good morning, Burglars," was his opening statement.

I was not a burglar, nor did I appreciate being called one, especially by a Municipal Official! I almost stood up and told him so. Instead, I just glared at him during his speech and he, in turn, glanced quizzically back at me - often.

The IRS (Internal Revenue Service) audited the company, one year. WJ and I were called to a downtown Chicago office and appeared before a middle-aged man who had been in the construction business with his father before they lost all of their money. I learned this by asking him about his background. Next, he had gone to work for the IRS, he told us, and, there, sitting at his desk in front of us, he was finding fault with my salary.

That the IRS could deny a portion of my salary was news to me. Asked what I did at the company, I told him I was involved in practically everything and also flew the plane.

The company had to reimburse the Internal Revenue Service for the taxes on 30% of my salary for one year. WJ did not offer to tell me this. I asked him about it, sometime later, and he told me.

The assumed right by the IRS to determine my salary was more discouraging to yours truly than anything I had ever encountered in this world - and it remains so. Not only did I feel that I had earned all that I was paid and more; I seriously questioned the right of the IRS to make that kind of a determination. And I still do!

Meanwhile, work on the I-80/I-65 interchange was progressing. Looking ahead, the next big job would extend I-65 south almost to U.S. Route 30 (Lincoln Highway). There seemed to be a corridor through which I-65 would pass. I obtained aerial photos of areas bordering the proposed right-of-way and began a systematic search for available properties from which we might obtain fill materials, should we win that next I-65 contract.

WJ left me alone, for awhile, but he was becoming impatient with my activities in the office that involved posting aerial photos on a wall and using thin adhesive tapes of various colors to outline available properties on the photos. I had no idea what the actual size of the job to come would be, but I sensed that it would be pretty big. I was driving back and forth to our Gary jobsite, to various properties I investigated as potential borrow pits, and to the Lake County Courthouse in Crown Point, to determine who the various property owners were. Then, I would contact them in person, if possible, to learn whether or not they would be interested in selling us an option to purchase their land in case we got the job.

WJ kept circling around. But finally one day, he couldn't stand it any longer. "How much are you gonna make on this job?," he asked me, in a surly tone of voice; like, you're wasting a lot of time and energy if it's not going to be a lot.

Without thinking, I blurted out, "A million dollars!" I had no idea what the size of the job would ultimately become, neither did anyone else. But WJ wasn't going to catch me unprepared, I thought. That seemed to satisfy his curiosity. His eyes registered that he was thinking it over. For the moment, at least, he went away and left me alone.

As that I-65 bidding date drew closer, I obtained a few more options, and WJ would remind me, WC, and also John Mooney, when we were in the same room together, "He says you're gonna make a million dollars on that job!" One thing everyone knew about WJ was that he would hold you to whatever you might have said to him. He could remind you of it over and over again if he had nothing else to say. So, now I was tagged with the promise of making a million dollars on a job we hadn't even received the plans for yet.

"Yep," I would answer him with consistency.

Another way to create a scene would be to try to change what you had previously said to WJ. He could change HIS story, but you couldn't change YOURS.

There was an International truck dealer in Chicago Heights named Wally Meidel who had a great sense of humor and was always fun to talk to. He had a son in the Navy and had given him this advice: When anyone approaches you, do something, anything, but look busy.

One day, Wally told me about a conversation he had had with WJ, whom he liked to call "Uncle Bill." Wally thought Uncle Bill had wanted to order some 10 tandem-axle trucks with concrete batch bin bodies, a good-sized order. So, Wally placed his order with the factory.

Sometime later, the trucks arrived at Wally's dealership and he arranged to have drivers for all of the trucks so they could be delivered to "Uncle Bill's" yard in sort of a parade. Wally drove over in advance of the truck arrivals and stood proudly beside Uncle Bill as the trucks began arriving. They just seemed to keep coming and then Uncle Bill asked Wally, "What's going on?"

"These are the trucks you ordered," said Wally.

"I didn't order any trucks. Get 'em the hell out of here," commanded Uncle Bill; and Wally had to take every one of them back.

Wally insisted, when he told me this story, that WJ, indeed, had ordered the trucks, but Wally had not obtained the order in writing, regrettably.

As the I-65 bid submission date approached, I had been able to obtain six-month purchase options on all of the available land areas between I-80 and Lincoln Highway for a total of about $35,000.

It was in 1965 when we flew to Indianapolis and checked in at the Claypool Hotel, downtown, near the State Office Building, where we would submit our bid, the next morning.

By having options to purchase all of the properties available for providing embankment material along the I-65 right of way, my strategy also included the possibility that other contractors would either not bid on the job, or have to bid quite a bit higher than Orr Construction due to not knowing exactly what the cost of fill materials would be. And if we didn't get the job, we could either go ahead and buy some or all of the lands and sell them back to whoever had gotten the job, or just let the options expire.

Usually, I would try to stay up all through the night during State lettings, but, this time, it was about 3:30 AM when I decided to go into the next room for a short nap. The Job had been totaled, including the $1 million (which turned out to have been a reasonable estimate).

Our room was near the top floor at the Claypool and had windows facing north. There were other buildings next to the hotel, but, lying on the bed, I could look up and see blue sky and a few clouds to the northwest. It was 5:30, and I had awakened with an overpowering premonition that our bid was $100,000 too high. As I lay there looking up at the sky, I tried to dismiss it; but the feeling became stronger: We were going to lose that job by bidding it $100,000 too high. Enough!

I got up and ventured back into the room where WC, John Mooney and Ralph, our calculator person and civil engineer, were sitting around trying to pass the time.

"Now, Bill, you're going to wonder about my sanity, perhaps, but I have just awakened with the premonition we are $100,000 too high," I announced for all to hear. "I don't know why or how I've developed this impression, but I'm convinced we're gonna lose this job if we don't lower the bid by a hundred."

"If we lower it by a hundred grand," I went on, "we'll only have a $900,000 profit potential; but, at least, we might get the job and have building it to look forward to."

If we lower it to 900, when we get home, WJ will begin to harp on both of us for not getting a million. "You said there'd be a million dollars in the job," he'll remind us, "and if we ever run into unforeseen difficulties, he'll have a field day with both of us."

"Bill, it's up to you," I announced, adding, "I am willing to accept the 900 and go back and face WJ for the length of the job; but I do not want to speak for you on this. If you are willing to put up with him for 900, OK; but if not, that's going to be OK with me, too. But I do truly believe that if we don't lower our bid, we won't get the job. If we lower it a hundred grand, we stand a good chance of getting it."

Our bid was left unchanged. As the bids were read off at the State Office Building later that morning, our bid was $90,000 over the lowest bid. In other words, if we had lowered our bid by $100,000, we would have gotten the job and only left $10,000 on the table. I don't remember the total amount.

There were no words, acrimonious or otherwise, spoken on the way back to Wings Field. After landing, I was the only one to head back to the office. WC drove off to his farm in Indiana; John Mooney left for his home in nearby Country Club Hills. I was tired and just wanted to go home. As usual, I assumed WC had phoned the result to WJ from Indy.

After I had entered the lower office, WJ came down the stairs from the offices above. I was just leaving, when he came up to me and wanted a full report on what had happened. I was tired and said I needed to go home for some rest. I offered to give him a full report in the morning. No, he insisted. He wanted it then and there.

"I'm too tired, Bill," I countered, as I went out the door and headed for my company car. "I'll tell you all about it in the morning." With that, I opened the car door, got in, closed it, and started the engine.

WJ followed behind me and then stopped beside the door of my car, which was parked under the carport roof, next to the office. Suddenly he reached out and grabbed the door handle, opened my door and demanded that I get out of "his" car.

"Give me the keys! That's MY car! Get out of it," he blurted out. I turned off the ignition and got out of the car. As I stood there facing him, he reached up and began hitting me on the chest with his hands and forearms. His face was red. I was beginning to wonder if he'd survive the tantrum.

As he continued pounding on my chest, I realized he wasn't about to calm down; so, in part to break the spell, I tried to look into his eyes while saying, "You've just lost yourself a good man," and then immediately backed away from him, went into the office, called my wife, and asked her to come and pick me up. I don't know where WJ went, but I waited alone until my wife came along, and she drove us back to our home in Flossmoor.

There had been a phone call or two between my wife and her mother so that by 9 AM the next morning, all four of us were seated in WJ's den to make amends. WJ fumbled around without really apologizing, but tried to, I think. Finally, attention turned to me for a response.

If WJ had shown me that he truly regretted his behavior, I might have wanted to stay and protect him. However, there was more involved than his angry outburst. He showed little or no genuine remorse, I thought, so it was not likely that he would welcome any more suggestions from me regarding company operations and activities, either. He wasn't going to change. He would just get tougher.

"As I told you yesterday, Bill," I said, "you've just lost yourself a good man." Those were my last words, repeated again for him.

Everyone quickly jumped up out of their seat and headed for a door.

When in fast company, instinct can become an important factor in determining one's actions. That instinct, of course, is largely derived from what the challenge is and from one's upbringing, education and life experiences to date.

I felt an opportunity had arisen unexpectedly for WC and me to take some of the reins away from WJ and in a way that WJ could have found agreeable and acceptable. Instead, WC had chosen not to - for whatever reasons. Perhaps he liked the status quo. Maybe he wasn't even aware of having a choice. He had once said to me, "WJ needs a place to hang his hat." I must give WC credit for that; but everyone has limits.

In hindsight, a choice had somehow materialized. WC was presented with a fair chance to act on it. I didn't know where I was headed, but I knew I was leaving Orr Construction Company. I doubt that WJ ever learned the truth about what had happened shortly before that bid was submitted.

CHAPTER 13

ACTION LISTINGS, AFR, TWA, CONTINENTAL

Lawrence Lessig, a professor of law at the Stanford Law School, wrote a book that was published in 2001 titled, "the future of ideas." In it, on page 318, he quotes portions of a memo written by Bill Gates intended to recommend the Microsoft strategy for responding to a new world of patents:

"The solution ... is patent exchanges ... and patenting as much as we can.... A future start-up with no patents of its own will be forced to pay whatever price the giants choose to impose. That price might be high: Established companies have an interest in excluding future competitors."

The mission I had in mind for the company I started in 1966, Action Listings, Inc., was for it to ultimately become the U.S. Patent and Copyright Exchange. On a very limited budget, I first sought to list airplanes and construction equipment for sale or lease; to be followed by patents and copyrights later, as future opportunities to do it became available. Bill Gates offered that "established companies have an interest in excluding future competitors." While that is often true, it can also be argued that established companies often can help themselves by acquiring rights to produce some new products and services developed by others, rights that may not be needed or wanted by the discoverers.

Before inviting anyone to invest in Action Listings, however, I first wanted to be certain of obtaining the necessary Service Marks (I called them trademarks, but my patent attorney insisted they were service marks). If an infringement arose, I might have to change the name of the company after getting started and spending a lot of money. I did not want my investors involved in anything like that. I would first obtain the applied-for Service Marks and then feel better about selling stock in the company. The patent attorney I engaged, by the way, was the same one from San Francisco with whom I had played golf. After all, he also hailed originally from Chicago Heights. Meanwhile, I would use my own limited funds to get the company under way. I knew it would be a difficult challenge, but I intended to do a lot myself - for free. My house and car were paid for, and I had about $10k in the bank. In 1966, that would have almost been enough to buy two new Cadillacs.

What I soon became aware of was the need to advertise. And, since I was attempting to list equipment and aircraft in the U.S., Canada, and Mexico, I needed to spend relatively large sums (for me) for advertising. So, I did. I worked out a series of ads that sort of began slowly and worked up to offering more.

When you "Action Listed" your airplane for sale, lease, or charter, we would carry your listing for a maximum of 12 months, or until cancelled within 12 months, for $100. The same applied to construction equipment of all kinds. Experienced contractors knew that nothing made getting a job done easier than using the right tools. I intended to make finding the right tools easier. Whatever would fit onto one of our standardized forms could be included in a listing.

Planes and cranes, let's say, were listed on special cards that had copper teeth affixed to their bottoms and were then placed on a machine with a keyboard at one end. An operator, when she took your call, would also refer to our complete listing of cities and towns in North America and look up the latitude and longitude of where you were calling from or where a plane or equipment was needed or parked. If you were calling from Reno, Nevada, to purchase a used Caterpillar 631 model scraper, for example, our operator would insert the latitude and longitude of Reno into the machine, press a button, and the 631 scraper listings closest to Reno would be recited first to a caller, followed by others gradually more distant.

One of the most prestigious listings we carried was one for Sammy Davis Jr.'s Lockheed JetStar that was available for charter flights. And while Mexico seemed like an impoverished country, there were people in Mexico City willing to pay big bucks for a used Beechcraft Baron, if they could only find one.

Magazines had long lead times, so it took nearly a year before anyone could know about Action Listings. Gradually, however, word started getting around and the phone began to ring - a little. Most of the callers were attempting to locate used airplanes of various kinds. It was taking longer to generate interest amongst contractors to buy, sell and lease construction equipment, it seemed.

As the planned sequence of ads advanced one step at a time in two magazines, the phone became busier, with callers looking for various kinds of aircraft to buy, mostly. If only we had had more listings, I thought. That would have helped to pay for some of the overhead, too.

One evening, WJ cajoled me at a social function and said he had heard from someone he considered knowledgeable that it would cost $250k to accomplish what I had set out to do. I just nodded my head. I was doing my best. In my own mind I thought an additional $25k would be enough for the new company to be able to start up and become able to support itself.

I still had not received Registered Service Marks from the Patent Office. A search completed before starting up company operations had revealed no potential infringements; but a Service Mark grant had not yet been received.

Regrettably, I gradually came around to realize that there were not enough listings coming in and that my personal financial resources were becoming insufficient to carry the company much longer. My last and best ad in the sequence of ads I had prepared was only about to appear.

Meanwhile, persons who owned an advertising firm in Batavia, Illinois, had begun calling on me from out of the blue and had been trying very hard to convince me that they could do a much better job with my ads. Eventually, they produced an ad totally different from mine and assured me it would be very successful.

Having initially signed up for two ads per month for twelve months, and having about the last two or three months available for the Batavia firm, I reluctantly agreed to let them take over and run their ads in place of mine, in those last few issues.

Upon publication of the last ad that I, personally, had prepared, the phones started ringing once more and a few listings began to dribble in. There was more activity in that office than ever. It would have been beneficial if that ad could have been continued from then on without changing it, as had been my initial intent.

Unfortunately, the very next ad was one the advertising firm had prepared. The silence in the office after their ad appeared was instant and deafening. Not a single listing or inquiry came in after that. Not one! The ad firm finally called and wanted to be paid.

I answered that their ad had essentially killed my business. But I made an offer: I'll pay for the ads if you will reimburse me for this business.

We never spoke again after that.

After two and a half years of effort, I was being forced to close.

IBM had rented a kind of word processor, which I was able to continue using. It was almost the size of a small upright piano and recorded onto a magnetic tape whatever was typed. Then, it could reprint from that tape onto whatever paper was inserted into the typewriter printer behind the keyboard. I used that machine to write letters to as many potential customers as I could, until all of the company stationery was used up. I had already run out of money to pay IBM's rental fees; but they had kindly allowed me to continue using that piece of their equipment without charge.

About that time, handyman Lawrence Bond showed up with a pick-up truck from Orr Construction. WJ sent him over to help me vacate the rented office. There were first-rate filing cabinets to move out, containing at least two brochures with specifications and descriptions of every crane, dozer, back hoe, end loader, bucket, and what have you, from every manufacturer of construction equipment in the U.S. A McGraw-Hill sales representative in Chicago who had handled my ads for one of their magazines even visited my office to see for himself, one day. With his wife along, I overheard him say to her: "I knew that someday, somebody would come along and build a library like this."

Lawrence Bond moved those file cabinets and files to my basement at my home in Flossmoor. Not long after that, a stranger came to the door and my wife, Peggy, called me to go to the basement with him. She insisted on selling those bright yellow filing cabinets - to that man, for something like ten cents on the dollar. I tried to dissuade her; but she was adamant. Unaware of it then, I was headed for a divorce.

It was summer when I came home and found no one there. Not even WJ and Mrs. Orr were around. Where was my 9-year-old son? Where was his mother? I learned from WC that WJ and his wife had gone to Las Vegas; but he didn't know the whereabouts of Peggy and my son and said WJ didn't know that either.

So I began calling hotels from San Francisco to San Diego to Phoenix to Miami to New York City. A contractor friend of mine in Chicago, Ernie Bederman, asked if I had driven much on the new Interstate highway system. No, I answered. He suggested that doing so might help me feel and think better.

Finally, in desperation, I got into the car and drove to Atlantic City, hoping, for some unknown reason, to find my wife and son there. Nope!

Then, it occurred to me. Pensacola! Of course!! From Atlantic City I called Sugar Heffernan at her home near Pensacola and asked if she had seen Peggy.

"Sure, she's just now backing out of the driveway and taking GW and (her son) Robert to the swimming pool."

"I'll be there as soon as possible," I said. Sugar sounded upbeat as ever.

After parking my car at the airport in Atlantic City, I boarded a plane and later checked in at a Pensacola motel that had a small outdoor swimming pool. I can still recall the fun my little son and I shared as we were reunited and able to swim and play in the warm clear blue waters of that little motel swimming pool, the next afternoon!

A few days later, Mrs. Heffernan accepted Peggy's invitation to return with her to Flossmoor and to stay with her for awhile.

We left on separate flights, as I had to fly to Atlantic City to retrieve my car.

When I finally returned to Flossmoor, I was not permitted to stay in my house while Peggy was in it. She was suing me for divorce. So I checked into a motel in nearby Homewood.

The next day, I drove to the Post Office in Chicago Heights and picked up my (accumulated) mail. After returning to the motel room, I opened one of the envelopes and discovered that the Patent and Trademark Office had finally granted the Service Marks I had applied for. The memory of that moment lingers. As I read that letter, I stood in a motel room with an afternoon sun streaming in through a window and hitting me from the waist down. "What I could have done with this if it had only arrived sooner!!" I thought. If anyone should want to hear reasons for speeding up the PTO, I can provide some. Just as quickly, I reminded myself that I was broke; and, unfortunately for Action Listings, I could see no way of raising sufficient capital to restart its operations. Besides, its reputation had been disrupted, if not, destroyed. I felt too tired and discouraged to even entertain such an idea at that time.

Eventually, Mrs. Heffernan returned to Brewton, Alabama; Peggy moved in with her parents in Chicago Heights; and I was allowed back into our house in Flossmoor to live with my son for as long as a Court order might permit and a freezer full of chicken capons could last. I wasn't much of a cook; but I knew how to barbecue capons outdoors on our patio. And Peggy had filled the freezer with them.

It was sometime around Labor Day in 1968 when my son returned to school. He didn't have far to go, as his elementary school was located almost kitty corner from our house, a short distance away.

Another year would elapse before our divorce became final. Peggy had made it clear to me that she didn't want to change the world and had also declared, "I'M NOT LEAVIN'!!" when I asked her if she would stay with me as I pursued some new endeavor.

Thus, I eventually arrived at having some personal time available, some time for myself at home. In turn, I soon wanted to put it to good use. What had I not had a chance or time enough to do or complete?, I wondered. After pondering that question for awhile, I came up with an answer.

Some six to eight weeks later, I finished writing and drafting a proposal for the FAA titled, "AFR - Automatic Flight Reporting." With jet aircraft being relatively new to aviation, I realized that probably few people had evaluated uses of the new airways to the extent that I had. So, I thought I should apply my experiences and whatever talents I could muster for suggesting new safety of flight equipment. I had flown jets AND small single engine aircraft in the U.S. I had had my share of mid-air close calls and felt motivated to try to do something about avoiding them. Skies, even then, were beginning to get crowded.

Two "black boxes" would be needed aboard each aircraft capable of instrument flight, I offered; one mandatory, the other optional.

The mandatory "black box" would be hooked up to a plane's navigational radio. Whenever a pilot tuned in a Vortac navigational radio station, for example, his new "black box" would then also automatically transmit back to that Vortac the identity of his aircraft and a repeat of the Vortac signals received.

Each plane would also telemeter its airspeed, altitude, rate of climb/descent, and compass heading data automatically to the Vortac station it was tuned to. Ground based computers could then input those signals, compare them with others received from other aircraft, and determine if any close calls were developing.

A second "black box" could be mandated for airliners, but would remain optional for other aircraft. That second "black box" could provide cockpit warnings of impending close approaches to other aircraft. By receiving warning signals from ground-based computers a few minutes in advance of other aircraft closing to within certain predetermined distances and altitudes, planes equipped with that second "black box" could be given time to investigate and maneuver away as necessary to avoid potential mid-air collisions.

Too much credence for avoiding mid-air collisions has been given to nose radars on airliners. Nose radars can be useful for spotting and avoiding thunderstorms generally up ahead, but they will not warn pilots of the most frequent and most difficult to avoid mid-air collision threats: aircraft that are descending from above; and aircraft that are climbing up from below. AFR proposed to handle that. Likewise, AFR would also make climbing out and descending much safer. AFR would lessen the needs and the times required for communicating with air controllers. Delays incurred by having to talk to Air Controllers could also be reduced or avoided.

After making copies and mailing the AFR proposal to the FAA, I felt relieved, somehow. Perhaps I had been carrying around a subconscious obligation to express to the FAA what I felt from my technical background to be possible and from my flight experiences to be needed for future flight safety.

Anyhow, I next turned to preparing and sending out a resume. My immigrant father pronounced it resume, as in to resume an activity.

He and my mother were shocked by my divorce and it is safe to say neither of them approved of it. There were times when I sensed having lost much of their respect as well.

Towards the end of 1968, a judge in Chicago evicted me from my house and I chose to move in with my parents in their small apartment. I offered to pay room and board; and my father accepted $250/month. Soon, I would have to sell my car for about half of its retail value just to keep up payments to my Dad.

Meanwhile, I tended to job opportunities that resulted from my resume mailings.

TWA was the only airline, at that time, that did not have a Safety Director. After being tested in Kansas City and interviewed in NYC, I was offered the job but at a salary that was about one-third of what I had been earning at Orr Construction. A fringe benefit would allow me to fly anywhere aboard a scheduled TWA flight free (except for having to pay any applicable taxes). As the Director of Safety, I figured I'd be flying a lot anyway, so my counter offer was that I would pay my own way if only my salary were raised. Working in a NYC highrise with a magnificent view of the East River would have been enjoyable (and expensive getting to and from work), but there was one more serious fly to enter the ointment, as the saying goes.

A copy of my AFR proposal had been previously submitted to TWA for review and was returned to me during my visit to my "potential" office floor overlooking the East River.

"What do you think?," I asked the man who handed it back to me and who had apparently read and understood it.

"It's do-able. The hardware exists right now," he said.

"Well then," I perked up, "how about if we get TWA to prod the FAA into adopting it for the airline industry?"

"Oh, no. We couldn't do that!," was his immediate reply. Turning away and seeming to duck, he promptly disappeared.

That's when I lost interest in TWA. I had had some reservations about going to work for them, but that little episode settled it. If a TWA Director of Safety could not defend the safety of passengers and airliners before the FAA, what real good could be expected of him?

Another job opportunity interview arose and I found myself in an office a few stories above Michigan Avenue, almost across from Chicago's Art Museum. The office had no windows, but it was quite large and had an unusual ceiling with indirect lighting.

Seated at a desk almost in the middle of the room was a well-dressed man who may have been a few years older than I. Today, they are commonly known as "head hunters," but, back then, he was identified more as an employment agent. I had presented myself to him in hopes that he could find someone in industry who might be looking to hire an employee like me.

He seemed to hesitate a lot before saying anything. Finally, he muttered something about my paying him $3,500.

"Are you asking me to pay you $3,500 to find me a job?," I asked him directly.

"Well, yes," he answered, peering at me from behind his big desk.

"Look," I said. "If I had $3,500 I wouldn't have to be here with you looking for a job. But I expect you can charge whatever you want to a company you can find that is looking to hire someone like me if and when they hire me. But understand, I'm not going to pay you to find me a job," I concluded.

On my way to his office, I had passed through a room filled with little booths with desks, chairs and people in them. Windows at the far end of that long, dark room faced towards Lake Michigan. Employees were interviewing job applicants, I assumed. So, I sensed what the head hunter's offer held in store when he offered me a job there. "No thanks," I said, and left.

Continental Airlines wanted to interview me out in Los Angeles. I remember being aboard a flight approaching the Rockies and the Captain about to be honored with a candle lit cake in the isle in the middle of the passenger cabin. It was his last flight before having to retire due to age.

Just then, I was invited to the cockpit. The pilot and I must have crossed paths. I don't remember ever seeing him. However, his seat was empty when I arrived up front and I was invited to sit in it. The co-pilot and engineer were as cheerful as capable pilots usually are, and I sat for a moment in the pilot's seat to scan the instrument panel. The sun was getting low directly ahead in the west, but the hood protruding out from atop the instrument panel made it possible to duck down a bit to avoid the sun and see the instruments better. That was the same hood I had blamed airline pilots for hiding behind in the past when they had failed to see me or my flight leader in a close mid-air encounter.

The automatic pilot was engaged, of course, and the co-pilot wanted me to feel at home. An old question suddenly came to mind, and I decided to settle it then and there. That cockpit crew probably thought I was a little nuts. I never did explain my actions to them.

Back in my Navy flying days, I had been vectored by the carrier's radar operator to intercept and identify a bogey that had apparently come out of Hong Kong and was headed towards the carrier. It was almost a head-on situation when

I was finally turned and eventually approached what turned out to be an airliner. I approached it from low on its starboard quarter. I don't remember the identity of the airline, just that I approached to within about 150 feet of it. Looking at the cockpit's starboard side window from slightly below the wing, I saw that the wing tip protruded out beyond my line-of-sight to the cockpit window.

The carrier's air controller then called the intercept completed. Instead of rolling right about 90 degrees and turning away from the airliner, I rolled to the left 270 degrees and turned away. Momentarily, it could have looked to someone on board the airliner that I was turning into the airliner; but the roll continued and, just as quickly, I was pulling away.

What had surprised me was that the airliner's wings, after holding steady for as long as I had been close enough to observe them had momentarily rocked when I initiated that roll to the left, and then returned to wings level again. I had wondered ever since how that co-pilot could have looked that far aft and seen me. Then, as I sat in the pilot's seat over the Rockies, I tried several times to look back; but I was not able to see any part of the wing. That meant my F8 Crusader would have been hidden from view when I executed that 270 degree departure roll. It remains a mystery as to why that airliner rocked its wings at the precise moment when I initiated that roll.

Continental offered me an opportunity to help start up their new cockpit simulators at their Los Angeles airport facility. A good beginning. I felt it was a creditable offer and the kind of activity I could have learned from as well; but I suddenly seemed to lose interest in Continental and in living again in California. For some reason, I just wanted to fly back to the Midwest and spend some time with my son. So, aboard another Continental flight, I promptly returned to Chicago.

CHAPTER 14

FOUND A HOME IN INDIANA

My parents' apartment that they shared with me for a short time almost overlooked the Bloom Township High School track and football field, where I had run and played only a little football for two years before going to Culver. It was Fall, just after Thanksgiving in 1968, when a letter arrived from Culver Military Academy with a questionnaire to alumni asking what each of us thought about Culver becoming a co-educational institution. Attendance and revenues were threatened and it had been suggested that allowing girls into the Academy could change that.

While recognizing the revenue needs, I also felt that introducing females to a previously all-male institution could detract from boys being able to fully concentrate on getting an excellent education and achieving some physical sports abilities. So, I voted "No," don't let the girls in.

As usual, money won. That's not necessarily what they tried to teach me at Culver; but, nevertheless, money won when push came to shove amongst the Culver Military Academy Foundation members when declining attendance and revenues were anticipated. Culver, today, is well attended and well funded, I am happy to observe. Lord knows what might have happened to it if it had attempted to remain a "boys only" institution. A feminist movement, after all, had started.

As I was interviewed for jobs in the Chicago area, I made a few observations. Most important, perhaps, was the impression that developed of being interviewed by personnel who probably had never met the company founders and whom the company founders would probably have let go immediately if even a chance meeting had occurred. What is more, I wondered if the founders, themselves, would have been hired by some of the employment managers I encountered. Why did they not first describe the tasks they needed new hires to perform, instead of asking people looking for jobs what they had done? I had done a lot; but what did they need me to do, exactly, and could I do that?

Another observation gained from attempting to respond to newspaper want ads was that I often suspected some want ads were placed in order to scare employees into wanting to keep their jobs. There were many long-running ads for jobs that were reported unavailable or filled when I inquired about them; yet the ads continued. If you were a company salesman, for example, and your company continued to advertise for a salesman, what would you be thinking?

During an interview, I was often asked, "How much do you want to be paid?"

My answer, usually, was, "Pay me what you think I'm worth."

That would result in the same question being asked again, "How much do you want to be paid?"

It never resulted in a salary offer that I can remember.

After a long interview, I could be told that I was "overqualified" for the job available, and that I wouldn't be happy for long doing it.

That I could understand. So, I would express gratitude for the interview and promptly leave.

One day, I felt like a blue-collar worker in a hiring hall. While waiting alone to be interviewed at the Caterpillar plant in Peoria, I found myself in what seemed like a painted concrete, high ceilinged, utility room, with frosted windows on one wall, lunch tables and a mass of pipes overhead. I was finally greeted. The person who made an appearance thanked me for my interest in Caterpillar, was polite, and that was about it. But, at least someone had been sent to meet with me, which was not always the case at some companies.

There were two instances where offices were empty during working hours and the lights were on when I arrived. One was at the office of one of the barge-moving companies near Joliet that pushed barges up and down the Mississippi River. Another was at the main office of Waste Management in Des Plaines on the outskirts of Chicago, when Waste Management was a relatively young company. There was not one person to be found in either office. I suppose I could have waited around for someone to show up; but I moved on.

One day, I was contacted and invited to be interviewed by a civil engineering firm in South Bend, Indiana. They were looking for a Chief Pilot to fly photogrammetry missions, mainly. South Bend was about 85 miles away and I thought that distance would be sufficient to get me out of town and away from my parents, and (soon to be) ex-wife and ex-in-laws; but yet be close enough to permit return trips to visit my son. By then, I also felt like flying again.

The interview went well. Within about a week, I was called and asked to come and join Clyde Williams & Associates in South Bend. Since Williams was a civil engineering firm, I also wondered if, by chance, the future could hold a possible merger with Orr Construction Company. I had noted that some of the larger construction companies had their own in-house civil engineering departments. So, what might the future hold for Williams and Orr, I wondered.

Being rated to fly only single-engine aircraft, I was promptly sent to a nearby Michigan City airport for a check-out and to become licensed to fly multi-engine airplanes. Clyde Williams had two twin-engine planes that were used for photogrammetry: a Piper Apache and an Aztec. Clyde Williams Senior had his own Aztec, but it was not rigged or used for aerial surveying.

The fact that I had flown in the Navy must have impressed my young check-out pilot. After a few days of flying and ground school, he probably thought that he could put us into any situation and that I would manage to safely get us out of it.

The twin engine Piper Apache "trainer" had excellent visibility from the front pilot and co-pilot seats. The problem with it, however, was that it was underpowered. On take-off with a full load, the loss of one engine would cause the plane to have to land. It could not maintain level flight on one engine when fully loaded. As the fuel and passenger loads were reduced, however, there would come a weight that one engine could support.

On my final check-ride, my young and eager check-ride pilot and I had flown enough to use up some of the fuel. As we headed back to the airport, I assumed from all that we had done that my check-ride was essentially completed and that I was merely flying us back to the airport office to fill out the necessary forms.

After lowering the gear, coming around in the landing pattern and almost getting ready to flare for a landing, that young pilot sitting in the right seat next to me reached over and pulled the throttle back to idle on the left engine and then shouted at me to simulate another airplane being on the runway directly in front of us and to execute a waveoff!

Adding full power on that starboard engine, raising the gear handle and gently pulling us out of a descent to level flight at about five feet off the deck at near stall speed, I allowed that starboard engine to pull us around to the left a bit, if only to keep from losing any more airspeed and altitude from using the rudder to keep us headed along the runway. Using ailerons to keep the wings level was enough. As it was, we wound up turning left some 30-40 degrees and I still had my hands full trying to at least pick up a little airspeed to climb with. The airport office had about a 10-foot high antenna sticking up from the center of its roof, and we were headed directly for it.

Airspeed finally began to pick up. That low powered starboard engine gradually pulled us to slightly above minimum lift-off speed and we barely made it over the office and its antenna. After that, the instructor kindly restored power to the port engine, we gained airspeed enough to quickly get back up to pattern altitude, into the landing pattern, and to land.

I passed. Others in that airport office only smiled at the check-out pilot and me as we walked by. That building must have shook and been pretty noisy when we passed overhead. I was issued a multi-engine license and promptly headed back to my new employer in South Bend.

The next day, I was sent to Indianapolis to deliver something or other, as I recall. What I remember most vividly was being alone on a bright sunny morning and leveling off at altitude after departing from the South Bend Airport. Reflecting on my situation, I was flying an expensive twin-engine airplane that I did not have to own or rent and I was getting paid to do it! Wow!

Next day, I was assigned to carry passengers somewhere and I had to hurriedly return my Hertz rent-a-car to the airport check-in counter while my passengers waited for me. A dispute arose about the bill.

When I departed Chicago Heights, I had no car of my own so I rented one from Hertz for a week from a filling station in Homewood at a "negotiated discount rate." Then, using my American Express credit card to pay for it at the airport, the Hertz counter person did not want to recognize and honor the "negotiated discount rate."

What could I do? I was in a hurry so I had to sign for a much higher amount than had been negotiated. Eventually, I received the American Express billing and tried to talk AE into paying Hertz only the "negotiated" amount. Nope. They wouldn't do that. So, I paid the full amount and enclosed my cut-in-half American Express card with the check. I have not had another AE card since, though a new one has been offered many times.

A motel room near the airport became my residence and "place to sleep," as I was gone during most of the daylight hours. It was expensive, but within walking distance of the company office and hangar. I had no car, so that was a saving. I was essentially broke until payday, and payday never seemed to come.

After the first week, I expected a paycheck, but it did not come. I learned that paychecks were issued only every two weeks. OK, so after the second week, where was my check? Ans: The office was still getting my account set up and, before issuing any payment, they wanted to know how much of my salary I wanted to invest in the company's interest payment plan. As I recall, now, a portion of one's salary that one might choose to invest could automatically be invested in Clyde Williams & Associates with about a 3-5% return. All of that was fine and good; but I was flat broke and needed money! Finally, after some three weeks, I received a paycheck. Not one day too soon, either!

Photogrammetry is interesting. Abe Lincoln had been a land surveyor at one time. I wondered what he might think of photogrammetry. The land area he had required a day to survey could likely be covered by two overlapping pictures taken from an airplane in a few seconds.

A 12- to 18-inch diameter hole was cut in the floor of the plane behind the pilot. A large camera was mounted on gimbles in that opening so the camera operator, sitting on one of the rear seats, could peer straight down through an eye piece, focus the camera, keep it vertical and lined up, while also adjusting for speed variations over the ground.

The film came in 250-foot rolls and was about a foot wide. The pictures were large and developed onto glass. My cameraman, Harold, often had to use airport restrooms with the lights turned off, with me standing guard outside to prevent any entries, for changing films in camera cassettes in the dark, when we were away from South Bend.

Overlapping pictures were taken automatically as we flew along so the net result would allow three-dimensional views of the ground surfaces afterwards, as projected onto sheets of white paper atop drafting tables. Once set up, focus adjustments were made and variations in ground elevation contours became distinct enough to be traceable. Even a 3-inch curb height, for example, was detectable.

If you've ever noticed a big white + mark on a street, sidewalk or on the ground, at the center of that + can be found a survey marker indicating the known elevation above sea level of the top of that marker. That known elevation (determined from previous surveys made the hard way on the ground, many conducted in Lincoln's time) can be brought into focus on the drafting table, elevation dials adjusted and set, then various elevation contours can be drawn from there. Survey field crews emplace the white + markers.

Soon, I had a planeload of field crew members as we headed south to Fort Lauderdale, Florida. Our ultimate destination was Grand Bahama Island, some 85 miles east north east of Fort Lauderdale. About one-third of the island was to be surveyed from the air and field crews needed to place those big + markers at various locations on the island. Also needed were high and low tide beach pictures, and aerial views of the casino complex.

England had freed Grand Bahama earlier, but Islanders had learned that newcomer developers and business owners were more likely to bring along their own personnel than to want to hire islanders. Native islanders were left poor and unemployed, as they watched newcomers work and prosper.

Williams had had an office on Grand Bahama. When the field crew and I arrived in the afternoon on March 4, 1969, an affable Williams representative greeted us, walked with us around downtown Freeport, then went with us to dinner at a lively restaurant. The weather was about as good as it gets anywhere. The smallest Holiday Inn sign in the world could be seen in front of a Holiday Inn along the beach.

Gradually, I learned about changes taking place on the island. The natives were getting a little restless about not being hired by the newcomers with money. The Williams office had some unnecessary equipment that it was thought best to remove and ferry back to the mainland. Work permits seemed to be on the horizon. In order to be able to work on Grand Bahama Island in the future, one would have to obtain a work permit from the government there. Such permits, in addition, would go first to island natives.

The next day, I left the field crews to their assignments and departed with as much office equipment in the plane as the Williams representative could give me. I also decided to fly in and out of Fort Lauderdale, instead of Freeport, to avoid any unwanted encounters with Grand Bahama authorities. There was no customs check. We merely brought what we had off the street to the plane and loaded it.

After about a week, our missions were accomplished and I returned to Freeport to pick up the field crews. All went well until shortly after taking off. The tower called, but I changed radio frequencies and flew off to Fort Lauderdale.

Not many months later, the Williams office in Freeport was closed. I recall reading a WALL STREET JOURNAL article shortly after that about a man from London who had gone to Freeport and purchased several businesses there, before the Permit requirements were imposed. The man from London then sold everything he had owned in London in order to pay for his new Freeport purchases. Unfortunately, upon his return to Freeport, he was refused a work permit to work in his own businesses. Amazing.

One of the images that had been portrayed to me of the Grand Bahama natives was that they could work very hard for a week until payday. Not being accustomed to receiving such relatively high wages, however, they usually were overcome by prosperity and did not want to return to their jobs until they needed money again. Employers came to consider them unreliable when they did not show up for work on Monday mornings, after Friday paydays.

A short hop over to Miami International Airport with films that were then flown to Chicago and South Bend had allowed capable Williams photo lab personnel to quickly review the results of our Grand Bahama efforts. Once notified that no re-takes were necessary, we left Freeport and returned to South Bend.

It's 1,000 nautical miles by air to South Bend from Fort Lauderdale, about 6.5 hours in a Piper Aztec. (From my Navy flight planning days, I remembered it was also 1,000 NM by air from Whidbey Island, near Seattle, to San Diego, but only about 2.5 hours in an F8 Crusader.)

As soon as I had amassed enough money, I bought a little 1964 2-door Chevrolet Corvair and moved into a furnished one-room apartment near Notre Dame and downtown South Bend. In a new complex of mostly studio apartments with a small outdoor swimming pool, my "apartment" was almost twice as large as the motel room I had been staying in; but quite a bit smaller than my red brick 2-story colonial house in Flossmoor, with its tall white columns in front. I was al-lowed to visit my son on weekends; and once a month I could bring him to South Bend on a Saturday and return him to his mother in Flossmoor the next day. During the forthcoming 4-5 years, I was destined to make about 60 round trips per year from South Bend to Flossmoor plus many more excursions to Chicago and elsewhere. I did try my best to be available and to be a good father to my son.

Across the driveway from my ground floor apartment, I could look out the picture window and see the 2-story brick home that belonged to an older gentleman who bought, re-stored and sold antiques of many kinds. His two-car detached garage where he restored and sold his antiques was set between his house and my apartment. His name was Leonard "Jake" Jaqua and he claimed to have been one of Vincent Bendix's first twenty employees. "Jake" and I got along, even though his rough voice and manner sometimes frightened other people.

At first, I managed to buy a restored carpenter's level from him by promising to leave it on display in my apartment window so he could look at it every time he drove in and out of his garage. "Jake" had made two small U-shaped pieces of wood to hold the level in a slightly raised position for display on a flat surface. The U-shaped pieces needed somehow to be held about 18 inches apart. Why not with two brass rods?, I asked. I'll be right back, I told him.

A welding shop a few miles away gladly sold me two of their thickest brass rods. After I returned, "Jake" filled me in on some of his activities at Bendix during WWII.

First, when he saw me coming with the rods, his eyes opened wide and he praised me for so quickly resolving the problem. "You would have been good at my job at Bendix during WWII," he said. His job, he went on, had been to get machinery running again as quickly as possible after breakdowns. All sorts of problems had to be resolved - and in a hurry. There was a war on!

Another item purchased from "Jake" that I still have is a cabbage cutter. What's special about it is that the cutting blades will never rust. "Jake" took them out to the Bendix plant and had the blades electroplated with a silver colored material that "would have cost a lot had he not known the boys out there at the plant."

Vincent Bendix had invented, patented and mass produced electric starters for cars in the 1920s and became a very rich man. Later, he produced brakes for cars. The Bendix Trophy Air Races marked his entry into promoting aviation.

Unfortunately, Bendix was apparently not content to merely supply parts to other car makers. Sometime in the early 1930s, he secretly designed and had produced a single 4-door sedan that was later unveiled and seen for the first time at the 1934 World Trade Exposition in Paris. That car was later observed to resemble a 1934 Chrysler Airflow. The connection to the Chrysler Airflow design is unknown; but assembly of the secret Bendix automobile had been started in the South Bend area in 1932.

The design was stunning for its time; but it caused other major U.S. automakers to turn against Bendix, to view him more as a threat than as a parts supplier.

By the start of WWII, Vincent Bendix had lost nearly all of his Bendix Corporation stock and his money and to keep up appearances was allowed to live in only a few of the rooms in his South Bend mansion, which he had also lost. He died in 1945, but the corporation he created prospered during WWII and afterwards, making brakes and brake systems for cars, trucks and airplanes, fuel controls for jet engines and landing gear and wheels for many commercial and military aircraft.

That Bendix car was found by accident in someone's garage in or near Michigan City, Indiana, and has since been completely restored and put on display in the Studebaker Museum in South Bend.

Shortly before I was hired, Clyde Williams had completed building a test section of pavement for Bendix at the old Studebaker proving grounds, west of town. It was perfectly flat and was used for testing what we now know of as ABS (nonskid) brake systems. The pavement could be sprinkled with water and made slippery. A truck equipped with experimental ABS brakes would then drive along and the driver would apply the brakes to have the ABS system kick in. The perfectly flat pavement would stay wet, since there was no slope for water to run down, and it made accurate instrument readings possible. Some of the Williams engineers were very proud of that Bendix pavement.

A few other highway interchanges and river crossings in South Bend were also a source of pride that I heard about. Clyde Senior had promoted and laid out a new industrial park area adjacent to the airport. He lived long enough to witness some of the street and utility installations, and he would no doubt be quite proud of it today. It is almost completely occupied.

Meanwhile, photogrammetry assignments continued. Harold, the cameraman, and I were kept busy with flights over piles of coal at power plants in Wisconsin (to measure the amounts of coal in the piles), farm fields to measure crop yields in Nebraska, we flew over and took pictures of the General Motors proving grounds in Michigan, the Port Clinton, Cedar Point, Sandusky peninsula and island areas plus other parts of Ohio, vast areas of Kentucky for the U.S. Geodetic Survey, and other parts of Illinois and Indiana. There was even a time when a bid had to be prepared and submitted for quickly taking pictures of the Florida orange groves so as to be able to quantify the crop.

Then, one day, Clyde Senior called me over to a map that was opened and spread out on one of the office drafting tables. Flight lines had been drawn running east and west over an island. It was Grand Cayman Island, south of Cuba. I had never been there, but Clyde Senior had. He was going to build an office there and wanted some aerial photos.

There are occasions when taking a few moments to think about something can save you a lot of time and effort in the long run. That became one of those moments.

The island was about 20 miles long and some 10 miles wide at its western end. Otherwise it was perhaps 2-3 miles wide, on average. The way the Williams engineers had drawn the proposed lines of flight would require that I fly some pretty long distances from east to west and west to east. Clyde Senior then happened to mention that puffs of clouds would usually develop sometime during the day. Clouds, of course, could spoil our pictures.

It helped to trust in Clyde Senior's knowledge of the Island or I would not have thought to ask him, "Is there a prevailing wind and which way does it blow?"

"From southeast to northwest," he answered immediately adding, "It blows steady and usually in the same direction."

As much work as the engineers had already done on the map in front of us, I realized that changing the flight lines to shorter north-south lines would give us a better chance of avoiding any clouds. North-South flight lines being shorter, if a cloud did happen to develop under us while we were taking pictures, we would not lose as much film when having to do it over. Clyde Senior agreed and new lines were drawn on another map. We would take both maps along, however.

Fidel Castro's government had to be notified a day in advance of our flight in order for us to fly over Cuba; but, instead, I elected to fly around the western tip of Cuba and over the Yucatan Channel between Cancun and Cuba. On a sunny day at 7,500 feet, both land masses were easily kept in sight as we flew southeastward between them.

Grand Cayman's low frequency radio navigation beacon was strong and steady. Eventually, the Island appeared on the horizon and gradually grew larger as we approached it. The tower operator then called us on the radio and I answered, thus letting them know we were OK and within radio range. I decided to fly around the Island before landing. We found a rusting ship hull that had apparently run aground at the very eastern end of Grand Cayman where an opening in the reef had apparently been misjudged as deep enough but wasn't. By now, that hulk may have rusted away completely and disappeared.

After landing on Grand Cayman, Harold and I were taxiing onto the parking apron when, before us, a huge 4-engine turboprop plane began to move out. It was a Hercules C-130 belonging to Great Britain's RAF and was painted in camouflage colors that looked to have been polished and waxed. Harold and I were informed, later, that the Hercules had been there for three weeks to obtain an aerial survey of the Island but finally had to give up and go home. Grand Cayman had never been surveyed using aerial photos and the RAF Hercules had been sent there to do it. Apparently, they had tried to fly the east-west flight lines but were interrupted repeatedly by unexpected puffy cloud formations. Hmmm. Our north-south flight lines were to come in handy!

It was April 15, 1969. After parking the plane, we walked to the open, tin roofed, terminal area that had a couple of painted horizontal two by fours atop some posts set in the ground to walk between. There was gray-colored crushed stone or shells to walk on. And that was it. No Customs. In fact, there was no one there at all; just the base of the tall airport tower structure, nearby.

Grand Cayman had only two banks at that time. In 2000, according to Moodys, it had 570 Bank & Trust companies.

Harold and I checked into the Holiday Inn and I sensed immediately that we would have to start the job and keep at it, or we'd soon become one of the vacationers. What a relaxing climate! Air temperatures seemed to hold steady in the high seventies to low eighties. The water temperature was actually higher than the air temperature, as I recall. The water temperature a few feet out from the water's edge along the beach was 90F. We had to measure and report it to our photo lab. The bay area across the road from our Inn was touted as one of the world's best skin diving sites. During our stay, we did see a few tourists with their diving equipment standing around in the lobby, apparently waiting for transportation to a diver boat landing, nearby.

The Island can be visualized as shaped somewhat like a boot with the leg of the boot extending eastward and with the toe pointing north towards Cuba. The airport and most of the Island's population lived in the heel area, a community called George Town. The Holiday Inn was in the arch. The toe had another smaller population of Islanders. What we were told was that the two groups of Islanders did not associate with each other. Why? We did not learn the answer to that.

Clyde Senior's building site was located south of the airport runway, near the heel of the boot. The only port facility, what there was of it, also was at the bottom of the heel. The concrete slab floor had been poured, but the next step had Clyde a bit worried. He had purchased a used flatbed semi-truck trailer and had loaded the prefabricated building parts onto that trailer for shipment to the Island. What arose as a matter of concern was the realization that that trailer would have to be pulled along one-lane roads with drainage ditches on both sides and then around at least two right-angle corners. The trailer was far too long to be able to make it around those corners. I don't know how he did it. Harold and I were back in the States, by then. But the Williams Office was eventually finished and opened for business.

By the time Harold and I approached Key West on our return to the States, the sun was setting behind us and we saw lights coming on in Key West. It grew darker and became black as we entered over the Everglades National Park. A lot of swampland down there, I thought. Not a good place to have to land. It seemed like a long time before lights in Fort Lauderdale appeared on the horizon and the Air Controller allowed us to commence making a descent.

We were still over the Everglades but getting closer to the lights ahead of us when unexpectedly there was a loud WHACK! Something had hit the windshield, the part of it in front of Harold who was sitting in the right seat.

The next day, inspection revealed that a bird had been hit and if it (the bird) had been an inch or so higher and large enough, it might have passed right through the windshield and hit Harold. As it was, there was a raised metal frame for holding the plastic windshield that the bird had struck before glancing upward and following harmlessly along the contour of the windshield. A jungle down there.

On July 2, 1969, an event caused me to think I should quit flying. I had been doing a lot of it, had enjoyed it, true; but I was starting to grow a little tired of it. In the Navy, right or wrong, we often kidded about our fates: If it wasn't your turn yet, just be patient. Your number will be called. The only pilots who haven't landed gear up are the ones waiting for it to happen, etc., etc.

On July 2, I was returning to Columbus, Ohio, from what was to be three hours in the air doing photogrammetry over Kentucky. It was a bright, sunny day and sometime in the afternoon. I radioed the tower that I was about 5 miles south-west and approaching for a landing.

The tower had no sooner answered "Roger," than another pilot speaking broken English with a Mexican accent called and reported his position as 6 miles southwest and that he was inbound for a landing.

That put him directly behind me, I thought, and closing. He was flying a twin-engine airliner and was undoubtedly flying much faster than I. With his head in the cockpit much of the time, he could drive right up my tail and not even know it, I thought.

It was a first time for me, but, instead of continuing on, I pulled up a few hundred feet and moved over to the left. Looking down on the starboard side moments later, I saw the airliner moving along and passing right where I had expected it to be. I then dropped back down and followed it in to the Columbus Airport. I had had many close calls in my flying days that I'd known about; plus many more, probably, that I'd not been aware of. If I didn't have to fly anymore, perhaps I should think about improving the odds. It was just a thought, but it came at a time when my divorce hearing was almost imminent.

Odds or no odds, I WOULD continue flying if I could somehow arrange to invite my wife (still) to come and live with me in South Bend. But to manage that, I'd have to have a raise in pay. So, ultimately, I asked for a raise.

"How much do you want?," Clyde Junior asked me. When I told him, his mouth dropped open and he almost whispered, "There isn't anyone in this BUILDING making that!" It wasn't that much. Really.

"I guess that answers that," I replied and started to get up to leave.

"Wait a second," said Junior, while Clyde Senior, who suddenly appeared out of nowhere, moved closer to me. "Would you consider running the new Cayman office?," Junior asked, with Senior looking on.

A few thoughts ran through my head. I would be out of the U.S. and anything could happen to me down there. In fact, there could be some folks interested in having me down there and unable to get back.

"No," I answered. "But you have some difficult flying over Kentucky to complete that I will finish for you, if you want."

"That won't be necessary," said Junior.

The meeting was adjourned.

Afterwards, Clyde Senior asked me if I would fly him to the Piper Aircraft plant in Lockhaven, PA.

"Sure," I said.

Clyde Senior was one of the few men I've ever met who consistently seemed able to lead without pushing. Whatever he wanted, you were always willing and glad to help him. He died of cancer a few years after that. Junior also died of cancer some years after his father passed away. I met Mrs. Williams Senior at the Post Office a few years ago as she emerged from her car. She had always flown with Senior.

"I see you're still driving," I told her.

Instantly, she looked me in the eye and said, "I'm 91 years old and the driving part is easy. It's getting in and out of the car that's hard!"

More power to you, Dorothy!

By September, my divorce had been declared official in Court in downtown Chicago. What really hurt was when the Judge instructed my almost eleven-year-old son to leave my side and to go and be with his mother on the other side of the empty Courtroom. I'll admit it. I was hurt; and a few tears came into my eyes.

Back in South Bend several months later, I was having a martini before dinner one afternoon at the Town Tower, a frequented watering hole, when a young Bendix employee came over to me. Someone had apparently informed him of my recent divorce and he said to me, "So you pick yourself up and start all over again. Right?"

Right. He WAS right. But it would take me a little more time yet to "get over it."

CHAPTER 15

SPEED-UP

One confession I can make is that I had never committed adultery. My ex-wife had acknowledged as much during the last months of our marriage by telling me, "You're the truest husband...." For her to have volunteered that admission almost under her breath and one other, "You're the salt of the earth," left me feeling a little better about myself during and shortly after the divorce proceedings.

So, I intentionally resolved to not even date any other women for awhile. I busied myself with the stock market. I had accepted the settlement that had been offered to me via the attorneys without argument and proceeded to learn about and "play" the market. The only regret I had later was giving my ex-wife complete control over our son's education. He came from reasonably wealthy parents, both college educated, but he does not have a college degree. That should not have happened. There are people who have been born and raised in foreign countries and who have come to the U.S., learned the language and graduated from college. OK, I'll be fair. There also are American college grads who still can't connect the dots. Even simple ones.

To relate all that happened during the next 10-15 years as I researched, charted, bought and sold various stocks could fill another volume. I even went to New York and was allowed onto the floor of the NY Stock Exchange, one day. I witnessed how stock purchase and sell orders were telephoned onto the floor. A floor trader from my brokerage firm could look up and, if his numbered plaque was displayed on the wall, he was to pick up his phone, receive an order, and then walk over to the specialist handling whatever stock he was to buy or sell and negotiate a transaction. That floor trader would then return to the phone and inform his NY office of what had been done. The NY office would then telegraph the office from whence the trade had originated giving the transaction details. Next, the local stock broker would be informed and that broker would then inform me, the customer. On a busy day, it was easy to account for trading delays, of which there were many. And a 20 million share trading day was one of the records set, back then.

Computer trading has greatly increased the market's capacity for handling transactions. But, in October 1987, it got out of hand.

As I indicated at the beginning of this chapter, I could write another book about my stock market experiences, but I want to keep it short, here. So, I'll only mention the crash in October 1987 as I observed it and as no one else seems to have reported it. It was disturbing and costly to many investors, including me.

The NYSE often spoke with pride of successfully fulfilling its fiduciary duty by maintaining an orderly market. By 1987, however, it had allowed something new onto the trading scene: computer trades by institutional investors that involved trading so-called baskets of stocks. The minimum institutional entry fee reportedly was $1 million.

As these baskets of stocks were traded with increasing frequency, they gradually began to influence the Dow Jones

Industrial Average which, in turn, began to influence the NYSE in general. That "orderly market" began to disappear. The Dow would swing up and down during the day and gradually attained bigger movements upward and downward. But, at the end of those trading days, the Dow would usually close on the upside, sometimes a little, sometimes a lot; but, normally, to the investing public's satisfaction.

As this was happening, investors faced sweeping changes in the tax law enacted in 1986 that effectively raised the tax rate on all capital gains by requiring that such gains would have to be taxed as ordinary income starting in 1988.

Capital gains selling had increased towards the end of 1986 as investors took advantage of the old, lower, 20% tax rate that would no longer apply in 1987. After selling had abated, for awhile in 1987 the market had risen again in active training, due partly to rumors that Congress might reinstate a 20-25% capital gains tax. Also, October or November was felt to be a better time to sell, when the market usually topped out. Just the same, long-term investors took note in the summer of 1987 of what they considered a "sell" signal (for tax purposes).

As October finally came around, many investors were getting ready to sell; but daily stock price swings had dramatic increases attributable to the influence on the Dow of program trading. Gains were often astounding, at least they were in my portfolio. I had made money in the market, but never that much that quickly, and it continued day after day. As long as portfolios were increasing from day to day, who would want to sell and miss out on the next day's windfall?

Well, the market appeared to be topping out by the close of trading on Friday, October 16 - finally. So, when Monday, October 19, rolled around, those capital gains sellers entered the market in a big way and were joined by short-term traders and, ultimately, by those having to sell or be sold out to make margin call payments to brokerage firms. With a preponderance of sell orders, the Dow Jones Industrial Average closed down some 500+ points on a record 604.33 million shares. Trading on the NYSE had to be halted for several days to sort things out.

Aside from the New York Stock Exchange having failed to maintain an "orderly market," what also seems generally overlooked by many retelling this "crash" story is the capital gains aspect of it. Blame Congress? Partially. But the NYSE had precipitated the eventual market crash by not maintaining an "orderly market." Computer trading of baskets of stocks had been allowed to get out of hand and for that the NYSE was directly responsible. The biggest losers were margin accounts forced into selling out.

As I write this, a (Oct. 2003) TIME magazine article headline reads, "Big Board, Big Payday - As CEO Dick Grasso takes a $140 million cashout, the New York Stock Exchange takes the heat." The NYSE was a non-profit organization and got off scot-free after the Oct. 1987 market "crash," as far as I know.

Serious problems can develop when people serving on blue ribbon panels and boards choose merely to "go along," even when an emperor stands naked before them. It's the same as when civil servants refuse to make waves fearing for their pensions instead of "risking" doing the right thing.

That little kidney-shaped swimming pool at my apartment complex had concrete decking surrounding it to allow towels or chairs for sunning. A great place to get some tanning rays. One young female began to catch my eye. I tried to ignore her, but, after awhile, I wanted to be with her.

Finally, on February 5, 1971, I came around to asking Sharon Elizabeth McCall if she would help me insert 537 individually addressed 2-page letters into appropriate envelopes also individually addressed to each Member of Congress plus one each to President Nixon and Vice President Agnew.

Without hesitation, that first-grade teacher helped me out, and we began what developed into courtship...and, in August 1974, marriage.

How lucky I was and continue to be as our 30th anniversary approaches!

Here is a true copy of that letter to Washington:

"I must inquire into a matter for which the U.S. Congress bears responsibility. I seek your reply to a question posed at the end of this two page letter. I will respond promptly.

"Article 1, Section 8, Paragraph 8 of the Constitution empowers Congress 'To promote the progress of science and useful arts, by securing for limited times to authors and inventors the exclusive right to their respective writings and discoveries.'

"It has been my experience during the past fourteen years that the Patent Office, with its inability to respond QUICKLY to requests for searches and applications, FAILS to uphold the requirements of the Constitution, as set forth above, and that it does, in fact, DO INJURY to those who would seek legitimate claims.

"The effect is, in part, to limit the progress of science and useful arts. But, even more important, I feel, is the IMPACT which the DISCOVERY of such inadequate service can have on the citizens who endure the rigors of bringing something new, better and more desirable into the world, only to find that, while the Patent Office conducts its time consuming operations, and while the applicant holds back on progress outlays, awaiting word from the Patent Office, someone ELSE, or ANOTHER organization can introduce the same, or a similar improvement... And at times, with a 'Pat. Pending' label yet!

"There are products that can be manufactured and sold to the point of SATURATION before the Patent Office can complete and forward the results of an infringement search!

"There are people who can get 'hung up' on ONE project for YEARS and not progress beyond it for having to wait on the Patent Office!

"My experiences with Patent ATTORNEYS indicate that they are NOT motivated towards initiating Patent Office improvements. After considering that they are paid, usually, on an hourly basis by their clients, it seems logical to presume that they can find the lack of SPEED at the Patent Office to be convenient and useful, while attaching their OWN claims to time requirements, for purposes of meeting overhead and profit demands. I do NOT wish to begrudge Patent Attorneys of a means of making a livelihood, nor, even, a solid profit, either, but I HAVE been in hopes (and to no avail) that they would do SOMETHING to speed up Patent Office operations!

"It becomes apparent, then, that like the Post Office, responsibility for Patent Office operations rests FULLY on the shoulders of the Federal Government and its CONGRESS!

- FURTHER, it becomes evident that a SLOW, OUT-DATED, OUT-MODED, BEHIND-THE-TIMES PATENT OFFICE will CONTINUE to reflect UNFAVORABLY upon the Federal Government and its CONGRESS! - ESPECIALLY to those having the EXPERIENCES of looking to the Patent Office to fulfill its CONSTITUTIONAL obligation of caring PROPERLY for Patent Rights!

"To COMPUTERIZE Patent Office Operations - Like at the CIA, DOD, NASA, IRS and others - so that PATENT Attorneys can perform THEIR SEARCH and APPLICATION functions in terms of MICRO-SECONDS (And from their respective offices), stands to not only GUARANTEE adequate safeguards against fraudulent disclosures (because of the shortened exposure time element), BUT it stands to UNWIND the GIANT sized bundle of RED TAPE which BUREAUCRACY is currently STRANGLING Creativity with in America; It stands to re-kindle the fires of HOPE and RESPECT FOR LAW AND ORDER in America; It stands 'To promote the progress of science and useful arts' and to secure 'for limited times to authors and inventors the exclusive right to their respective writings and discoveries' as is GUARANTEED by the CONSTITUTION; It stands to be a worthy EXAMPLE for the OTHER NATIONS in the world to EMULATE; And, I dare say that it stands to IMPROVE on the Rights to the Pursuit of Happiness, the well being, habits, living standards and the employment opportunities of MOST AMERICANS!

"Now, my question to each and all of you distinguished members of CONGRESS is: 'HOW LONG DO YOU ESTIMATE THAT IT WILL TAKE TO DO IT?'

"Because of the Patent Commissioner's, the Senate's and the President's reluctance to answer prior inquiries concerning this matter, and because of the apparent lack of meaningful Patent Office Reform Programs in the Congress, it is my intention, currently, to publicize your reply, or the lack of one, as I deem it necessary to arouse public interest in and/or support of Patent Office Improvements.

"President Nixon, Vice President Agnew, Senator ———, Congressman ———, I await and look forward to your reply."

Signed: "Sincerely and respectfully,

G.S. Jenson"

There were many replies. I answered every one of them.

The commissioner of patents, at that time, was William E. Schuyler Jr. In a previous response to me on behalf of President Nixon he had stated the following: "As to searching by computer, Mr. Jenson may be advised that since about 1954 studies have been conducted, experiments made, and pilot systems inaugurated leading, it is hoped, to automatic or machine searching of patents. This work has been conducted not only by the Patent Office but also by other Government and private industrial organizations. The problem is exceedingly complex, and only limited success thus far has been achieved."

Commissioner Schuyler had responded to Congressman John Brademas who represented my 3rd District in Indiana with a little more information: "We have pointed out in our letter to the Congressman that studies have been undertaken by my predecessors and have been continued under my administration seeking to find ways by means of machines to improve our services. The backlog of patent applications, approximately 180,000 at the present time, accumulated following World War II. Notwithstanding various administrative improvements, and the provision by Congress of budgets adequate to deal with the proper management of our workload, it has been possible to make only minimal inroads on the inventory of applications, which at one time approached 240,000 cases. The reasons for our inability to make a more rapid reduction of the inventory include, among others, the continuing high filing rate of applications, the increasing mass of technology to be searched, and the loss of trained examiners to industry and other private endeavors as fast as eligible technical personnel could be recruited. We have indicated that the problem is exceedingly complex, and a solution not only by the Patent Office but by others who have examined our operations, has not yet been proposed or adopted."

The Administrative Assistant to Vice President Agnew made another offer. He wrote: "I can only reiterate the suggestion that Commissioner Schuyler has made to you in previous correspondence: If you will write to his office concerning the patent in which you have an interest, every effort will be made to expedite an investigation. Included in your request should be the filing date and serial number of your application."

My reply was the same to all such offers, of which several were made: "I DO appreciate your willingness to assist me with a particular patent application; however, my interest is in promoting reforms at the Patent Office itself."

"At your convenience during August 1971, I respectfully request an audience with you in D.C. If you will kindly notify me of a satisfactory time and place, I will make travel arrangements accordingly," I wrote to Commissioner Schuyler on July 17, 1971.

Margaret McCarthy, Secretary to the Commissioner, later responded: "At the time of the receipt of your letter dated July 17th, Commissioner Schuyler was out of the country and did not return until recently. In the Commissioner's absence, I asked Mr. William Nugent, our newly appointed Assistant Commissioner for Search Systems Development ... as to his availability in speaking with you. He indicated to me that he would be very pleased to see you and will make himself available at your convenience...."

On Thursday, August 26, 1971, I met with Mr. Nugent in his office, with my 12-year-old son along. It dawns on me now for the first time, as I review records to write this, that the Honorable Robert Gottschalk had become the Acting Commissioner on the day before my meeting with Nugent, replacing William E. Schuyler Jr. Later, on Monday March 27, 1972, Gottschalk would be sworn in as the new Commissioner of Patents. He had joined the Patent Office as the Deputy Commissioner on May 20, 1970. There would be many exchanges between us.

I also toured the Patent & Trademark Office in Arlington during that visit. What I saw first-hand of the PTO really opened my eyes.

Located in Crystal City, Virginia, (in Arlington), the PTO had mirror-like windows in a several-story building that was surrounded by open areas of concrete. It was beautiful and ultra-modern looking from the outside. Inside, one stepped down a few steps onto a huge carpeted main floor rotunda where off in the distance and away from any windows could be seen a small group of wooden filing cabinets with drawers like ones used in public libraries. You had to search those files to learn where to find a patent in its manila folder on one of the adjustable steel shelves on one of the floors above.

Upstairs, I could look out the darkened windows almost directly into the sun. Turning around, I found one lone patent in its manila folder on a shelf. The other shelves and spaces around it were empty. The sun shone on it, but the tinted glass no doubt offered some ultra-violet protection. A string was tied around the manila folder to keep the many papers of all sizes that I could observe from falling out. It was one of about 3.6 million patents on file at the PTO.

My son and I met with William R. Nugent, the assistant commissioner for Search Systems Development. We spent at least an hour with him. An average patent, he told us, would require approximately 27,000 bytes of storage. He promised to write when he had more to inform about.

Almost ten months later, I had not heard from Nugent, so I wrote to him and received the following quick response:

U.S. DEPARTMENT OF COMMERCE
Patent Office

June 15, 1972

Dear Mr. Jenson:

Thank you for your letter of June 12. I recall with pleasure the visit you and your son made to my office last year and your strong interest in Office automation activities.

We did meet our scheduled deadline of December 1971 for our first demonstrations of computer search systems, including an on-line retrieval and display of chemical compounds. We demonstrated a search of 22,000 compounds in three seconds, and the regeneration of two-dimensional chemical structure diagrams on a computer display terminal. Another demonstration of interest was a manual simulation of a computerized patent classification system, that showed potential of 1,000 to 1 savings in cost and time with respect to manual methods. The first component of a full-text retrieval system was also developed, and our tests in Optical Character Recognition showed that cost savings of up to 7 to 1 could be attained, with respect to manual keyboarding, in the conversion of patents to machine form.

In brief, 1971 was a highly productive year. In January 1972, however, funding for our program was cancelled, and two days ago this cost center and my position were abolished.

We have demonstrated, however, that the Patent Office can have an automated search system in any year it wants one. I regret that one is not wanted in 1972.

Yours sincerely,

Signed - William R. Nugent
Assistant Commissioner for Search Systems Development

Copies of Nugent's letter were then sent to each and every senator and representative who had responded in some way to my appeals.

On August 18, 1972, I received a telephone call from the Commissioner of Patents, Robert Gottschalk. We spoke for about an hour.

Gottschalk had come to realize that the chemical patents which represented almost half of the 3.6 million patents on file could be logged onto computers, but not the other remaining patents. Therefore, he did not think it would be fair to only do the chemical patents; and due, further, to an expected lack of comprehensive cross reference capabilities.

My suggestion was to be grateful for having an opportunity to log chemical patents onto computers and that the PTO would likely learn more by doing it than anyone could otherwise imagine. Sometimes, the most difficult part of a venture is to begin it, to get started, I said. Compare it to opening a savings account. It may take a long time to open one, but, once it's done, all sorts of savings plans can evolve that could not have even been imagined beforehand.

Then, the commissioner expressed concerns about funding. It was my impression that he did not want to go before the Congress to ask for the additional funds that the computer operations would need. I advised him to do so. The average patent required about 27,000 bytes of storage. According to Nugent's findings, about $38.5 million would be needed to complete the chemical patent entries. After that, less than $2 million would be required annually to maintain storage of those 1.6 million patents on computers.

Total PTO operational funding, at that time, was less than $57 million.

My appeals to Patent Commissioner Gottschalk were continued by letter on November 26, 1972:

"Perhaps Congressman Helstoski of New Jersey was correct when he wrote to me on February 18, 1971, and said, 'In my opinion Congressional action is not needed to modernize the operations and procedures of the Patent Office. It could be done by a vibrant and forward-looking Patent Office administration with the sanction and support of the President.'"

My letter continued: "On May 4, 1961, almost twelve years ago, a previous Patent Commissioner testified before Congress saying, 'I am not at all pleased by the fact that we are in arrears in our work.' He favored mechanization, but there was none available, as witnessed by his further testimony:

" 'Research efforts during the year were directed towards expanding the number of patents which could be mechanically searched. Success in the phosphorous compounds and steroids was sufficient evidence to encourage a vigorous pursuit of mechanization. No breakthrough was made which would suggest that one day soon the voluminous files of the Patent Office would be reduced to automation. This remained the biggest problem and the major goal for the Patent Office.'

"Now, it appears, that goal is in sight and it should be attained," I wrote to the commissioner. "Its name as far as I can perceive is 'Project POTOMAC.' It is at least a beginning - and a sizable one at that. 1.6 million patents filed on computers by the end of FY '78 will represent over 38% of a possible total of 4.2 million patents on file by that time.

"If 'Project POTOMAC' were adaptable theoretically, to the entire Patent Office search file of the projected and forthcoming 4.2 million patents," I added, "the entry cost would be about $100 million, not 'a quarter of a billion dollars,' as you indicated.... The annual maintenance costs would dwindle to 4.2 million dollars afterwards.

"Also, in your November 6th correspondence, Commissioner Gottschalk, you stated the following in conclusion:

" 'The major part of the pendency time is taken up, not by searching, but by the 6 to 10 months the Patent Office waits upon the applicant for responses to official communications and for payment of final fee, and by the several months necessarily taken up by the printing and other processing procedures. If we could induce faster responses from the applicant, we could reduce the pendency times by a factor significantly greater than any major reduction in search times and for significantly less costs.'

"As of June, 1972, Commissioner Gottschalk, you reported to me that the average pendency time had been reduced to 25.3 months. I find it easier, now, to understand that if one deducts the 6 to 10 month period mentioned above from 25.3 months, the average pendency period could be reduced immediately to from 15.3 to 19.3 months, or, say, an average 17.3 months. Your 18 month pendency goal would be achieved, the Patent Office would NOT be automated to any degree, but I would still be here making appeals, as I am now, for Patent Office improvements.

"During the past several months, Commissioner, you and I have discussed many of the problems besetting the Patent Office with a view towards reducing pendency times. You have stated to me that Patent Office funding problems have arisen because of budget cuts made by the Commerce Department and the Office of Management and Budget to the amounts requested originally by the Patent Office. The Congress has gone on to approve those budgets, but they have been insufficient to begin with because of the cuts.

"You have indicated, also, that 'Project POTOMAC' had to be terminated when it became apparent that normal Patent Office operations could not be funded and maintained while funds from normal operations were diverted for automation purposes. What the Patent Office apparently needs is enough money to operate 'Project POTOMAC' in tandem with normal operations until it or another program proves itself. Therefore, I am initiating, today, an appeal to the President and the Secretary of Commerce to come to your assistance.

"My appeal includes forwarding copies of this correspondence and that of Mr. William R. Nugent, the former Assistant Commissioner for Search Systems Development, addressed to me on June 15, 1972, of which you are cognizant.

"I will forward copies of your November 6th letter and this letter, as well, to the office of Congressman Begich of Alaska, as promised. He was interested in having your goal of 18 months pendency reduced, and his staff is maintaining on-going office operations as, I am sure, Congressman Begich would approve of.

"Commissioner Gottschalk, I hope you will look upon this action as an opportunity to assemble temporary additional Patent Office funding for automation purposes..."

Signed: "Sincerely yours, G. S. Jenson"

Regrettably, on October 16, 1972, Alaska's Representative-at-Large, Nick Begich, House Democratic Leader, Hale Boggs, of Louisiana and two others were lost on a flight from Anchorage to Juneau, Alaska. Heavy snow and bad visibility forced cancellation October 29 of the search for their plane. More than 70 aircraft had performed an intense but vain search over a 56,000 square mile Alaska area.

Before leaving on that campaign trip, Congressman Begich had written to me on September 13, as follows:

"The enclosed material was sent from the Patent Office in response to my inquiry concerning the length of pendency and their apparent intent not to use more modern methods of patent search.

"As you can see from Mr. Gottschalk's letter, the Commissioner is also concerned that the Patent Office give the best and most efficient service to its clients. According to the Commissioner, the cost of the contemplated system was excessive considering the small amount capacity the final system would have, and that further funding of the project would have meant deterioration of the conventional classification past the stage of any type of efficient operation. With this facing him, it is understandable that Mr. Gottschalk would make the decisions that he has.

"From the enclosed materials, and his letter, Mr. Gottschalk appears to be moving toward reduced pendency as quickly as possible, given the limitation his office faces. I would appreciate hearing your comments on the letter and will be most happy to continue this investigation if you feel it is necessary. I look forward to your comments.

"Best regards.

"Sincerely," signed NICK BEGICH

Congressman Hale Boggs, the Majority Leader, who was on the plane with Congressman Begich, had responded to my appeal on February 17, 1971, as follows:

"Thank you very much for giving me the benefit of your views on the need to streamline the procedure by which we protect intellectual property.

"The Congress is continually examining these subjects, and I assure you that I will have your views in mind as they are brought before us.

"In the meantime, let me again thank you for taking the time to write me. I look forward to hearing from you at any time on matters of interest or concern.

"With kindest regards and best wishes, I am sincerely, HALE BOGGS, M.C. Majority Leader."

Another Member of Congress from Louisiana's 6th District, sent an official certificate with the Capitol dome pictured and that declared I was an Honorary Aide-de-Camp on the staff of Representative John R. Rarick.

"To all to whom these presents shall come, Greetings. Be it known that Gunnar S. Jenson Because of evidenced patriotic activities in behalf of Constitutional Americanism and in defense of liberty, and because of confidence and trust demonstrated in the Member of Congress representing the Sixth District of Louisiana, It is my pleasure and privilege to confer with the above-named Patriot the Title of Honorary Aide-de-Camp on the Staff of Representative John R. Rarick, Member of Congress. Given under my hand in Washington, D.C., this 28th day of March in the year of our Lord, one thousand nine hundred seventy-two."

Signed, "John R. Rarick, MEMBER OF CONGRESS."

On February 16, 1971, the Congressman had written: "Thank you for your letter of February 5th and for sharing your views with me regarding the inadequate service and the length of time involved in obtaining the necessary patents.

"I can only agree with you in every respect and join you in not wishing to begrudge Patent Attorneys of their means of making a livelihood, but I see no reason for them to milk their clients either.

"Not being a computer expert, or even a programmer of computers, I can't answer your question as to how long it would take to computerize Patent Office operations, but it does seem like a good idea."

Signed, "Sincerely, John R. Rarick, Member of Congress"

Michigan Senator Philip A. Hart, Chairman of the Antitrust and Monopoly Subcommittee, wrote an interesting response on February 22, 1971, and another some 2 years later.

"Your letter touches upon a fundamental problem with the Patent Office that I agree needs prompt reform. The gap between an individual Senator's belief and action is rather wide, since Congress is primarily a reactive body rather than a creative one. It is especially difficult to obtain reform when that reform tramples upon the vested interests of special interest groups. We have been attempting to pass a revision of the Patent Code for several years with little success. If enough citizens bring pressure for reform, we might be able to finally achieve it.

"Your specific question of how long will it take simply cannot be answered with a set date. The members of the Patents, Trademarks and Copyrights Subcommittee have been working on the problem for several years; yet, lobbying against reform continues to block action. I would suggest that pressure for reform is building, since the courts are adopting the same view you have toward the Patent Office and are invalidating more and more patents because of incompetent granting of the patents. Unfortunately, my only prediction is that reform will only take place when we are faced with disaster. While I don't urge you to help bring the disaster about, in all honesty, I can give you no better estimate of how long it will take nor can I give you any better suggestion of how to bring it about.

"Please be assured that I shall continue to labor for reform of processes and procedures followed by the Patent Office. You must also gain the support of 99 other Senators and 435 Congressmen."

Signed, "Sincerely, Philip A. Hart,
Chairman, Antitrust and Monopoly Subcommittee"

Some 2 years later, on April 5, 1973, Senator Hart wrote again:

"Recently, I came across your letter respecting Patent Office pendency times. You may be interested in the Patent Reform Act of 1973, which I recently introduced – S. 1321. Specific objectives of the bill include speeding up and improving Patent Office procedures, reducing costs and increasing efficiencies, and the utilization of modern technology within the Office."

Signed, "Sincerely, Philip A. Hart, Chairman."

I regretted having to answer Senator Hart, but did so promptly on April 11th:

"Your letter dated April 5th with enclosure (Patent Reform Act of 1973 – S. 1321) is appreciated. Your continuing interest in Patent Office improvements is acknowledged, and your recent introduction of what is obviously a comprehensive Patent Reform plan is commendable. As much as I would like to, however, I cannot offer support of S. 1321.

"While recognizing your good intentions towards patent procedures improvements, I find S. 1321 an unacceptable plan and one which stands to discourage registrations rather than encourage them.

"The objective which I have attempted to convey to Members of Congress has been for them to pursue measures which will 'speed-up' Patent Office operations. The Congress, meanwhile, seems to overlook the many constructive reforms and improvements which are inherent in the pursuit of that objective, and appears capable of drafting reform legislation which accepts, and, in some cases, even provides for extended pendency periods.

"S. 1321, for example, proposes that 'Examination could be deferred for up to 5 years after filing.' Respectfully, Senator Hart, and with due regard for European patent problems, I submit that persons and corporations should either file and obtain their patent grants, or not file.

"The proposed reduction of patent grant protection to 12 years is an obvious 'retraction' of rights granted by the Constitution. Copyrights are good for life, and, I believe, can be inherited, even. Why should there be such a vast difference between patent rights and copyrights?

"To propose that 'Beginning in the fourth year after a patent issues, the maintenance fee thereon shall be no less than $1,000.00, and shall increase annually by at least 25 per centum each year' will, no doubt, impose hardships on patent holders of limited means, regardless of appeal and other provisions."

NOTE: During the Reagan Administration, a similar maintenance fee schedule was indeed enacted, along with raising PTO charges, significantly. I have argued against it because there are likely many discoveries that will not be recorded due to inventors not being able to afford the fees necessary to give notice of their inventions. How can the PTO remain a reservoir of data if inventors cannot afford to register their discoveries?

I even appealed to Federal Reserve Board Chairman, Paul Volcker. He agreed that, while it was important to reduce federal spending across the board, there were some exceptions that needed to be taken into account, notably and certainly, the PTO. (However, not even Volcker's advice was heeded.)

My letter to Senator Hart is continued, below:

"To propose that 'an oath would be required to assure that all material information which would adversely affect the issuance of the patent is brought to the attention of the [Patent] Office' by the applicant seems like a reversal of responsibilities and obligations. Furthermore, that 'a person shall not be entitled to a patent if the subject matter sought to be patented was known or used by others in this or a foreign country' leaves me in doubt that even a single person or a corporation on Earth will be able to qualify itself for a future patent grant; especially in view of the apparent reversal of responsibilities and obligations mentioned above, and especially when one evaluates the capabilities and limitations of current patent search systems and equipment.

"To propose that a new function of the Patent Office should be to evaluate between 'patents which are frivolous and fanciful with little or no redeeming public good' and those considered of 'high quality' appears to represent a departure from attempts to provide for system equality and greater ease of searching.

"The comments, above, are all I can provide from a sketchy analysis of S. 1321. Time allowances do not permit me, at the moment, to proceed with a more detailed review of S. 1321, unfortunately. I am satisfied, however, that I do not support passage of S. 1321.

"Senator Hart, I do appreciate your writing April 5th, and, again, I am grateful for your obvious interest in the U.S. Patent Office. Please be assured that I wish to be able to continue to correspond with you concerning Patent Office reform matters."

Signed, "Sincerely yours, G. S. Jenson"

A copy was sent to Patent Commissioner Gottschalk.

Three days later, I wrote again to Senator Hart:

"As a brief follow-up to my recent (April 11th) letter to you, I would like to present one additional concept for your evaluation and considerations.

"While proposing and enacting legislation dealing with Patents, Congress would do well, I feel, to consider imposing a requirement that U.S. Patents cannot be granted to foreign residents until said foreign residents have first obtained and do continue to maintain the same patents in their native lands.

"In calendar year 1970, for example, 47,073 U.S. Patents were issued to residents of the United States, while an additional 17,354 U.S. Patents were issued by the United States to residents of Foreign Countries. Foreign residents, therefore, received over 26% of the U.S. Patents granted in calendar year 1970.

"Foreign participation in the U.S. Patent System is certainly welcomed. With international trade activities increasing, however, I feel the U.S. should recognize and move to preserve the patent system as it may find opportunities to do so.

"A 'speeding-up' of U.S. Patent Office operations, meanwhile, will minimize the effects of any similar moves by foreign nationals, and improve on American industries' abilities to react competitively to products imported for sale in the U.S.

"I hope these additional comments are helpful."

Signed, "Sincerely yours, G.S. Jenson; with a copy to Patent Commissioner Robert Gottschalk."

Senator Hart answered by letter on May 7, 1973:

"Thank you for your recent letters commenting on S. 1321 – the Patent Reform Act. You may be assured that your suggestions will be considered by the Subcommittee.

"Best regards."

Signed, "Sincerely, Philip A. Hart, Chairman."

Regrettably, Senator Hart died of cancer on December 26, 1976.

"Thank you for your letter discussing the problems of the Patent Office.

"I am sympathetic. My wife applied for a patent some time ago and still hasn't received notification."

Signed, "Yours sincerely, J. EDWARD ROUSH, Member of Congress, 4th District, Indiana."

There were many responses and many who didn't respond. Altogether, some 22 senators responded (and 78 did not); while 51 Members of the House of Representatives responded (and 384 did not). A total of 18 states gave no response at all. In alphabetical order, they were: Arizona, Delaware, Idaho, Iowa, Kansas, Kentucky, Mississippi, Montana, New Hampshire, North Dakota, Oklahoma, Oregon, Rhode Island, Tennessee, Utah, Vermont, Wisconsin and Wyoming.

On May 29, 1973, Patent Commissioner Robert Gottschalk resigned.

There was one memorable statement from a Member of Congress that I could not find while reviewing communications for this chapter; but I can at least paraphrase it here. I don't recall whether he was a Representative or a Senator. But I do distinctly remember what he wrote: "Only two or three Members of Congress have ever experienced applying for and obtaining a patent. Therefore, it should be no surprise that it will be difficult for Members of Congress to appreciate the needs for and want to do anything about speeding-up PTO operations."

One final bit of irony, perhaps, came some years later, after former Patent Commissioner Robert Gottschalk had returned to practicing patent law. In Florida, a retired friend of mine living in Winter Haven at the time mailed a newspaper clipping to me that quoted Gottschalk in a speech. Gottschalk complained that PTO operations were too slow.

CHAPTER 16

THAT DREAM

By December 12, 1973, thanks to a helpful XEROX sales office in South Bend, I had been able to make copies of all correspondence and enclosures described in Chapter 15 and then some. Next, those copies were bound and made into several hard-cover books. One copy was sent to Ed Lowe, the founder of Kitty Litter, who had corporate offices in South Bend. He was known for promoting entrepreneurs and enterprises, so I wanted to invite him to consider funding a Patent Exchange. Nothing happened except that he had the book returned via UPS after having it for about a week. Entitled, "UNCLE SAM - DAVID, OR GOLIATH? - (BIRDIE, PAR, OR BOGIE?)," another copy was sent to Congressman John Brademas, my representative in Washington from the 3rd District in Indiana. After making it available to any interested Members of the House and Senate, I asked that he send it along to Mr. Edward J. Brenner, executive director, Association for the Advancement of Invention & Innovation in Arlington, Virginia, who, in turn, returned the book to me. Here is how it began:

PREAMBLE

The total population of the Earth was estimated to be 3,580,000,000 persons as of January 1, 1970. 204,300,000 were residents in the United States of America.

For every "David" or "Goliath" living in "Uncle Sam's" America, therefore, there were about 16.5 other persons in other areas of the world who were probably organized and living under something considered less beneficial to mankind than what Americans refer to as the United States Constitution.

An easier way to understand the comparison, above, might be to think of an 18-hole golf course with one world player on each fairway. An American plays on one of them. He uses U.S. Professional Golfer's Association (PGA) rules. The other 17 players on this imaginary world course each have their own equipment and rules. Some do not even use golf clubs. Everyone has a golf ball, however, and appears to be playing golf. Thus, life appears to continue, globally.

Excluding Antarctica and the Arctic Polar Ice Region, there are about 52,362,548 square miles of land, of which about 33,588,038 square miles is considered fertile, on Earth.

Returning to our imaginary 18-hole golf course, we can translate those numbers into observing that each world player has a fairway averaging about 9.4 acres in size, with about 6 acres of that considered fertile land. (A football field, including end zones, covers about 1.3 acres)

The fairway being played on by that long ball hitting, low handicap, birdie putting American out there is about 11 acres in area, of which about 5.2 acres IS, indeed, farmland.

The shortest hole (and smallest fairway) award goes to the European who has only about 3.9 acres to play on.

The largest fairway is enjoyed by an Australian who has over 152 acres to himself.

Besides making it apparent that there would not be enough land on Earth for each and every person in the world to have his own, private, standard size 18-hole golf course, the comparisons, above, are intended to assist in describing the world we live on in more meaningful terms. (If Americans, for example, were to double in population and double their farmland areas accordingly, there would be very little acreage left for them to even stand on without stepping on farmland.)

Humanity is traveling through space on a world planet which offers challenges, diversities and satisfactions of all sizes and descriptions. To Free Men everywhere, however, Nature offers a particular challenge, and to Americans, especially, opportunities for gaining financial rewards.

It is the United States Constitution and the U.S. Patent Office which has separated the American from his counterparts on this world planet in the past and which has permitted him to "begin" to enlarge upon his understandings and uses of Nature for the benefit of himself and mankind.

Many Americans will have already expired by the time July 4, 1976, rolls around and we celebrate our 200th Birthday. While we have certainly "proven" ourselves, America, still, will rank as, and be considered, a relatively "young" nation.

For example, on July 4, 1976, one will be able to compare America's 200-year life span to the passage of time since Christ's death, 1,976 years, and find that America's 200 years is about the same as 2 hours and 26 minutes of a 24 hour day. Similarly, since the Marmes Man roamed the Snake River in the state of Washington some 13,000 years ago, America's 200 years represents only about 22 minutes of a 24-hour day. The earliest known instance of mining, predating copper mining activity in Yugoslavia, took place in South Africa, considered the first homeland of modern man's ancestors and in the forefront of technological invention. That mining took place between 80,000 - 100,000 B.C. America's 200 years of progress represents only about 3 minutes and 10 seconds of a 24-hour day when compared with the passage of time since about 90,000 B.C. Compared to the estimated age of the Earth, 4.5 billion years, America's 200 years is only .00384 seconds of a 24-hour day. So you can see that Americans and their Constitution are, indeed, "young."

This book could be devoted to selling the idea of adopting constitutional governments outside the U.S. Instead, it deals with one of America's long-term assets that has become a problem in need of solution as soon as possible.

Briefly stated: The U.S. Patent Office is too slow! It is outdated, out-moded and behind-the-times when compared to American capacities to create new products and services.

Thirty years ago, here is more of what I dreamt:

UNCLE SAM - DAVID, OR GOLIATH

Ever stop to think of what might have happened to David if he'd missed? Well, he did have four more rocks, and the target, undoubtedly, would have moved closer and grown larger ... and David could have tried and tried again.

In the Bible, I. Samuel tells of Goliath, who stood more than 9 feet tall and was dressed in armor head to foot. His coat, alone, weighed over 156 pounds. The point on the end of his spear weighed almost 19 pounds. He carried a sheathed sword. Out front was his shield carried by a shield bearer, no less. Behind Goliath stood the Philistine army.

From under a brass helmet, Goliath had voiced his challenge to the men of Israel, "Choose you a man ... If he be able to fight with me, and kill me, then will we be your servants; but if I prevail against him, and kill him, then shall ye be our servants."

David, as we know, got the message and volunteered to defend the men of Israel even though he was considered a mere youth. After delivering an armful of cheese, bread and grain to the army men of Israel, David enlisted and went on to convince their leader, Saul, that he had previously killed lion and bear in defense of his father's herd of sheep. The challenge of dealing with Goliath seemed only similar. Even more, it would be for a cause.

To young David, Goliath was "an uncircumcised Philistine" who "defied the armies of the living God" like a lion or a bear attacking a herd of sheep. David believed that Jehovah would protect him from Goliath, just as he had protected him from the lion and bear. Though reluctant to send a "mere youth" into a conflict with Goliath, Saul gave his approval, finally, and he attempted to dress David for battle by lending him his own armor. But David, after trying it on, chose to go without it, because he was unaccustomed to it. Instead, David picked up 5 smooth stones from a brook, his bag and sling, and sallied forth to meet the challenger.

David and Goliath approached each other, exchanged verbal threats (each promised to feed the remains of the other to the birds and beasts), and proceeded to close the distance between them.

Finally, David reached into his bag, pulled out a stone, inserted it into his sling and launched it towards and into Goliath's head. Goliath fell flat on his face, armor and all. David advanced, drew Goliath's sword and slew him.

*   *

Sound like an ordinary day in an American's 20th Century battle to accumulate a nest-egg? At times, it has reminded me of my battle to speed-up Patent Office operations, I can say that much.

Times change, and so do people, the story goes, and in America we seem to have more room for error than in any other nation on Earth. God Bless Us for that, at least!

At any rate, when a point is reached from which we cannot return, we often arrive somewhere else, wondering, hopefully, why anyone would want to return to that previous point, anyhow! That, in a manner of speaking, can be a partial description of human progress.

So it goes until one day, we find ourselves older and wiser (perhaps too old and wise too late, sometimes), and we begin to realize that our hopes and aspirations in a complex society of Millions of People, Big Government, High Taxes and Certain Death are, perhaps, not to be realized unless we apply ourselves more towards doing something about them.

My parents are naturalized American citizens. They immigrated from Sweden while in their 20's. As a youngster, I heard them speak, repeatedly, of America as being the "Land of Opportunity." They and their immigrant friends spoke often of the wonderful opportunities one could enjoy in America through the Patent system. Why, to me, it sounded as if a person could patent a new product and become financially rewarded for the rest of his life!

America, where I was born, was quite a country, indeed! I began to feel privileged to be a part of it. Even more, I resolved to become a working, financially rewarded part of it! I chose not to deprive others of their ownership rights and to somehow eventually invent and patent something myself for the benefit of mankind and for the financial benefit of Gunnar S. Jenson and his family. After all, it did make sense to believe that if one invented something, it would not be stolen from someone else, because no one else would have had it to begin with! To invent something would afford one an opportunity to give, not steal. What an equal-opportunity privilege America presented to everyone by having a Patent Office to keep track of all the new inventions! I was really impressed! ... and motivated! America and Nature may have seemed like two Goliaths, but the presence of a Patent Office seemed to make it possible for me, or anyone else, to be a David!

By July 1952, at the age of 18, I had become somewhat more cognizant of the U.S. Constitution and its role in providing for America's welfare. Upon entering the Naval Service as a Midshipman, I took an oath at the U.S. Naval Academy to uphold the Constitution against all enemies, foreign and domestic.

As you would be, or have been already, I became interested in learning more of what I had sworn to uphold. In reading the Constitution, Article 1, Section 8, Paragraph 8 came into focus more clearly than ever. It was the one part of the Constitution which I felt the proudest of, had relied on most heavily for motivation in the past, and it spelled out in brief terms the legality of what my parents and their immigrant friends had described previously. There WAS a provision for a Patent Office, and there WERE exclusive rights given to authors and inventors for their writings and discoveries.

The Constitution does not mention, of course, anything about monetary rewards, capital requirements, marketability, production, inventory, distribution, advertising, public relations, quality, and some of the other elements essential to achieving public acceptances and purchases of new products, services, writings, entertainment, art, medicine, and all else that can be created and called New in America. Having knowledge of the existence of Creator's Ownership Rights in Constitutional printed form, however, was reassuring and made serving in the Naval Establishment a contributing, worthwhile, stimulating experience; until around the middle of 1957.

By 1957, I had graduated from the Naval Academy, married, and was serving aboard a Destroyer in the Pacific. Long Beach, California, was our home port in the U.S., and my new bride made the most of our meager beginnings there. I came to want to look after her more as time and attention away from my Naval Service obligations would permit.

We had traveled together frequently, and I came to realize that she had no place to pack her shoes, except in her suitcase amongst an already crowded array of other items. I, likewise, had the same problem.

Paper bags and shoe trees were available, of course, but I tried to think of something better and came up with an idea. I designed a standard container which could hold a pair of shoes, of any reasonable size, men's or women's, securely to its sides with the twist of a wrist. Stacking was included, also, in the design, so that one or several shoe containers could be carried as one unit, or stored in a closet.

Having in mind not only the solution to my family's shoe transport problems, but, also, the possibilities of royalties from luggage manufacturers, I employed the services of a Long Beach patent attorney and engaged a small Pasadena plastic manufacturing establishment to produce a pair of containers.

The containers were quickly and easily fabricated, but obtaining the services of that Patent Attorney started a chain of events which has led me, now, to the writing of this book.

The attorney was congenial enough, truthful enough and willing to do his part to preserve the rights of a new enterprise enough, but he was not going to be able to be FAST enough. The Patent Office, he explained, could require several YEARS to handle an infringement search and patent application. Further questioning revealed that extended patent pendency periods were commonplace, had been so ever since he could remember, and would probably remain so for as long into the future as he could imagine. What a dilemma!

I felt like a David who had missed the first shot, and Goliath was coming on strong!

I could have instructed the attorney to file the necessary search and application papers, and then proceeded to attempt a sale of the (patent pending) invention to a luggage manufacturer. I could have even tried to form a company for the purpose of selling and distributing the shoe containers, using the Pasadena facility as a manufacturing source. A number of options began to appear, but my chief concern became, "What if it were found later that I had infringed on someone else's patent rights, even though unknowingly?" As a Naval Officer, I wanted no part of that! Furthermore, I could not imagine that any luggage manufacturer would want any part of it, either. In fact, it became apparent that attempting to sell anything short of an actual Patent would be like making a trip to give away an idea.

David, my boy, SPEAK to me!

Down? Sure, I was down, and I had spent a lot of money in the process. I was grateful, though, for the experience. I considered myself fortunate to have had at least some inventive "luck" in the private sector, which was quite removed from the realm of my sworn duties to the Naval Establishment. The Navy had me and my mind substantially preoccupied with Naval interests; and I had appreciated the good fortune of stumbling upon a new and workable idea outside of those preoccupations. Additional time for such extracurricular activities, for me, however, was running out. In a few months, I was to be transferred to Florida for flight training. To stay alive, I intended to be fully preoccupied with the Navy's Flight Training Program from start to finish.

By the Fall of 1962, I had completed over 6 years of Active Duty. I would come out of Uncle Sam's Navy swinging.

Service time in the Armed Forces can be a rewarding experience, especially when one believes that Constitutional requirements are being upheld by civilian authorities on the home front. I met and served with some excellent people in Uncle Sam's Navy, but the memory of that encounter with a Long Beach patent attorney lingered on. It bothered me to think that it was a fact that the U.S. Patent Office actually required YEARS to perform its services. What if the Military Establishment required YEARS to prepare a nuclear counter-attack? It would be like not having a Military Establishment! That syllogism could apply to the Patent Office, as well, I felt. Something would have to be done about it, but who would do it? Golf is like living, in a way. The more you play, the better your score. If you shoot a par, or birdie hole and step up to the next hole thinking you've got it made, look out! You will probably bogie, or double bogie the next hole or holes until you return to working at it again. I was beginning to relate my life to a game of speeding-up Patent Office operations. It was becoming apparent that I would have to pay attention to the game even more than I wanted to. The course was full of traps and hazards, apparently. But, then, it seemed like a worthwhile, constructive challenge!

I began thinking, "What if I HAD obtained that shoe container patent and SOLD it? I'd probably be as happy with the success of achievement as with the royalty or royalties."

Then I began to analyze my previous actions further. "What if I HAD been able to get a patent on the shoe container invention in, say, a week? And what if I had not been able, after that, to travel as necessary to sell the patent?"

What's more, I thought, suppose I had invented something else, and did not know where to go, or whom to attempt to sell it to? What if I had been a poor salesman? What if, after selling it, I had learned later that someone else would have paid more for it?

I was convinced that it was to be in our best national interest for the Patent Office to operate much faster than it did. It was beginning to dawn on me, further, however, that a Patent Exchange System similar to our Stock Exchanges around the world could lend considerable assistance to our patent system.

The game was getting even more interesting!

By late September 1962, my resignation from the Naval Service had been accepted and I became, once again, a civilian. I did not know for sure HOW to do it, but I felt compelled to somehow TRY to do what I could to speed up Patent Office operations. First, however, I would have to make a living and adjust to new preoccupations.

In focus at that particular time was the image of Americans being able to submit Patents and Trademarks to a central exchange for bids from all interested industrial and other commercial representatives. I had visions, even, of people in foreign countries rising to demand a Patent Office in their own countries where they had none, because of the eventual opportunities that would come from it, and as had been witnessed in America. Eventually, there could become a world network of Patent Offices and Patent Exchanges, leading to man's further utilization and understanding of Nature and to his just rewards therefrom!

My imaginations expanded even more and envisioned improvements to our patent search and application systems extending all the way back to the offices of patent attorneys themselves.

For example, it seemed entirely feasible that patent attorneys could equip themselves with electronic means, as stock brokers were equipped for obtaining current market information, which could enable attorneys to communicate with Patent Office files and with examiners, and it could all be done in terms of micro-seconds, electronically.

Instead of preparing a patent search application, for example, and "mailing" it to some student attorney working his way through Georgetown University, for the purpose of having him conduct a preliminary Patent Office search in his spare time and "mailing" it back, the attorney, instead, could, should and would (I hoped) have direct access to Patent Office files, himself, for search purposes and from his own office by means of some kind of electronic communications system. After a preliminary search, then, the attorney would be able, also, to "apply immediately," using the same electronic system, to a patent examiner for an "official" search and, hopefully, a patent or trademark grant. The grant, also, would be issued "electronically" and be received "in micro-seconds" by the attorney, with a follow-up, of course, of an official certificate and printed "mailed" copy.

It was beginning to appear that one day soon, one would be able to walk into a patent attorney's office anywhere in America and be able to expect a patent or trademark grant within, say, a week!

The attorney, naturally, would still have to take the time necessary to prepare an application based on information given to him by his client. After that, however, he could use his machine to interrogate the Patent Office files in prompt fashion himself, leading, ultimately, to a quick patent, trademark or service mark grant.

David, my boy, you DID it!

What a way for people to go from rags to riches in a "push-button, automated, leisure-time-oriented space age!" There were unemployed persons as well as employed persons who could benefit!

The best judge of manufactured products and services, after all, is the consumer who buys and uses them. If the consumer could benefit by suggesting improvements to industry which he, in fact, could support with a Patent offered for sale to a corporation, not only would the corporation benefit, but so would the purchasing public in receipt of its products and/or services!

Ever since childhood, as you know, now, from reading this book, I had placed considerable faith in the U.S. Patent Office to the extent that I had come to feel that I could afford to gamble (if you will) with life's activities, and hope for its benefits to be realized, eventually. Behind a willingness to "participate" in civilized society (which by many is referred to as a jungle), I believed that if times and conditions ever reached a point of futility, or failure, I would always have an opportunity via our Patent Office to salvage whatever I could by developing and patenting some sort of new invention and selling it. Thoughts of a Patent Exchange now seemed to coincide with that outlook.

While unemployed and poverty stricken persons would no doubt benefit from "timely" Patent Office functions, I imagined young people, even, while attending high school or college, being "granted" patents and "selling" them through a Patent Exchange and receiving royalties to pay even their own tuitions, if necessary. Teachers and professors, in time, could supplement their incomes and bolster their positions in the eyes of their students by lending their resources to industries through our Patent Office and a Patent Exchange and achieving laudable results. In short, it seemed that everyone would stand to benefit from improved Patent Office operations and the creation of a Patent Exchange.

For how many years and on how many courses does one have to maintain a zero handicap before entering a tournament?

Without consulting the Patent Office regarding their plans, or efforts to reduce pendency times, I proceeded, in 1966, to begin a business venture which I hoped would result, ultimately, in the creation of an American Patent Exchange. If that business venture would succeed, it would provide the financial, technological and marketing expertise needed for creating and maintaining an American Patent Exchange. I would pursue Patent Office improvements later, if necessary.

Now, when I say that I had not consulted with the Patent Office regarding their operations improvement plans, I mean that I had not made DIRECT inquiries, as you have witnessed already in this book. They were begun later in the 1970s.

I DID apply for corporate service marks; something I had never done before, something which I felt would be easier for the Patent Office to handle than a patent, and an action which I felt would provide a firsthand, current report on Patent Office pendency requirements. I would learn, firsthand, what the pendency time requirements were at that time by filing for and getting service marks.

About 2.5 years later, I was broke, separated from my family (and later divorced), my business was closed, I was looking for employment and then, finally, I became the recipient of several corporate service marks from the U.S. Patent Office. What a way to go!

When it had become apparent to me that the company would need more capital, and that it would have to come from outside sources, I made several efforts to acquire it, but not enough was obtained. I wished, all along, for those service marks to be granted, but I had to do my best without them.

Rights to service marks are maintained by use, which must continue if those rights are to be preserved. So said my lawyer, and I spent a considerable sum on advertising in an effort to fulfill that requirement ... too much, in fact. But, at the time, it seemed that I had no choice. At any rate, by the Fall of 1968, I had abandoned all activities related to Patent Office improvements. I guess you could say I was forced to. This time, I felt that I had paid a considerable price for the right to pursue what I still considered to be worthwhile objectives.

Ever try for a hole-in-one? - when you needed it to win? If the thought of it makes you uncomfortable, you're normal!

Upsetting as events in 1968 had been, I considered myself fortunate to be alive, physically able and, certainly, a considerable distance away from one of those prison camps in North Vietnam, which I felt I could very well have been in, had I remained in Uncle Sam's Navy. The thought often occurred to me that if I HAD been in a North Vietnamese prison camp, I would probably be anxious and frustrated over not being able to proceed with the very activities I was engaged in, at that time.

True, I had encountered misfortunes, but who hasn't? I had known from estimates by close friends and business associates, that my available resources and time were only a fraction of what their estimates indicated I would need. I fought the good fight just the same and met a number of persons along the way who confirmed the needs I had felt for speeding up Patent Office operations. Several, in particular, come to mind at this writing:

One was a farmer who had purchased a new tractor many years earlier and fabricated a useful attachment for it. Later, he had invited representatives of the tractor manufacturing firm to come and see his device, which they did. He took them into his barn, showed them what he had done to their tractor, and they, in turn, graciously observed. A year, or two later, that device appeared on the newer tractors manufactured by that same company, and the farmer never received even 10 cents for his contribution. He was really upset and disappointed.

Another was a road contractor who had been in the business a long time and was getting tired. He remarked at breakfast one morning that he wished he could invent a new construction tool and retire, "but who ever heard of getting a patent on time!"

There were many examples and results to hear of and observe which would cause one to testify that our Patent Office was failing to fulfill its obligations through inadequate operating standards, but there seemed to be no one interested in doing anything about it.

Ralph Nader, for example, if I can bring up a personality we have all had exposure to. If he were something more than a lawyer, in my judgment, he would recognize the importance of our patent system in lieu, to a degree, of choosing to seemingly defend everyone from the constructive contributions of many. Have you ever heard him even mention the Patent Office? I haven't.

His appeal, as far as I can observe, is directed towards an uninformed audience. Americans have benefited and thrived on finding better ways for anything and everything, but to listen to Ralph Nader, one would think that either he, or a government edict which he portents to arouse, will take care of things.

One evening, on March 25, 1971, to be exact, I attended a presentation at the University of Notre Dame given by Mr. John M. Swihart, Chief Engineer for Production SST Airplane Development, the Boeing Company. That was the very day, in fact, that Congress voted to terminate funding for the SuperSonic Transport Development Program.

It had been awhile since I'd heard it last, but Swihart made a comment before his Notre Dame audience which all Americans, I feel, should be proud of. He said, in effect, that "in America, one never knows from whom, or from where a good idea or an answer to a problem is going to come from." Amen. Reassuring as Swihart's remarks were, I found them in stark contrast to a mid-1950s statement by a West Point graduate Army general. I don't remember his name. At the time, I made a point of trying to forget it. And if I knew it now, I would probably still not want to remember it. At any rate, he proposed, at the time, that the U.S. should gather what it considered to be its "top brains," and form them into groups here and there for purposes of creating all of the new products and services that Americans would ever need.

It seems we have tried to do just that ever since! Now, therefore, we have a Ralph Nader AND a Presidential Assistant for Consumer Affairs, bored production line workers, the highest federal spending deficits in our history, inflation, exaggerated union activities, drug, youth, divorce, drinking and disease problems, welfare, urban renewal, unemployment, tax payment, environmental and, even, energy problems! The list seems endless, and, to some, it probably is, but I really cannot believe that Americans will tolerate being impoverished financially, or otherwise, indefinitely! It should be considered enough to understand and appreciate that Nature surrounds us everywhere, and that it is for the benefit of humanity that we should allow ourselves opportunities to investigate, discover and enjoy its offerings constructively! A means towards that end definitely requires improvements to a slow, out-dated, out-moded, behind-the-times Patent Office - and soon!

We're not talking about having to spend an exorbitant amount of money to improve the Patent Office, either.

For example, in Fiscal Year (FY) 1971, total Patent Office expenditures were $56,073,224. Income from fees and deposits received totaled $27,505,543. So the net operating cost to taxpayers of the U.S. Patent Office in FY 71 was only $28,567,681. That's actually less than 14 cents of the more than $1,029.45 per person living in the U.S. on January 1, 1970, which was expended [in total] by our Federal Government in the same

FY 71. (The Federal Government reportedly had total expenditures "excluding net lending" of $210,318,388,000.).

To "mechanize" at least a portion of our Patent Office files, a plan named "Project POTOMAC" was initiated in 1971. It provided for 1.6 million patents - of a total 3.6 million U.S. patents on file then - to be put on computers by the end of FY 78. "Project POTOMAC" would have added an estimated ($38.43 million) $7,686,000 annually (less than 4 cents per person) to Patent Office expenditures for five years. As you have witnessed earlier in this book, "Project POTOMAC" was cancelled. What bothers me most is that it was not replaced by any other computer-oriented improvement program!

In reading through communications I have had with members of the 92nd Congress, you may become aware, as I am, that Congress, in general, seems to have relieved itself of its responsibilities for Patent Office operations as assigned to it by the Constitution. Instead, the Patent Office seems adrift and subject mostly to the decisions of the President, the Secretary of Commerce, the Office of Management and Budget, and, of course, the Commissioner of Patents.

Ladies and gentlemen, I am grateful for this opportunity to make an appeal to a relatively "young" nation for support of measures that will effectively "speed-up" Patent Office search and registration procedures. The equipment and personnel are available to make that possible. What seems to be needed is for Americans to insist on having the kind of services provided which our Constitution requires and which, in fact, CAN be provided.

Wanting a Patent Exchange system is a new public request, as far as I know. I hope for its eventual development and successful utilization by current and future generations.

Finally, I must also suggest that if an overwhelming majority of Americans should choose NOT to favor Patent Office improvements, I believe they should identify themselves and move quickly to amend our Constitution so as to actually remove or nullify Article 1, Section 8, Paragraph 8.

At the moment, we seem to have a Patent Office that performs services for some who can afford its slow and expensive responses. For others, however, in need of a more rapid turnover of new products and services while catering to the whims and needs of today's marketplaces, the Patent Office presents merely a threat of lawsuits from patent (and other rights) holders, whose rights may have "unknowingly" been infringed upon. To continue such folly could, should and probably will bring damaging results even to the United States of America!

In closing, I thank you for this opportunity to appeal for help in defending one of America's most vital interests, its Patent system.

                                     *   *

During subsequent years, International Trade competition has intensified, presenting new problems that cannot be dealt with appropriately by a slow U.S. Patent Office. It is difficult, for example, for American industries to react competitively (and in time) to foreign imports when literally "years" are required for Patent clearances alone.

With International Trade increasing, opportunities are presented for turning World attention away from the basic habit of men to kill for survival, in favor of a more advanced notion which renders Nature a "beneficial challenge" and "profitable element" to be studied, utilized and accommodated. Our Patent System is a recognized "motivator" and an important "instrument" of "organized" free and civil societies whose full impact the World has yet to experience.

Meanwhile, many foreign residents have been and continue to be granted U.S. Patents. While their participation in the U.S. Patent System is welcomed, certainly, I would hope for our Congress to move to preserve and enhance the Patent System on a World scale. As you have noted in one of my appeals to Michigan's Senator Hart and Patent Commissioner Gottschalk, Congressional legislation to require foreign residents to first obtain and be maintaining in their own native lands those same patents which they call upon the U.S. Patent Office to grant them, has been suggested. By mere "local U.S. legislation," therefore, foreign governments could be influenced towards finding it in their own best interests to establish (where necessary) and to maintain their own Patent Offices.

In my original letter to Congressman John Brademas who represented my Third Indiana District, I made a special appeal: "At considerable personal expense, I have prepared and forwarded letters as enclosed herewith to all of the Members of the Senate and House of Representatives. While I DO trust the Post Office Department to deliver all mails, I would find it reassuring if you would read your copy into the Congressional Record."

On March 4, 1971, Mr. Brademas wrote back, in part as follows: "Because of the wide spread circulation of your letter, I
feel that it would be unnecessary and redundant at this point to
insert it into the Congressional Record."

By letter dated September 5, 1972, Commissioner Gottschalk
thanked me for sending him a copy of the summarizing book
to read. "I found this most interesting and I am certainly impressed by the dedication and interest reflected by this volume," he wrote. "I am very glad we had the opportunity to
discuss, in some detail, the matters we did. You can be sure
that these will continue to receive close and careful attention. -
Again, thanks for your thoughtfulness in keeping me
informed. - P.S. Your book is being returned under separate
cover." Signed: "Sincerely, Robert Gottschalk, Commissioner
of Patents."

If I had made any progress, it probably wasn't much. It
reminded me of comedian Bill Carty telling an audience in the
early 1960s: "I got up on the First Tee today in a Tournament
at Boca Raton. The announcer said, 'Will somebody tell that
idiot Carty to get back behind the tee markers?' And Carty
yelled back, 'Will somebody tell that idiot announcer this is
my second shot?!'"

In a letter to Ted Turner on January 7, 1992, I wrote that
"As bad as conditions might have seemed for me to onlookers,
I don't regret having tried - and failed; though I would have
preferred success.... I know that I did the best I could with what
I had at the time. Today, someone more capable could replace
me in this activity. Might it be you, Ted Turner? Next to a free

press and a Constitution and Bill of Rights guaranteeing it, I can think of no greater long-term benefit to mankind than the world respecting Article 1, Sec. 8, Par. 8 of our Constitution. Can you? Without inconvenience to you, I will be grateful for any reply." Enclosed was a copy of Nugent's June 15, 1972, letter.

Turner wrote back on January 9, 1992: "Thank you for your interesting and informative letter. However, between my ranch and office in Atlanta, my current activities keeps (sic.) me quite busy. Therefore, I cannot offer my support to you at this time."

At least Turner answered and considered the matter, which was more than Henry Ross Perot did, and we attended the same U.S. Naval Academy in Annapolis together, for one year, anyhow. Despite several mailings, Perot has never answered.

After applying for and receiving some Trademarks and design patents in the 1970s, I eventually decided not to bother the PTO with any more applications. The copyrights to this book, of course, will be an exception.

Perhaps the time will come when future generations can be served as they should be by Congress and the PTO. I hope so. As I conclude this memoir on February 4, 2004, the average patent pendency time reportedly stands at 22 months.

Inexcusable.

"We hold these truths to be self-evident,
that all men are created equal,..."

Thomas Jefferson

ALL MEN MAY BE CREATED EQUAL;
BUT VIA PERFORMANCE
CAN BECOME DISTINGUISHED.

Gunnar S. Jenson

Made in the USA
Lexington, KY
03 February 2011